PASSWORD 2

A Reading and Vocabulary Text

Linda Butler

Holyoke Community College

PEARSON
Longman

Dedicato ai miei amici in Italia con un abbraccio

Password 2

Pearson Education, 10 Bank Street, White Plains, NY 10606

Vice President of Multimedia and Skills: Sherry Preiss
Executive editor: Laura Le Dréan
Senior development editor: Joan Poole
Development editor: Mykan White
Production editor: Andréa C. Basora
Vice president of domestic marketing: Kate McLoughlin
Vice president of international marketing: Bruno Paul
Senior manufacturing buyer: Dave Dickey
Photo research: Dana Klinek
Cover design: Tracey Cataldo
Text design: Ann France, Patricia Wosczyk
Text composition: Elm Street Publishing Services, Inc.
Text font: 11/13 Palatino
Photo credits: See p. xiii
Illustration credits: Jill Wood pp. 3, 7, 17, 18, 19, 22, 23, 40, 41, 48, 57, 64, 65, 78, 79, 80, 82, 87, 95, 121, 133, 130, 158, 159, 166, 170, 174, 175, 184, 198, 199, 206, 208, 211, 215, 216, 224, 225; Hilary Price pp. 13, 42, 55, 63, 80, 86, 97, 139, 157, 165, 168, 185, 200, 223
Dictionary entries from *Longman Dictionary of American English*

Library of Congress Cataloging-in-Publication Data

Butler, Linda, 1952-
    Password 2: a reading and vocabulary text / by Linda Butler.
        p. cm.
    Includes index.
    ISBN 0-13-048467-9 (pbk.) —ISBN 0-13-140892-5 (pbk : CD)
    1. English language—Textbooks for foreign speakers. 2. Reading comprehension—Problems, exercises, etc.
3. Vocabulary—Problems, exercises, etc. I. Title: Password two. II. Title.
PE1128.B8615 2003
428.6′4—dc22

                                                                2003021632

ISBN: 0-13-048467-9   5 6 7 8 9 -CRK- 07
ISBN: 0-13-140892-5 (book with audio CD)   6 7 8 9 -CRK- 07

Printed in the United States of America

Contents

Scope and Sequence

UNIT/CHAPTER/READING	READING SKILLS	VOCABULARY BUILDING	DICTIONARY SKILLS
UNIT 1: STARTING OUT IN A CAREER			
CHAPTER 1 *A Dentist?* *Oh, No!*	• Scanning • Thinking about the main idea	• Guessing meaning from context • Studying parts of speech: nouns (common and proper)	
CHAPTER 2 *A Cool Job*	• Reading for details • Summarizing	• Studying collocations: *pay attention*	
CHAPTER 3 *Ready for Action*	• Scanning • Reading between the lines	• Studying parts of speech: verbs	
CHAPTER 4 *Life Is Full of Surprises*	• Reading for details • Understanding cause and effect	• Studying phrasal verbs	
UNIT 1: Wrap-up		• Expanding vocabulary: adjectives; word families	• Using guidewords • Finding compound words and phrasal verbs
UNIT 2: IT'S ALL IN YOUR HEAD			
CHAPTER 5 *Food for Thought*	• Scanning • Thinking about the main idea	• Studying collocations: adjective + *amount (of)*	
CHAPTER 6 *Your Memory at Work*	• Understanding topics of paragraphs • Summarizing	• Studying parts of speech: adverbs	
CHAPTER 7 *Sleep and the Brain*	• Reading for details • Summarizing	• Studying word grammar: *affect, effect*	
CHAPTER 8 *In Your Dreams*	• Distinguishing between fact and opinion • Summarizing	• Studying collocations: phrases with *right*	
UNIT 2: Wrap-up		• Expanding vocabulary: prefixes and suffixes	• Finding adverbs that end in *-ly* • Understanding word families

About the Author

Linda Butler is an independent ESL materials writer and editor and the author of several textbooks for learners of English, including *Password 1*. She began teaching English in Italy in 1979 and currently teaches part-time at Holyoke Community College in Massachusetts.

INTRODUCTION

To the Teacher

The *Password* series is designed to help learners of English develop their reading skills and expand their vocabularies. Each book in the series offers theme-based units with engaging readings, a variety of activities to develop language skills, and exercises to help students understand, remember, and use new words.

Any book in the series can be used independently of the others. *Password 1* is for high beginners assumed to have an English vocabulary of about 600 words; *Password 2* assumes a vocabulary of about 1,000 words; and *Password 3*, assumes a vocabulary of about 1,500. With each book, students will learn more than 400 new words and phrases, all of them high-frequency in American English. The *Password* series can help students reach the 2,000-word level in English, at which point, research has shown, most learners can handle basic everyday oral communication and begin to read unadapted texts. The vocabulary taught in the *Password* series has been carefully chosen. Target word choices have been based on analyses of authentic language data in various corpora, including data in the Longman Corpus Network, to determine which words are most frequently used and therefore most likely to be needed by students. Also targeted are common collocations and other multi-word units, including phrasal verbs. Most of the target vocabulary has been determined not by the topic of a chapter but rather by the frequency and usefulness of the words across a range of subjects.

While becoming a good reader in English does involve more than knowing the meanings of words, there is no doubt that vocabulary is key. To learn new words, students need to see them repeatedly and in varied contexts. They must become skilled at guessing meaning from context but can do this successfully only when they understand the context. For that reason, the sentence structure and vocabulary in the readings have been carefully controlled. The vocabulary used in the readings is limited to those 600 or 1,000 or 1,500 high-frequency words that the learner is assumed to know, plus the words and phrases to be targeted in the chapter and those recycled from previous chapters. The new vocabulary is explained and practiced in exercises and activities, encountered again in later readings and tasks, and reviewed in oral drills and self-tests. This emphasis on systematic vocabulary acquisition is a highlight of the *Password* series.

OVERVIEW OF *PASSWORD 2*

Password 2 is intended for low-intermediate students. It assumes a vocabulary of about 1,000 English words and teaches about 400 more. Sixteen words and phrases from each reading passage are targeted in the exercises for that chapter and recycled in later chapters. Because of the systematic building of vocabulary, as well as the progression of reading skills exercises, it is best to do the units and chapters in the order in which they appear in the book.

Most of the target words are among the 1,500 most high-frequency words in English—the vocabulary that students need to build a solid foundation in English. Other less high-frequency words have been targeted for their usefulness in discussing a particular theme. For example, the first unit, "Starting Out in a Career," includes the target words *career, boss, training,* and *interview.*

Organization of the Book

The book contains six units, each with four chapters followed by a Wrap-up section. After Units Three and Six, there are Vocabulary Self-Tests. At the end of the book, you will find the Index to Target Words and Phrases.

UNITS   Each unit is based on a theme and includes four readings that deal with real people, places, ideas, and events. Students need to understand the content, they need to speak and write about it, but they are not expected to memorize it. Each of the readings and each list of target vocabulary has been recorded on audio CD.

CHAPTERS   Each of the four chapters within a unit is organized as follows:

Getting Ready to Read   Each chapter opens with a photo or illustration and pre-reading questions or tasks. These are often for pair or small group work but may be best handled as a full-class activity when students need more guidance. *Getting Ready to Read* starts students thinking about the subject of the reading by drawing on what they already know, eliciting their opinions, and/or introducing relevant vocabulary.

Reading   This section contains the reading passage for the chapter. These passages progress from about 450 to about 750 words by the end of the book. Students should do the reading the first time without dictionaries. You may wish to have them reread while you read aloud or play the audio, as listening while reading can be helpful to students' comprehension and retention. It is also helpful for students to hear the pronunciation of new words. The reading is followed by *Quick Comprehension Check,* a brief true/false exercise that lets students check their general understanding. It is a good idea to go over the *Quick Comprehension Check* statements in class. When a statement is true, you may want to ask students how they know it is true; when it is false, have students correct it. By doing so, you send them back into the reading to find support for their answers. Try to avoid spending time explaining vocabulary at this point.

Exploring Vocabulary   Once students have a general understanding of the reading, it is time to focus on new words. In *Thinking about the Vocabulary*, students are asked to look at the list of Target Words and Phrases and circle (both on the list and in the reading) those that are new to them. Then they reread, noticing the uses of these particular words. From the beginning, learners are asked to examine the context of each unknown word and see what information the context gives them. They may need to work on this first as a whole class, with your guidance; later they can discuss new word meanings in pairs. *Using the Vocabulary* follows, with three exercises of various types, to help students understand the meanings of the target vocabulary as used in the reading and in other contexts. These exercises can be done in class or out, by students working individually or in pairs. In *Building on the Vocabulary*, you will find a word grammar or collocation exercise. Grammar exercises include study of the most common parts of speech and phrasal verbs. The collocation exercises focus students' attention on how words combine with others, given that knowing about possible word combinations is an important aspect of learning new vocabulary. For example, students will see that *make*, not *do* or *give*, goes with *an effort*, and that while *gain, earn*, and *win* may be similar in meaning, they combine with different nouns. Only after working through all the exercises in *Exploring Vocabulary* should students turn to their dictionaries for further information, if needed.

Developing Your Skills   In this section are tasks that require students to focus again on the reading. The exercises include work on scanning, answering comprehension questions, summarizing, understanding cause and effect, reading for details, paraphrasing and quoting, comparing and contrasting, using context clues, and stating the main idea. You will also find a fluency-building exercise: *Discussion, Sharing Opinions, Role-playing*, or *Interviewing*. The exercise *Using New Words* has pairs of students working productively with the target vocabulary orally and/or in writing. When students choose new words to use in sentences, encourage them to choose ones they need to learn more about. The chapter ends with *Writing*. Sometimes there will be a choice of two or more topics related to the content of the reading. These writing tasks may lend themselves to journal entries or more formal compositions. How you wish to use them will depend on your goals for the course.

UNIT WRAP-UPS   Each unit ends with a four-part Wrap-up section that brings together the vocabulary from the four chapters. The unit Wrap-up provides a key follow-up to the initial learning of the vocabulary—to consolidate and enrich students' understanding of new words. The first part is *Reviewing Vocabulary*, with varied exercises to review word meanings; the second is *Expanding Vocabulary*, with exercises on word families, word parts, and collocations; the third is *Playing with Words*, a crossword or word search puzzle; and the fourth is *Building Dictionary Skills*, using excerpts from *Longman Dictionary of American English*.

VOCABULARY SELF-TESTS   Two multiple choice vocabulary tests appear in the book, the first covering Units 1–3, the second Units 4–6. The answers are given at the back of the book, as these are intended for students' own use. (Unit tests can be found in the Teacher's Manual.)

TEACHER'S MANUAL

The Teacher's Manual for *Password 2* contains:

- The Answer Key for all exercises in the book
- Six Unit Tests with answers
- *Quick Oral Review,* sets of prompts you can use for rapid drills of vocabulary studied in previous chapters. These drills can be an important part of the spaced repetition of vocabulary—repeated exposures to newly-learned words at increasing intervals—that helps students remember the words they learn. For tips on how to use the prompts, see the Introduction in the Teacher's Manual.

To the Student

Welcome to *Password 2!* This book will help you improve your reading in English and expand your English vocabulary. The articles in it are about real people, events, ideas, and places from around the world. I hope you will enjoy reading, writing, and talking about them.

Linda Butler

References

Nation, Paul. *Teaching and Learning Vocabulary.* New York: Newbury House, 1990.

Schmitt, Norbert, and Michael McCarthy, eds. *Vocabulary: Description, Acquisition, and Pedagogy.* Cambridge, UK: Cambridge University Press, 1997.

Schmitt, Norbert, and Cheryl Boyd Zimmerman. "Derivative Word Forms: What Do Learners Know?" *TESOL Quarterly,* 36 (Summer 2002): 145–171.

Acknowledgments

I would like to thank first the people who shared personal stories with me so that students could enjoy them in this book: Mahmoud Arani, Kazumi Funamoto, Charles Lane, Brandon Middleton, Stephen Roy, and Bruce Yang. For their help with research, I would like to thank Craig Butler, Maggie Butler, Vitek J.P. Kruta, Siok Kuan Lim, Jim Montgomery, Miles and Clare Montgomery-Butler, Gail Mueller, Beatrice Romano, and Lynn Stafford-Yilmaz. Thanks also to my students at Holyoke Community College in Holyoke, Massachusetts, for their helpful feedback on the materials, especially to Julissa Garib and Lisandra Zeno, for the use of excerpts from their journals, and to readers Mayra Colón, Catherine López, Nasir Maqbool, Mónica Pérez, Jocelyn Sanchez, Luz Serrano, and Tatyana Skovorodina.

I would also like to thank the reviewers whose comments on early drafts of this book were very helpful: **Marsha Abramovich**, Tidewater Community College, Virginia Beach, VA; **Allan Aube**, Canadian Education Centre, Seoul, Korea; **Kathy Burns**, EF International Language School, Miami, FL; **Leslie Corpuz**, Tidewater Community College, Virginia Beach, VA; **William W. Crawford**, Georgetown University, Washington, D.C.; **Laura Freeman**, Oedae Language School, Kyonggi-Do, South Korea; **Elena Lattarulo**, Cuesta College, San Luis Obispo, CA; **Craig Machado**, Norwalk Community College, Norwalk, CT; **Denise Selleck**, City College of San Francisco–Alemany, San Francisco, CA.

A great many people at Longman helped in the making of this book, most of all Executive Editor Laura Le Dréan. Her experience as an editor and as a teacher, her good judgment and good humor, and her unfailing support were invaluable. I would also like to thank Assistant Editor Dana Klinek, Development Editors Joan Poole and Mykan White, Production Editor Andréa C. Basora, and artists Hilary Price and Jill Wood.

Photo Credits

p. 1, © Ted Horowitz/Corbis; p. 2, Photo by Linda Butler; p. 10, Photo by Linda Butler; p. 18, © Reuters NewMedia, Inc./Corbis; p. 26, Photo by Karl Sklar; p. 38, © Dale O'Dell/Corbis; p. 39, © John Henley/Corbis; p. 47, © Jose Luis Pelaez, Inc./Corbis; p. 76, © Carol Kohen/Getty Images; p. 77, © Royalty-Free/Corbis; p. 94, © Bettmann/Corbis; p. 102, © Stanley Fellerman/Corbis; p. 119, © Herrmann/Starke/Corbis; p. 120, Photo courtesy of Bruce Yang; p. 128, © Andrew Holbrooke; p. 136, Photo by Nancy Carbonaro, Carbonaro Photography, Wellesley, MA; p. 144, © H. Prinz/corbisstockmarket.com; p. 156, © Duncan Smith/Getty Images; p. 173, left: © Firefly Productions/Corbis; top right: © Myrleen Ferguson Cate/PhotoEdit; bottom right: © George Obremski/Corbis; p. 182, © Patrick Darby/Corbis; p. 196, © Ed Honowitz/Getty Images; p. 197, National Institute of Standards and Technology, Boulder Laboratories, U.S. Department of Commerce; p. 206, © Massimo Mastrorillo/Corbis; p. 214, © Photo by JC Bourque; p. 223, © Forrest J. Ackerman Collection/Corbis

STARTING OUT IN A CAREER

CHAPTER 1

A Dentist?
Oh, No!

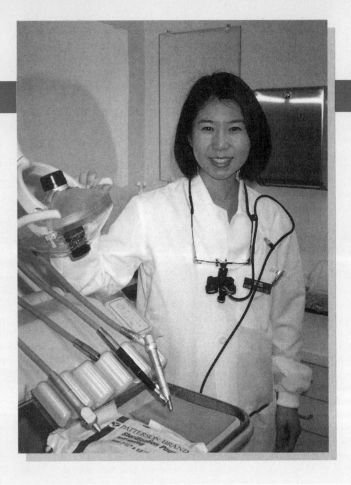

Dr. Kazumi Funamoto, dentist

GETTING READY TO READ

Talk with a partner or in a small group.

1. How often do you go to the dentist?
2. How do you feel about going to the dentist?
3. How many years of schooling does a dentist need?
4. Is being a dentist a good job? Tell why or why not.

READING

Look at the words and pictures next to the reading. Then read without stopping. Don't worry about new words. Don't stop to use a dictionary. Just keep reading!

A Dentist? Oh, No!

1   When people ask Kazumi Funamoto, "**What do you do?**" she answers, "I'm a dentist." Then she watches for the look on their faces. The same thing almost always happens. She can see that they are thinking, "I don't like dentists." She understands how they feel. They are thinking about **needles** and drills[1] and pain.

2   Kazumi does not want her patients to be afraid. She takes time to talk to them and ease[2] their **fears**. She tells them, "It's going to be OK. I'm going to be as **gentle** as I can. I don't like pain myself!" She always explains what she is going to do. She helps her patients feel **calm** and **relaxed**.

3   When she was a child, Kazumi did not like going to the dentist. She never expected to become one herself. She used to think about becoming an interpreter.[3] She was **interested** in other languages, and she liked talking to people from other countries. Kazumi chose a different **career**, but **communication** is still a big part of her job. She needs to talk with her patients and with the people who work in her office. They need to understand each other well.

4   Growing up, Kazumi talked about careers with her aunt. She says, "My aunt was a medical technician,[4] and she had a big **influence** on me." This aunt sometimes took Kazumi to work with her. Kazumi liked being in the lab.[5] There were doctors and technicians working there. She liked watching and listening to them.

5   In college, Kazumi had to get braces[6] on her teeth. "That was no fun, but the results were wonderful!" she says. Then she started to think about becoming a dentist. So, she spent some time helping in a dentist's office. She learned what a dentist's job was like. This experience helped her **make up her mind**. She decided to go to dental school after college.

6   Today, Kazumi feels great about her career. She gives three reasons why she is glad to be a dentist. First of all, she

continued

[1] a dentist's *drill*

[2] *ease* = make (a problem) smaller or not so bad

[3] an *interpreter* = a person who repeats someone's words in another language

[4] a *medical technician* = a worker who knows how to use machines or do tests that help doctors

[5] a *lab* = (short for) a *laboratory*, a room where scientists do careful tests

[6] *braces*

knows that she makes her mother happy. Her mother is glad that Kazumi can **support** herself. She told her daughter, "You won't have to depend on a husband. Good for you!"[7] Kazumi also likes working with her hands. A dentist needs a gentle touch and great control of very small **movements.** "I think I have good hands for this kind of work," she says. Finally, she likes learning new things. As a dentist, she learns from experience and from talking with her **boss.** At the end of the day, they often talk about difficult **cases.** She asks him questions about problems that **come up** with her patients' teeth, and she gets his advice. Kazumi says, "I feel like I'm growing each and every day."

[7] *Good for you!* = said to show you are happy about something that someone did

Quick Comprehension Check

Read these sentences. Circle T (true) or F (false).

1.	All her life, Kazumi Funamoto wanted to be a dentist.	T	(F)
2.	She doesn't usually talk to her patients.	T	F
3.	She used to go to work with her aunt.	T	F
4.	Kazumi's mother is happy that Kazumi is a dentist.	T	F
5.	Kazumi works alone.	T	F
6.	She is happy to be a dentist.	T	F

EXPLORING VOCABULARY

Thinking about the Vocabulary

Guessing Meaning from Context

We use words in a **context.** The context of a word is the words and sentences before and after it. These other words help you guess a word's meaning. For example, look at the context of *boss:*

> As a dentist, she learns from experience and from talking with her **boss.** At the end of the day, they often talk about difficult cases. She can ask him questions about problems that come up with her patients' teeth, and she gets his advice.

The context of *boss* tells you this is a person and it is someone at work. A boss can answer questions and give advice. *Boss* means the person who gives someone a job or tells a worker what to do.

Look at the target words and phrases. Which ones are new to you? Circle
them here and in the reading.

Target Words and Phrases		
What do you do? (paragraph 1)	**interested** (3)	**support** (6)
needles (1)	**career** (3)	**movements** (6)
fears (2)	**communication** (3)	**boss** (6)
gentle (2)	**influence** (4)	**cases** (6)
calm (2)	**make up her mind** (5)	**come up** (6)
relaxed (2)		

Read "A Dentist? Oh, No!" again. Look at the context of each new word and phrase.
Can you guess the meaning?

Using the Vocabulary

Ⓐ These sentences are **about the reading**. Complete them with the words
and phrases in the box.

career	cases	come up	fear	gentle	influence
interested in	make up her mind	movements	relaxed	support	

1. Many people have a _____ fear _____ of dentists. They are afraid of
   going to see a dentist.
2. Kazumi says, "I'm going to be as _____ as I can." This means
   she will be very careful in the way she touches her patient.
3. She doesn't want her patients to be nervous. She wants them to feel
   _____.
4. Kazumi liked learning about other languages. She was _____
   them.
5. First she thought about a _____ as an interpreter. Then she
   decided on a different kind of work.
6. Kazumi learned from her aunt while she was growing up. Her aunt had a
   big _____ on her.
7. After college, Kazumi needed to decide on a career. She had to
   _____.
8. As a dentist, she makes enough money to live. She can _____
   herself.

9. When Kazumi's hands are in a patient's mouth, she needs to move them carefully. She has to use very small _____.

10. Sometimes patients have special problems with their teeth. Kazumi talks about these difficult _____ with her boss.

11. "Problems that _____" are problems that happen, often suddenly, when someone isn't ready for them.

B These sentences use the target words and phrases **in new contexts.** Complete them with the words and phrases in the box.

came up	career		cases	fear	gentle	influence
interested in	made up my mind		~~movements~~	relaxed	support	

1. The doctor tested the ___movements___ of my eyes: up, down, left, and right.

2. He needs a job so that he can _____ himself and his family.

3. They're lying on the beach listening to music. They look very _____.

4. He had a 50-year-long _____ in business.

5. I like the new president. He'll have a good _____ on the country.

6. They aren't _____ money. They don't care about it.

7. It was hard to choose which shoes to buy, but finally I _____.

8. He planned to leave work early, but something _____, so he couldn't.

9. Be careful with the baby! You must be _____ with babies.

10. _____ of flying is common. Many people won't get on a plane.

11. In some _____, the dentist has to pull a tooth out, but sometimes the dentist can save a tooth.

C Read these sentences. Write the **boldfaced** target words or phrases next to their definitions.

a. A family needs good **communication**. People have to talk to each other.

b. You work for the college, right? **What do you do?** Do you teach?

c. Police and firefighters must stay **calm** so that they can think clearly.

d. A doctor uses a **needle** to give someone a shot of medicine or a drug.

e. The **boss** let the workers leave early.

Target Words/Phrases   Definitions

1. _____*boss*_____ = the person who gives you a job or tells you what to do

2. _____ = What is your job?

3. _____ = a very thin piece of steel

4. _____ = relaxed, not angry or nervous

5. _____ = giving and getting information (by speaking, writing, and so on)

A syringe with a *needle*

A sewing *needle*

Building on the Vocabulary

Studying Word Grammar

The **parts of speech** are the different kinds of words, such as nouns, verbs, and adjectives. A **noun** is a word for:

a person	*dentist, aunt, Kazumi*
a place	*home, school, Africa*
a thing	*tooth, book, Volkswagen*
an idea	*time, education, music*

Most nouns are **common nouns** (such as *dentist, home, tooth*). A **proper noun** starts with a capital letter and names one special person (*Kazumi*), place (*Africa*), or thing (*Volkswagen*).

A **There are one, two, or three nouns in each sentence. Circle the nouns.**

1. She has good (communication) with the (players) on her (team.)

2. Are you afraid of needles?

3. The police are working on a difficult case.

4. The boss is moving into a new office.

5. Did his family have an influence on his career?

6. John is going to the airport by bus.

7. My friend is in Australia right now.

B Write the nouns from Part A. Some nouns can go in more than one place.

Nouns are words for:

People	Places	Things	Ideas
players		team	communication

DEVELOPING YOUR SKILLS

Scanning

Sometimes you need to find a piece of information in a reading. To do this, you **scan** the reading. *Scan* means to read very quickly and look for just the information you need.

Read these statements about "A Dentist? Oh, No!" Scan the reading for the information you need to complete them.

1. Kazumi tells her patients, "I'm going to _____ be as gentle as I can _____."

2. Kazumi also thought about a career as an _____.

3. Communication is important in her work. She needs to talk with _____ and _____.

4. Kazumi had two experiences that helped her decide on a career as a dentist: first, _____; then, _____.

5. Kazumi gives three reasons for liking her work: **a.** _____,

   b. _____, and

   c. _____.

Thinking about the Main Idea

A A reading is about someone or something. That person or thing is the **topic** of the reading.

What is the topic of "A Dentist? Oh, No!"? Circle 1, 2, or 3.

1. Going to the dentist
2. A dentist and her family
3. Kazumi Funamoto and her career

B The **main idea** of a reading is the most important information about the topic.

What is the main idea of the reading in this chapter? Circle 1, 2, or 3.

1. Kazumi Funamoto knows that people don't like to go to the dentist.
2. A dentist needs to have good hands and a gentle touch to help patients stay calm.
3. Kazumi Funamoto didn't always plan to be a dentist, but now she is happy in that career.

Discussion

Talk about these questions with a partner.

1. How did Kazumi's aunt have an influence on her?
2. Who had the biggest influence on you when you were a child? Who has an influence on you now?
3. Name five to ten jobs in which a person works with his or her hands. Would you like any of these jobs? Explain.

Using New Words

These questions use some of the target words and phrases. Ask and answer these questions with a partner. Then tell the class something about your partner.

1. Is it sometimes hard for you to **make up your mind**? When?
2. When you pick up a newspaper or magazine, what are you **interested in**?
3. Would you like a **career** as a dentist? Why or why not?
4. How would you finish this sentence? A good **boss** is a person who . . .
5. What do you do to stay **calm** and **relaxed** at difficult moments?

Writing

Write a paragraph about a time when you had to make an important decision. Answer these questions:

- What did you decide? Why?
- Did anyone have an influence on your decision?
- How do you feel about your decision now?

Example:

My big decision in life was to come to the United States with my family. My husband and I made this decision together. We wanted to do it for our children. It wasn't easy because we had no other family here. Now I am glad we came.

CHAPTER 2

A Cool Job

Charles Lane

GETTING READY TO READ

Talk in a small group or with the whole class.

1. What video games can you name?
2. Do you ever play video games? Tell why or why not.
3. Charles Lane works for a video game company. His first experience in this area was working as a video game tester. Does this sound like a good job for you or anyone you know? Tell why or why not.

READING

Look at the words next to the reading. Then read without stopping.

A Cool Job

1   Charles Lane loves playing games, all kinds of games. He has loved games all his life. He has always been interested in computers, too. Today, his love of games and his interest in computers come together in his work. Charles works for a company that makes video games.

2   Charles did not really plan on this career. "It all started **by accident**," he says. "A friend of a friend worked for a video game company. He knew how much I loved games, and he told me about a job. It sounded like fun." It was a job as a video game tester.

3   When a video game company has a new game, they give it to testers. Testers play the game and look for bugs in it. The word *bug* usually means an **insect**, but a bug can also be a problem in a computer program. "For example," says Charles, "you're playing a war game, and you're flying a plane. You drop a **bomb** on a building, but nothing happens—the building is still standing. The bomb didn't work, so you know there's a bug." The company wants to find and fix any bugs before they sell the game.

4   Video game testers need to have good computer **skills**. They need to understand how computers work. They have to install[1] new **hardware** and **software**. Charles did not have great computer skills when he went to the **interview** for his first job, so he was nervous. **However**, the interviewer said, "That's OK. We can teach someone to use a computer, but we can't teach someone to love games."

5   Testers must have strong communication skills, too. They have to write very clear **reports** on the bugs they find. They have to describe **exactly** what is wrong in a game. Oral[2] communication skills are important, too. Testers are part of a team. Every day, they talk with other people on the team, such as the game designers[3] and programmers.[4] They all want to make their game fun and easy to use.

[1] *install* = put in place and make ready to use

[2] *oral* = spoken, not written

[3] *designers* = people who plan what things will look like and how they will work

[4] *programmers* = people who write computer programs (the instructions that make computers do their jobs)

continued

6   In his first job as a tester, Charles sometimes had to check **certain** parts of a game. At other times, he just started at the beginning and played the game, looking for bugs. He tried to **imagine** all the things that a player at home might do in a game. He played hour after hour, day after day. He always had to **pay attention** to **details**. Did he ever get tired of playing? "You bet!"[5] says Charles. "After 60 hours of testing in a week, you do not want to play games when you get home."

7   Charles spent three years as a video game tester. Now he is a video game producer. This means that he works on every part of **developing** a new game. He really enjoys his work. Charles says, "It's a great **field** to be in."

[5] *You bet!* = (informal) a strong yes

Quick Comprehension Check

Read these sentences. Circle T (true) or F (false).

1. Charles always planned to work for a video game company.   T   F

2. Testers check new games to look for any problems.   T   F

3. Testers need to know something about computers.   T   F

4. Testers don't need to be good writers or speakers.   T   F

5. It usually takes a team of people to make a new video game.   T   F

6. Charles wants to change to a different career.   T   F

EXPLORING VOCABULARY

Thinking about the Vocabulary

Look at the target words and phrases. Which ones are new to you? Circle them here and in the reading.

Target Words and Phrases			
by accident (2)	hardware (4)	reports (5)	pay attention (6)
insect (3)	software (4)	exactly (5)	details (6)
bomb (3)	interview (4)	certain (6)	developing (7)
skills (4)	however (4)	imagine (6)	field (7)

Read "A Cool Job" again. Look at the context of each new word and phrase. Can you guess the meaning?

Using the Vocabulary

 A Label the pictures. Write *a bomb, computer hardware, insects,* and *an interview.*

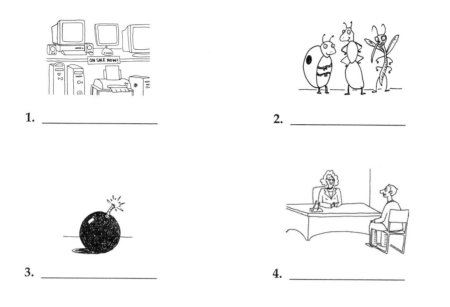

1. _____

2. _____

3. _____

4. _____

B These sentences are **about the reading.** Complete them with the words and phrases in the box.

by accident	certain	details	develop	exactly	field
however	imagine	pay attention	report	skills	software

1. Charles's career in video games started _____. He didn't plan on it.

2. Video game testers need to know how to use computers. They need computer _____. Charles developed these abilities at his first job.

3. Testers sometimes have to install computer _____. These programs tell a computer what to do.

4. Charles didn't have great computer skills, so he was nervous at his interview. _____, his interviewer said, "Don't worry."

5. A tester has to tell people at the company about the bugs in a game. The tester writes about the problems in a _____.

6. Testers have to describe a bug _____. They have to tell every little thing about it.

7. Sometimes Charles didn't test all of a game. He tested _____ parts only.

8. Charles thought about game players at home. He pictured them in his mind. He tried to _____ everything they might do in a game.

9. You can't think about other things when you test a game. You have to _____ to the game.

10. Testers look at every little part of a game. They pay attention to

    _____.

11. It takes a team of people to _____ a new video game. It is hard for one person working alone to make a good game.

12. Charles likes the video game business. He says it is a great _____ to work in.

C These sentences use the target words and phrases **in new contexts.** Complete them with the words and phrases in the box.

by accident	certain	details	developing	exactly	field
however	imagine	pays attention	report	skills	software

1. I wonder if it will rain. Let's watch the weather _____ on TV.

2. You need good driving _____ to pass the test for a driver's license.

3. I didn't expect to see her. We met _____.

4. The boss bought some new _____ for use on the office computers.

5. I remember something about the case, but I forget the _____.

6. Bob gets bad grades in school. He never _____ in class.

7. Scientists are _____ new drugs to fight AIDS.

8. What time is it? It is _____ 4:31.

9. Close your eyes, relax, and _____ lying on a beautiful beach.

10. He has classes on _____ days. I don't know which ones.

11. I expected her to be angry. _____, she seemed very calm.

12. Teachers work in the _____ of education. (This target word can also mean an area of land used for playing a sport, planting vegetables, **etc.**)

Common Abbreviations
Etc. is short for the Latin words *et cetera*. This abbreviation is often used at the end of a list. It means "and other people or things of the same kind."

Building on the Vocabulary

Studying Collocations

Collocations are words that we often put together. Some words can go together and some cannot. For example, we can say, *He never **pays** attention,* but we can't say, *He never **gives** attention.*

Note that *pay attention* is often followed by *to* + (someone/something): *Pay attention to your driving!*

Choose the correct sentence. Cross out the sentence with the mistake.

1. The teacher told them to pay attention. / ~~The teacher told them to give attention.~~

2. I gave no attention to the news. / I paid no attention to the news.

3. Please pay careful attention about this. / Please pay careful attention to this.

4. Sorry, I wasn't paying attention. / Sorry, I wasn't giving attention.

DEVELOPING YOUR SKILLS

Reading for Details

Read these sentences. Then reread "A Cool Job" for the answers. If the reading doesn't give the information, check (✓) It doesn't say.

	True	False	It doesn't say.
1. Charles loved games when he was a child.	✓		
2. He was interested in computers when he was a boy.			
3. He got his first job with a video game company after reading about the job in the newspaper.			
4. Video game testers need writing skills.			
5. Charles had an interview for his first job as a tester.			
6. He finished college before becoming a tester.			
7. Video game testers look for bugs in games.			
8. They sometimes work more than 50 hours a week.			
9. They make a lot of money.			
10. Charles still works as a video game tester.			

Summarizing

A **summary** tells the important parts of a reading again, but it has only the main ideas, not the details.

A **These six sentences make up a summary of the reading. Number the sentences in order.**

_____ **a.** They also need good communication skills.

_____ **b.** They need good computer skills and a love of video games.

__1__ **c.** Charles Lane works in the video game business.

_____ **d.** Today, Charles is a video game producer.

_____ **e.** His first job in this field was as a video game tester.

_____ **f.** Testers check new games for bugs.

B **Write the sentences from Part A as a paragraph.**

_____
_____
_____
_____
_____
_____
_____

Sharing Opinions

Think about the questions. Then talk in a small group.

1. A friend of a friend helped Charles get his first job with a video game company. Some people say, "When you are looking for a job, it's _who_ you know—not _what_ you know—that matters." What does this statement mean? Do you agree with it? Why or why not?

2. Why do video game testers need strong communication skills? What other jobs need these skills? Which of these jobs do you think are good jobs? Why?

Using New Words

Work with a partner. Choose five target words or phrases from the list on page 12. On a piece of paper, use each word or phrase in a sentence.

Writing

Write a paragraph about your first job. Maybe it was a job you had two years ago—or twenty-two. Where did you work, what did you do, and how did you feel about this job? Or maybe your first job is still in your future: When will you get a job, and what would you like to do?

Example:

My first job was in a supermarket. I was 16 years old. I worked there as a cashier. When I started, I didn't like the job because I didn't know anything about cash registers. I felt stupid. But day by day, I learned, and now I know everything about using a cash register.

CHAPTER 3

Ready for Action

A crew of firefighters

GETTING READY TO READ

Talk with a partner or in a small group.

1. Look at the photo. What kind of firefighters do you think these are? What are they doing?

2. Do you carry your books in a backpack?[1] If so, how much does it weigh?

3. How long would it take you to hike[2] three miles? (That would be almost five kilometers.) What about hiking three miles with a 45-pound backpack? (That would weigh about 20 kilograms.)

[1] a *backpack*

[2] *hike* = take a long walk in the country, in the mountains, etc.

18

READING

Look at the words and pictures next to the reading. Then read without stopping.

Ready for Action

1   When most people leave for work, they know exactly where they are going. They usually know what time they will get home, too. Brandon Middleton never knows for sure. He might **end up** working for eight hours, ten, or sixteen. Maybe he won't even get home that same week. But that is fine with him. It is all part of being a firefighter for the U.S. Forest Service.

2   Fighting **forest** fires is dangerous work. It can also be very exciting. Imagine being out in a forest, far from any city or town. (Maybe you're a "smoke jumper" and you jumped out of a plane to get there!) You are on your way to fight a fire. The air is heavy with the smoke from the burning trees. As you get closer, the sound of the fire fills your ears like the sound of a train rushing **toward** you. You know that **ahead of** you is the fire. It is like a monster[1] that you and your team must **destroy**.

3   Is being a firefighter always exciting? Brandon says no. The first thing he will tell you about the job is, "It's all about **patience**." He and his crew[2] spend a lot of time waiting and a lot of time getting ready. Each one is **in charge of** his or her own equipment.[3] They have to make sure their **tools** are **sharp**. They need to have all the right clothes, such as a helmet,[4] **leather** boots, and fire-resistant[5] pants and shirts. Each firefighter will carry a backpack that weighs 25–45 pounds (12–20 kilograms). Firefighters have to be ready to move quickly. They never know when the phone will ring.

4   Three years ago, Brandon was in college. He wanted a job just for the summer. His mother told him that the Forest Service had some jobs **available**. Brandon loves forests and being **outdoors**, so he decided to **apply** for a job as a firefighter. He did not go back to college that fall.

5   After getting the job, Brandon had to pass a test. He had to do a three-mile hike with a 45-pound pack on his back, and he had to do it in less than 45 minutes. Then he needed

continued

[1] a *monster*

[2] a *crew* = a team of workers

[3] *equipment* = things needed to do a job, play a sport, etc.

[4] a *helmet*

[5] *fire-resistant* = hard to burn

training, so he went to fire school. There he started learning about things like using tools, watching the weather, and staying safe. "But fire school is only one week. The real training is on the job," he says. "That is where all the learning happens—out in the forest. You have to trust the people with more experience, and you learn for yourself as you see more fire."

6   What is next for Brandon? He is thinking about applying for a job on a Hotshot crew. The name *Hotshot* **refers** to working in the hottest area of a forest fire, but *hotshot* also means a person who is very skilled and very confident. Hotshot crews go to all the big fires, and they get the most difficult jobs to do. During the fire **season**, they have to be available 24 hours a day, seven days a week. Not everyone could do this kind of work. Not everyone would want to. "But if this is what you like to do," says Brandon, "you'd love it."

Quick Comprehension Check

Read these sentences. Circle T (true) or F (false).

1. Brandon Middleton loves his work.   T   F
2. He does not work the same hours every day.   T   F
3. Being a firefighter is always exciting.   T   F
4. Firefighters have to carry heavy backpacks.   T   F
5. Brandon learned how to fight fires in college.   T   F
6. He is planning to return to college soon.   T   F

EXPLORING VOCABULARY

Thinking about the Vocabulary

Look at the target words and phrases. Which ones are new to you? Circle them here and in the reading. Then read "Ready for Action" again. Look at the context of each new word and phrase. Can you guess the meaning?

Target Words and Phrases

end up (1)	**destroy** (2)	**sharp** (3)	**apply** (4)
forest (2)	**patience** (3)	**leather** (3)	**training** (5)
toward (2)	**in charge of** (3)	**available** (4)	**refers** (6)
ahead of (2)	**tools** (3)	**outdoors** (4)	**season** (6)

Using the Vocabulary

A These sentences are about the reading. What is the meaning of each **boldfaced** word or phrase? Circle a, b, or c.

1. Firefighters like Brandon cannot depend on working eight-hour days. They sometimes **end up** working much longer. *End up* means:

   a. make something finish or stop
   b. like or enjoy something
   c. have a final result you didn't expect

2. If a fire is moving **toward** you, the sound gets louder. *Toward* means:

   a. because of
   b. away from
   c. closer to

3. If a fire is **ahead of** you, you are looking and moving that way. *Ahead of* means:

   a. in front of
   b. in back of
   c. on top of

4. Each firefighter **is in charge of** his or her own things and must take care of them. *Be in charge of something* means:

   a. feel relaxed about it
   b. be responsible for it
   c. forget about it

5. Brandon wasn't interested in an office job. He likes to be **outdoors** in the fresh air. *Outdoors* means:

   a. at home
   b. at school
   c. outside and away from buildings

6. Brandon **applied for** a job as a firefighter. *Apply for something* means:

   a. tell people about it
   b. ask for it (in writing)
   c. disagree with it

7. New firefighters get their first **training** at fire school. They continue to learn on the job. *Training* means:

   a. traveling by train
   b. trying to get a job
   c. learning the skills for a job

8. The word *Hotshot* **refers to** a certain kind of firefighter. *Refers to* means:

   a. is about or means
   b. comes from
   c. is the opposite of

9. Some firefighters have to be **available** when they are needed. *Available* means:

   a. gentle
   b. free to do something
   c. certain

10. Firefighters work hardest during the fire **season**. *Season* means:

    a. the time of year when   **b.** a place for learning   **c.** an interview
       something happens   to do something   for a job

B These sentences use the target words and phrases **in new contexts**. Complete them with the words and phrases in the box.

ahead of	apply for	available	ended up	is in charge of
outdoors	refers to	seasons	toward	training

1. He's the boss. He _____ everyone who works here.

2. The question "What do you do?" _____ the kind of work you do.

3. She finally made up her mind to leave the company, and she began to _____ other jobs.

4. Doctors study for many years. They need a lot of _____.

5. Mr. Lee is busy now, but after lunch, he'll be _____ to talk to us.

6. Canada has four _____: summer, winter, spring, and fall.

7. I tried to install the new software by myself, but I _____ calling Customer Support for help.

8. We wanted to eat _____, but it was raining.

9. She is _____ him.

10. She is running _____ him.

C Read each definition and look at the paragraph number in parentheses ( ). Look back at the reading to **find the target word** for each definition. Write it in the chart.

Definition	Target Word
1. a place where many trees cover a large area of land (paragraph 2)	forest
2. break or hurt something so that it cannot continue or be used (2)	
3. made of animal skin that has been prepared for use in shoes, belts, etc. (3)	
4. having a very thin part that can cut or pass through things easily (like a knife or a needle) (3)	
5. the ability to wait for a long time without becoming nervous or angry (3)	
6. things that are useful for doing a job (3)	

A firefighter may use these *tools:*

an axe

a saw

a shovel

Building on the Vocabulary

Studying Word Grammar

Remember: The parts of speech are the different kinds of words, such as nouns, verbs, and adjectives. A **verb** is a word for an action. For example, *go, fly, run,* and *play* are verbs. The words *have* and *be* are also verbs. Sometimes a word can act as a noun *OR* a verb. For example:

We can't stop now. We're in a **rush.** (noun)

We **rushed** *out the door to catch the bus.* (verb)

Are the boldfaced words below nouns or verbs? Write the abbreviation
n.* or *v.

1. a. I like to travel by **train**. _____n._____

    b. He is going to **train** the new horse. _____

2. a. He **supports** his wife and four children. _____

    b. The president thanked the voters for their **support**. _____

3. a. I have a job **interview** on Friday. _____

    b. How many people did they **interview**? _____

4. a. The plane dropped a **bomb**. _____

    b. Will the planes **bomb** the city? _____

DEVELOPING YOUR SKILLS

Scanning

**Read these questions about "Ready for Action." Scan the reading and
write short answers. You do not need to write complete sentences.**

1. Paragraph 2: What two words describe the work of fighting forest fires?
    ____dangerous____ and _____

2. Who first told Brandon about jobs with the Forest Service?

    _____

3. What test did he take? _____

4. Where did he learn to fight fires? _____ and _____

5. What is a Hotshot crew? _____

Reading Between the Lines

**You cannot scan the reading for quick answers to these questions. These
are inference or opinion questions. To answer them, you must put
information from the reading together with what you know or believe.
Write complete sentences.**

1. Why does the Forest Service give a test to new firefighters? Maybe the
    Forest Service wants to see how strong the new firefighters are, or
    maybe the test is to show the new people how hard the job is.

2. Why does Brandon say, "It's all about patience"? _____

    _____

    _____

3. Why do you think Brandon wants to join a Hotshot crew? _____

_____

_____

Discussion

Talk about these questions in a small group.

1. Fighting forest fires can be exciting. What other jobs do you think are exciting?
2. What do people in your country think of firefighters?
3. How would you feel if your husband or wife were a firefighter? Why?

Using New Words

Work with a partner. Take turns asking for and giving information. Then tell the class something about your partner.

1. When and where do you like to be **outdoors**?
2. What do you have that is made of **leather**?
3. Name two **tools** that you use to do your schoolwork.
4. Name two jobs that you would *NEVER* **apply for**.
5. Name two things that make you lose **patience**.

Writing

Brandon learned about firefighting from people on the job. He says, "You have to trust the people with more experience." Write a paragraph about learning from other people and their experience. You can write about:

- a time when you learned something this way, or
- using your own experience to teach someone else.

CHAPTER 4

Life Is Full of Surprises

Mahmoud Arani in the classroom

GETTING READY TO READ

Talk in a small group or with the whole class.

1. Mahmoud Arani is from Iran. Do you know where Iran is or anything about its history? Tell what you know about Iran.

2. Many people leave their countries to study or to work. List some reasons why people do this.

READING

Look at the words next to the reading. Then read without stopping.

Life Is Full of Surprises

1   Mahmoud Arani is a **professor** at a small American college. He did not expect to end up in the United States, and he did not expect to teach. He grew up in Iran, and he planned to be a doctor. However, as people say, life is full of surprises.

2   Mahmoud was born in Iran near the city of Tehran. At school, he was an excellent student, the best in his class, and he was planning to study **medicine** in college. First, he had to take the university entrance exam.[1] He needed to do well to **get into** a **medical** school. Out of 50,000 high school students taking the test, only 1,000 would have the chance to study medicine in college. Mahmoud missed the **score** he needed by a few **points**. His teachers were very surprised. He took the test again. Again the news was bad. "I was **disappointed**," he remembers, "but I said, 'That is my fate.'"[2]

3   Mahmoud was also interested in languages, so he chose to study English. After college, he decided to go to the United States for an **advanced** degree[3] in this **subject**. A few months later, he entered an English as a Second Language (ESL) program. It was in Buffalo, New York, at the state university. Mahmoud was one of half a million international students who entered the United States to study that year. But he **managed to** do something that few others could. In less than two years, he went from studying ESL to teaching it at the same school!

4   On a visit home from New York, Mahmoud had an interview at a university in Tehran. They offered him a job, and he accepted it. The university made an **agreement** with him. Mahmoud said he would return to Buffalo to finish his degree, and they agreed to support him. After he finished, he would come back to teach. So Mahmoud went back to New York feeling great. He thought his future was **secure**.

5   Then something happened. There was a revolution[4] in Iran. It **caused** great changes in the country. Soon Mahmoud received a letter from his university in Tehran. It said, "We don't need any English teachers." Suddenly, his support was gone, and his future was unclear.

[1] an *entrance exam* = a test someone must take to be able to enter a school

[2] *fate* = the things that will happen that a person cannot control

[3] a *degree* = what a student gets for completing a program at a college or university

[4] a *revolution* = a time of great and sudden change in a country, often by force

continued

6   Mahmoud decided not to **give up**: He would keep working toward his degree. After much hard work, he reached his **goal**. Then, after teaching ESL in Buffalo for a while, he accepted a job at Saint Michael's College in Vermont. His students there report that he is an excellent teacher.

7   Now Mahmoud is married. He and his wife, Roya, have two children. Roya is also from Iran, and she is a doctor. Mahmoud is still interested in medicine, too. "I could go to medical school now," he says, "if I had the patience!" He does not plan to make a career change at this **stage** in his life. However, he adds, "I know that life is full of surprises. . . ."

Quick Comprehension Check

Read these sentences. Circle T (true) or F (false).

1. Mahmoud was born and grew up in Iran.   T   F

2. He wanted to study medicine and become a doctor.   T   F

3. He traveled to the United States to study medicine.   T   F

4. He expected to teach at a university in Iran.   T   F

5. The Iranian revolution happened while he was at home   T   F
    in Tehran.

6. The revolution changed his life.   T   F

EXPLORING VOCABULARY

Thinking about the Vocabulary

Look at the target words and phrases. Which ones are new to you? Circle them here and in the reading. Then read "Life Is Full of Surprises" again. Look at the context of each new word and phrase. Can you guess the meaning?

Target Words and Phrases			
professor (1)	score (2)	subject (3)	caused (5)
medicine (2)	points (2)	managed to (3)	give up (6)
get into (2)	disappointed (2)	agreement (4)	goal (6)
medical (2)	advanced (3)	secure (4)	stage (7)

Using the Vocabulary

 A These sentences are **about the reading.** Complete them with the words and phrases in the box.

agreement	caused	disappointed	get into	give up	goal
managed to	medicine	points	stage	subject	

1. Mahmoud wanted to study _____ so that he could become a doctor.

2. Mahmoud had to do well on a test to _____ medical school. The test decided which students could enter the school.

3. Mahmoud's test results weren't high enough. He needed a few more _____.

4. Mahmoud had to change his college plans. He couldn't do what he had hoped to do. He felt _____.

5. In college, he took many English courses. English was the _____ that he studied most.

6. Mahmoud was able to do something unusual. He _____ do something that few international students could do.

7. Mahmoud and the university made an _____. Each side made promises.

8. Great changes happened in Iran because of the revolution. The revolution _____ these changes.

9. It was hard for Mahmoud to keep going, but he didn't _____. He never stopped trying.

10. Mahmoud finally got what he wanted. He reached his _____.

11. At one time, Mahmoud wanted to become a doctor. But at this _____ of his life, he is happy as a professor.

B These sentences use the target words and phrases **in new contexts.** Complete them with the words and phrases in the box.

agreement	caused	disappointed	gave up	get into	goal
managed to	medicine	points	stages	subjects	

1. Two companies made an _____ to develop software together.

2. Children go through different _____ as they grow.

3. College students can take courses in math, history, education, and many other _____.

4. There was an accident on the road ahead of us. It _____ traffic problems.

5. I kept calling, but your phone was always busy, so finally I _____.

6. You need good grades if you want to _____ a good college.

7. I couldn't open the door, but I _____ get in through a window.

8. Doctors, dentists, and nurses all work in the field of _____.

9. I was _____ when my team didn't win.

10. Jack's main _____ in life is to make a lot of money.

11. In basketball, a player usually gets two _____ for getting the ball in the basket.

C **Read these sentences. Write the boldfaced target words next to their definitions.**

a. I didn't get a good **score** on the test, so I was disappointed.

b. The **professor** is available to talk with students during her office hours.

c. He can relax and stop worrying about money. He has a **secure** job now.

d. You can get good **medical** care at that hospital.

e. We are both studying Spanish, but I'm a beginner and he's in an **advanced** class.

Target Words   **Definitions**

1. ___professor___ = a teacher at a college or university

2. _____ = not expected to change or be in any danger

3. _____ = relating to a school subject at a difficult level

4. _____ = relating to medicine and the care of people who are sick or hurt

5. _____ = the number of points someone gets on a test or in a game

Building on the Vocabulary

Studying Word Grammar

Give up is a **phrasal verb.** Phrasal verbs have two parts: a verb (such as *give, get, turn*) and a particle (such as *up, out, off*). The meaning of the phrasal verb is different from the meaning of the verb alone.

A In Unit 1, you learned the phrasal verbs *come up, give up, end up,* and *get into.* Use them to complete these sentences.

1. He couldn't _____ the class; it was already full.

2. The team was losing, but they didn't _____.

3. I try to get to bed early, but I often _____ watching a late movie.

4. Call me if any problems _____.

B On a piece of paper, write three sentences with the phrasal verbs in Part A.

Example: My friend got into college when he was only 16.

DEVELOPING YOUR SKILLS

Reading for Details

Read these sentences. Then scan "Life Is Full of Surprises" for the answers. If the reading doesn't give the information, check (✓) *It doesn't say.*

	True	False	It doesn't say.
1. Mahmoud was born in Iran.	✓		
2. He studied English in college.			
3. He went to the United States to look for a job.			
4. Mahmoud's visit to Iran lasted for six months.			
5. The revolution in Iran happened while he was there.			
6. He received a degree from the state university in Buffalo, New York.			
7. He is a husband and a father.			
8. He and his wife are both professors.			
9. He is now planning to enter medical school.			
10. All of Mahmoud's family is in the United States.			

Understanding Cause and Effect

Sentences with *because* explain why something happens. Complete the following sentences using information from "Life Is Full of Surprises."

1. Mahmoud's grade on the exam surprised his teachers because <u>he was</u> <u>the best student in his class, but his score wasn't high enough for</u> <u>medical school.</u>

2. Mahmoud decided to study English because _____
   _____.

3. He went to the United States because _____
   _____.

4. As an international student, Mahmoud was unusual because _____
   _____.

5. He lost the chance to teach in Tehran because _____
   _____.

6. He doesn't plan to start medical school now because _____
   _____.

Discussion

Talk with your class about these questions.

1. How many people in the class agree that "life is full of surprises"? Are surprises a good thing in life? Why or why not?
2. How many people in the class would like to teach English? What are some reasons why people in the class do and do not want to?
3. How did your teacher become a teacher of English?

Using New Words

Work with a partner. Choose five target words or phrases from the list on page 28. On a piece of paper, use each word or phrase in a sentence.

Writing

Choose a topic. Write a paragraph.

1. Describe a time in your life when you set a goal and didn't give up. What were you trying to do? What made it hard? How did you reach your goal?
2. Think back to an earlier stage in your life. Write about a time when you wanted something very much. Did you get what you wanted, or were you disappointed? Explain.

Wrap-up

REVIEWING VOCABULARY

A Match these nouns with their definitions. There are two extra words.

agreement	detail	goal	hardware	~~insect~~
interview	report	skill	software	subject

1. _____insect_____ = a very small animal (such as a fly) that has six legs
2. _____ = something you want to do in the future
3. _____ = a promise made between two people or groups
4. _____ = a meeting to ask someone questions
5. _____ = one fact or small piece of information
6. _____ = a group of instructions that tell a computer what to do
7. _____ = a topic or an area that you study in school
8. _____ = an ability to do something, especially because you have learned it

B Complete these sentences. There are two extra words or phrases.

by accident	came up	exactly	fear
in charge of	leather	make up her mind	manage to
pay attention	refer to		

1. He should turn off the TV and _____ to his homework!
2. She has two job offers. Now she has to _____.
3. A problem _____, so I needed some advice.
4. The computer isn't working, but I'm sure Yoko will _____ fix it.
5. I took your book _____. Sorry, I thought it was mine.
6. The words *they* and *them* can _____ people or things.
7. I don't know the time _____, but it's about 10:00.
8. Who is _____ training the new workers?

EXPANDING VOCABULARY

A Remember: The parts of speech are the different kinds of words, such as nouns, verbs, and adjectives. An **adjective** is a word that describes a noun. Adjectives can come before nouns: *a nice person, a great idea.* They can also come after the verb *be* and linking verbs such as *feel, look,* and *sound: She wasn't nice to me. Your idea sounds great.*

There are one or two adjectives in each sentence. Circle the adjectives.

1. That knife is (new) and very (sharp.)
2. They looked calm and relaxed before the game.
3. He is available to meet with us at 4:00.
4. I was disappointed when I heard the final score.
5. The boss is interested in getting better software.
6. Certain kinds of birds cannot fly.
7. I worry that Ann's job is not secure.
8. She told the boys to be gentle with the little cat.

B Many words belong to **word families**. When you learn a new word, it is a good idea to learn other words in the same family.

Use words from each family in the chart to complete the sentence.

	Nouns	Verbs	Adjectives
1.	application	apply	
2.	communication	communicate	
3.	trainer training	train	trained

1. Before you can get an interview for the job, you must complete an _____.

2. People in business all over the world _____ in English.

3. a. Medical schools _____ doctors.

   b. His army career began with six months of basic _____.

   c. The hotel workers all seemed well-_____.

PLAYING WITH WORDS

Complete the sentences with words you studied in Chapters 1–4. Write the words in the puzzle.

Across

1. Most plural nouns in English end in -s, but certain_____ ones don't.

4. I closed my eyes and tried to i_____ being on a beach.

6. My shoes are made of l_____.

7. We expected him; h_____, he didn't come.

9. Forest fires d_____ trees.

11. I saw her coming t_____ me across the room.

12. Teachers and parents need a lot of p_____.

13. She had a long c_____ as a banker.

Down

2. These shoes are a_____ in four different colors.

3. They d_____ software for businesses.

5. She was standing a_____ of me in line.

8. We're developing a plan, but it's still at an early s_____.

10. They work hard to s_____ their families.

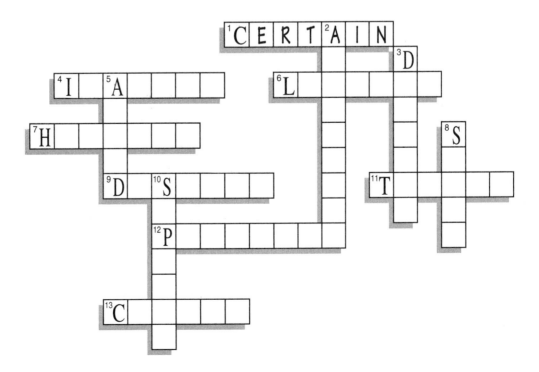

BUILDING DICTIONARY SKILLS

Finding Words in the Dictionary, Part 1

A **Guidewords** help you find words in the dictionary. Look at pages 114 and 115 below. The guidewords are *cater* and *center*. *Cater* is the first word on the left page; *center* is the last word on the right page.

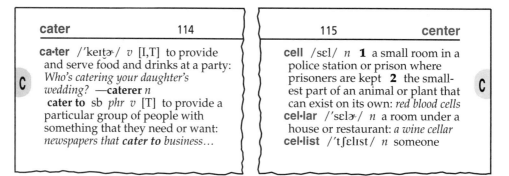

cater	114

C

ca·ter /ˈkeɪtɚ/ *v* [I,T] to provide and serve food and drinks at a party: *Who's catering your daughter's wedding?* —**caterer** *n*
cater to sb *phr v* [T] to provide a particular group of people with something that they need or want: *newspapers that cater to business...*

115	center

C

cell /sɛl/ *n* **1** a small room in a police station or prison where prisoners are kept **2** the smallest part of an animal or plant that can exist on its own: *red blood cells*
cel·lar /ˈsɛlɚ/ *n* a room under a house or restaurant: *a wine cellar*
cel·list /ˈtʃɛlɪst/ *n* someone

Will these words be on pages 114–115? Check (✓) *Yes* or *No*.

	Yes	No
1. certain		
2. cause		
3. calm		
4. cent		
5. CD-ROM		
6. central		

B A **compound word** is made up of two words. Some compound words are written as one word (*birthday, homework*); others are written as two words (*ice cream, good night*); and others are written with a hyphen (*good-looking, bird-brained*). The *Longman Dictionary of American English* treats these words as one word and lists them with other words in alphabetical order, for example:
good
good-bye
good evening
goodness

Write the following words in the order you would find them in the dictionary. (Note: In the examples below, the small numbers¹ and² after a word are superscripts. The dictionary entry for *outline*¹ gives the meanings of the noun *outline;* the entry for *outline*² gives the meanings of the verb *outline*.)

outer space	out¹	outdoors	outdoor
outline¹	outline²	out-of-state	outlive

1. _____out¹_____   4. _____   7. _____

2. _____   5. _____   8. _____

3. _____   6. _____

C **Phrasal verbs** do not have their own entries in *The Longman Dictionary of American English.* They are part of the entry for the verb.

Look at this entry for the verb *end.* Circle the two phrasal verbs.

> **end**² *v* [I,T] to finish or stop, or to make something do this: *World War II ended in 1945.* | *Janet's party didn't end until 4 o'clock in the morning.* | *Lucy decided to end her relationship with Jeff.*
> **end in** sth *phr v* [T] to have a particular result or to finish in a particular way: *The meeting **ended in** a huge argument.*
> **end up** *phr v* [I] to come to be in a place, situation, or condition that you did not expect or intend: *Whenever we go out to dinner I always **end up** paying the bill.*

UNIT 2

IT'S ALL IN YOUR HEAD

CHAPTER 5

Food for Thought

Morning coffee

GETTING READY TO READ

Talk in a small group or with the whole class.

1. How many people in the group drink:

   _____ coffee

   _____ tea

   _____ soda such as Coke or Pepsi

   _____ chocolate drinks

2. All the drinks in the list have caffeine.[1] Do you know any other drinks with caffeine?

3. When and why do people like drinks with caffeine?

[1] *caffeine* = a substance (in coffee, tea, and some other drinks) that helps tired minds wake up

READING

Look at the words and pictures next to the reading. Then read without stopping. Don't worry about new words. Don't stop to use a dictionary. Just keep reading!

Food for Thought

1   The foods you eat **supply** your body with energy. Your body needs energy to move and even to sleep. One part of your body uses a surprising **amount** of energy. This body part is small—only 2–3% of your total **weight**—but it uses 20–30% of the energy from your food. Can you guess what it is? It is your brain.

2   You already know that drugs **affect** the brain. Did you know that food affects it, too? Different types of food affect the brain in different ways. Sometimes we can feel the changes that food makes in our brains. For example, most people can feel an **immediate** change after drinking coffee. It is the caffeine in coffee that affects the brain. Caffeine usually makes people feel more **awake**. After a cup of coffee, a person can think and make decisions more quickly.

3   Other foods affect the brain in ways that we cannot see or feel. We don't **realize** how they influence us. However, everything we eat matters. Our food affects how **smart** we are and how well we remember things. It also affects how long we can concentrate.[1] For example, scientists know that:

1. Eating breakfast makes students do better on tests.

2. Spinach,[2] berries,[3] and other colorful fruits and vegetables help keep older brains from slowing down.

3. Eating large amounts of animal fat (in meat and cheese, for example) makes learning more difficult.

4. Fish really is "brain food." For years, many people believed that eating fish was good for the brain. Now scientists are finding that this is true.

4   For millions of years, the brains of early human beings[4] stayed the same size. They weighed only about one pound (400–500 grams). Then, during the last million years or so,

continued

[1] *concentrate* = think carefully

[2] *spinach* = a dark green, leafy vegetable

[3] *berries*

[4] *early human beings* = the first people who lived

there was a big **increase** in brain size. The human brain grew to about three pounds. This increase in brain size **meant** an increase in brain power. With bigger, stronger brains, human beings became smart enough to build boats and **invent** written languages. They developed forms of music and **created** works of art.[5] Some scientists say that these changes happened after people started to eat seafood.[6] Seafood **contains** a certain kind of fat, omega-3 fat. **According to** these scientists, omega-3 fat caused the increase in brain size. Today, brain scientists agree: This fat is still important for healthy brains. They also say that most of us are not getting enough of it.

[5] *works of art* = the things that artists make

[6] *seafood*

5   Did you know that the brains of adults continue to grow and change? The foods you eat affect how your brain grows. They affect how well you learn and remember things. Maybe you never thought about that before. **Luckily**, it is never too late to start **feeding** your brain well!

Quick Comprehension Check

Read these sentences. Circle T (true) or F (false).

1. Your brain is small, but it uses a lot of energy.   T   F

2. The foods you eat affect the way your brain works.   T   F

3. When a food causes changes in your brain, you can always   T   F
   feel it.

4. Maybe eating fish helped make the human brain bigger.   T   F

5. All kinds of fat are bad for your brain.   T   F

6. Children's brains grow and change, but adult brains don't. T   F

EXPLORING VOCABULARY

Thinking about the Vocabulary

Look at the target words and phrases. Which ones are new to you? Circle them here and in the reading. Then read "Food for Thought" again. Look at the context of each new word and phrase. Can you guess the meaning?

Target Words and Phrases			
supply (1)	immediate (2)	increase (4)	contains (4)
amount (1)	awake (2)	meant (4)	according to (4)
weight (1)	realize (3)	invent (4)	luckily (5)
affect (2)	smart (3)	created (4)	feeding (5)

Using the Vocabulary

A Complete the sentences. Write: *amount, awake, feeding,* and *increase.*

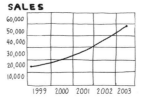

SALES

1. She's _____; he's not.

2. There was an _____ in sales.

3. He's _____ the baby.

4. Write the _____ on the check.

B These sentences are **about the reading**. Complete them with the words and phrases in the box.

according to	affects	contains	create	immediate	invented
luckily	meant	realize	smart	supply	weight

1. Food gives us energy. When we eat, we _____ our bodies with energy.

2. Your brain is not very heavy. It is only 2–3% of your total body _____.

3. Drugs influence, or cause changes in, the brain. Food _____ it, too.

4. Sometimes a drug or food affects the brain quickly and people feel the difference very soon. They feel an _____ change.

5. Many people know about coffee, but they don't _____ that other foods affect them, too.

6. The right food can make a person more intelligent. Our food influences how _____ we are.

7. An increase in the size of the human brain _____ more brain power. The increase led to that result.

8. People developed spoken languages first. Later, they _____ writing. People needed larger brains to think of this idea.

9. Early humans also began to produce music and art. They started to _____ these things.

10. Some scientists say that eating seafood caused big changes. _____ these scientists, seafood helped the human brain to grow.

11. There is omega-3 fat in seafood. Seafood _____ this kind of fat.

12. Maybe you never thought about eating "brain food" before. _____, it's not too late. You can start now, and that is a good thing.

C These sentences use the target words and phrases **in new contexts**. Complete them with the words and phrases in the box.

according to	affects	contain	create	immediate	invents
luckily	meant	realize	smart	supplies	weight

1. There was a car accident there today. _____, no one was hurt.

2. She's a _____ girl, and she does very well in school.

3. Fruit is often sold by _____—$1.00 a pound, for example.

4. There were no surprises in the report. It didn't _____ any new information.

5. The weather often _____ people's travel plans.

6. He needed _____ medical care, so we rushed him to the hospital.

7. She was already in bed when I called. I didn't _____ it was so late.

8. The company _____ its workers with all the tools they need.

9. We got a foot of snow, so that _____ we had no school the next day.

10. I have no more patience with them. They just _____ problems for everyone else.

11. When someone _____ a new machine, product, or way of doing something, we call that person an inventor.

12. _____ the newspaper, there will be a lot of jobs in that field in the years ahead.

Building on the Vocabulary

Studying Collocations

Remember: Collocations are words that go together. Certain adjectives go with the noun *amount.*

- Use *large* + *amount* but not "*big amount.*"
- Use *small* + *amount* but not "*little amount.*"

Use *amount* + *of* + a noncount noun (such as *energy, time, money,* or *work*).

Example: *I never carry large amounts of money.*

Write three sentences with *amount of.*

1. _____

   _____

2. _____

   _____

3. _____

   _____

DEVELOPING YOUR SKILLS

Scanning

Read these statements about "Food for Thought." Scan the reading for the information you need to complete them. Answers inside quotation marks (" ") must match the words in the reading exactly.

1. The foods you eat give your body _____.

2. The brain makes up only _____% of your body's total weight.

3. The brain uses _____% of the energy from your food.

4. The _____ in coffee makes people feel more awake.

5. Scientists know that:

   a. "Eating breakfast_____."

   b. "_____" are
      good for older brains.

   c. "Eating large amounts of animal fat _____
      _____."

   d. "_____ really is 'brain food.' "

6. Early human brains grew from about _____ to about
   _____.

7. With bigger, stronger brains, human beings were able to build
   _____, invent _____, and create _____.

Thinking about the Main Idea

Complete the main idea of "Food for Thought."

The foods you eat affect how _____.

Discussion

Talk about these questions with a partner.

1. At what times during the day do you think your brain works best? Why?
2. How much would you change the way you eat to make yourself smarter? What is one thing you would do? What is one thing you would not do?
3. What questions would you like to ask scientists about food and the brain? Make a list.

Using New Words

Work with a partner. Take turns completing each statement. Use one of the words or phrases in parentheses.

1. I'm (glad/sorry) that somebody **invented** . . .
2. I'm (usually/rarely) **awake** . . .
3. **Luckily**, (I/my family) . . .
4. **According to** my (parents/friends), . . .
5. (People/Children) often don't **realize** that . . .

Writing

Write a paragraph about something you like to eat or drink. When do you usually have it? How does it affect you? Do you think it's good or bad for you? Why?

CHAPTER 6

Your Memory at Work

Trying to remember . . .

GETTING READY TO READ

Talk with a partner or in a small group.

1. Look at the things in the list. Which ones are usually easy for you to remember? Which ones are hard?

people's names	colors	words to songs
people's faces	music	information from classes
numbers	new vocabulary in English	other: _____

2. When you MUST remember something, what do you do? How do you help yourself remember it?

READING

Look at the words and picture next to the reading. Then read without stopping.

Your Memory at Work

1   You have two basic types of memory: short-**term** memory and long-term memory. Things you see or hear first enter your short-term memory. Very little of this information passes on into your long-term memory. Does this mean you have a bad memory? Not at all.[1]

2   Your short-term memory has a certain job. Its job is to **store** information for a few seconds only. Your short-term memory is at work when you **look up** a phone number, call the number, and then forget it. You remembered the number just long enough to use it. Then it **disappeared** from your memory. That's really a good thing. Imagine if your memory held every number, every face, and every word you ever knew!

3   However, some information is important to remember for a longer time. Then it must pass from short-term to long-term memory. Sometimes we tell ourselves to remember something. We might also **practice** it: "OK, don't forget: 555-1212, 555-1212." Usually, we don't even think about it. Our brain makes the decision for us. It decides to store the information or let it go.

4   The brain seems to make the decision by asking two questions:

   1. Does the information affect our **emotions**? **That is,** does it make us happy, sad, excited, or **upset**?

   2. Does the information **concern** something we already know, so our brain can store it with something already there?

An answer of "Yes" means that the new information enters long-term memory. That means the brain creates new **connections** among brain cells.[2] These connections form in a **region** of the brain called the *cerebral cortex*.[3] It is the largest part of the brain.

5   After a piece of information enters your long-term memory, how do you get it back? Sometimes your brain may seem like a **deep,** dark **closet.** You open the door to look for

continued

[1] *not at all* = in no way

[2] *a cell* = in any living thing, the smallest part that can live by itself

[3] the *cerebral cortex*

something—you are sure it is in there somewhere—but you cannot find it. Maybe the information really is **not** there **anymore.** Information disappears when connections among brain cells become **weak.** They get weak if time passes and the connections are not used. That is why it is good to read your lecture[4] **notes** soon after the class. Don't wait too long to "look in the closet."

[4] a *lecture* = a long talk about a subject to a group or class

6   To keep the memory of something strong, think of it often. For example, look at those lecture notes the next day. Look at them the day after that, too. Every time you think about something, the connections in the brain get stronger. Then it is easier to remember the information when you need it.

Quick Comprehension Check

Read these sentences. Circle T (true) or F (false).

1. People have two types of memory.   T   F

2. Your short-term memory holds information for only a few days.   T   F

3. All information should go to your long-term memory.   T   F

4. We usually remember information that affects how we feel.   T   F

5. Information in long-term memory will always be there.   T   F

6. There are things you can do to help yourself remember information.   T   F

EXPLORING VOCABULARY

Thinking about the Vocabulary

Look at the target words and phrases. Which ones are new to you? Circle them here and in the reading. Then read "Your Memory at Work" again. Look at the context of each new word and phrase. Can you guess the meaning?

Target Words and Phrases

term (1)	practice (3)	concern (4)	closet (5)
store (2)	emotions (4)	connections (4)	not . . . anymore (5)
look up (2)	that is (4)	region (4)	weak (5)
disappeared (2)	upset (4)	deep (5)	notes (5)

Using the Vocabulary

A These sentences are about the reading. What is the meaning of each **boldfaced** word? Circle a, b, or c.

1. Information first enters your short-**term** memory. *Term* means:

   a. training   **b.** an amount of time   **c.** movement

2. Your short-term memory can **store** information for a short time only. *Store* means:

   a. cause   **b.** keep   **c.** sell

3. When you need a phone number, you can **look up** the number in the phone book. *Look up* means:

   a. come up   **b.** get into   **c.** try to find (information)

4. Some information leaves your brain quickly. It **disappears**. *Disappears* means:

   a. goes away completely   **b.** moves ahead   **c.** communicates

5. It is easier to remember new facts or ideas when they **concern** something we already know. *Concern* means:

   a. be about   **b.** destroy   **c.** end up

6. New **connections** form among brain cells when we learn something new. *Connections* means places:

   a. where nothing happens   **b.** where things come together   **c.** where something stops

7. The cerebral cortex is a **region** of the brain. *Region* means:

   a. a tool   **b.** a season   **c.** an area

8. Sometimes a fact was in someone's brain, but it's **not** there **anymore**. *Not . . . anymore* means:

   a. not . . . now   **b.** not . . . exactly   **c.** not . . . luckily

9. We forget things when connections among brain cells get **weak**. *Weak* means:

   a. sharp   **b.** not strong   **c.** secure

10. Students usually study their **notes** from class before they take a test. *Notes* means:

    a. information in writing   **b.** things to eat   **c.** professors

B These sentences use the target words and phrases **in new contexts.** Complete them with the words and phrases in the box.

concerns	connection	disappeared	looked up	not anymore
region	store	take notes	terms	weak

1. Students often _____ in class about things they want to remember.

2. I _____ the word *connection* in my dictionary.

3. We watched the plane until it _____ into the clouds.

4. He lives in a _____ where they get a lot of snow.

5. Where do you _____ your summer clothes during the winter?

6. At his university, there are two _____ in the school year: fall semester and spring semester.

7. I just received this letter from the bank. It _____ my credit card.

8. She gave up coffee. She used to drink ten cups a day, but _____.

9. Being sick for so long made him lose weight and feel _____.

10. When one fact, idea, or event affects another, we can say there is a _____ between them.

C Read each definition and look at the paragraph number in parentheses ( ). Look back at the reading to **find the target word or phrase** for each definition. Write it in the chart.

Definition	Target Word or Phrase
1. do something again and again to develop a skill (3)	
2. strong feelings such as love or hate (4)	
3. (a phrase meaning) "What I mean to say is . . ." (4)	
4. unhappy or worried (4)	
5. going far in or far down (5)	
6. a very small room where people usually hang clothes or store things (5)	

Building on the Vocabulary

Studying Word Grammar

Remember: The parts of speech are the different kinds of words, such as nouns, verbs, adjectives, and **adverbs**. An adverb can describe:

- a verb: *She **gently** <u>touched</u> my hand. Please <u>go</u> **ahead**.*
- an adjective: *I felt **very** <u>relaxed</u>. Is it <u>sharp</u> **enough**?*
- a whole statement: ***Luckily**, <u>it didn't rain much</u>.*

Circle the adverbs that describe the underlined words.

1. I (quickly) <u>realized</u> that it was a mistake.
2. Please be sure the door is securely <u>closed</u>.
3. She <u>spoke</u> calmly, but I knew she was upset.
4. He's a very <u>smart</u> boy.
5. By accident, <u>I took the wrong bus</u>.
6. We need to <u>leave</u> immediately.
7. The map <u>shows</u> exactly where to go.
8. The runner was too <u>weak</u> to continue.

DEVELOPING YOUR SKILLS

Understanding Topics of Paragraphs

A **Where is the information about these topics in "Your Memory at Work"? Skim the reading and write the paragraph number.**

__4__ a. How the brain deals with new information
_____ b. Types of memory
_____ c. Trouble remembering information
_____ d. Keeping connections among brain cells strong
_____ e. What short-term memory does
_____ f. Ways to pass information from short-term to long-term memory

B Write a sentence or two about each topic in Part A, beginning with the topic of the first paragraph and continuing in order. Use information from the reading, but do not copy sentences. Use your own words.

1. _The two basic types of memory are short-term and long-term memory._
   _____
   _____

2. _____
   _____
   _____

3. _____
   _____
   _____

4. _____
   _____
   _____

5. _____
   _____
   _____

6. _____
   _____
   _____

Summarizing

Complete the summary of "Your Memory at Work." Write one or more words on each line.

The two basic types of memory are ___short-term memory___ and
(1)

_____. Information stays in short-term memory for
(2)

_____. Then the information often _____.
(3)   (4)

When information is important to remember, it has to pass to

_____. When information enters long-term memory,
(5)

_____ are formed among brain cells. You make them stronger
(6)

each time you _____ the information.
(7)

Discussion

Talk about these questions in a small group.

1. What helps you remember new words in English?

2. How do you study vocabulary for a test?

3. What kinds of words are easy to remember? What kinds of words are hard?

Using New Words

Work with a partner. Choose five target words or phrases from the list on page 49. On a piece of paper, use each word or phrase in a sentence.

Writing

Choose a Discussion question above and write a paragraph about it. You can begin with:

- *Several things help me remember new words in English.*

- *I have several ways to study vocabulary for a test.*

- *Certain kinds of words are easier to remember than others.*

CHAPTER 7

Sleep and the Brain

Deep in Stage 4

GETTING READY TO READ

Talk with a partner or in a small group.

1. How many hours of sleep do you usually get?
2. Would you like to sleep more? Less? Explain why.
3. Do you think these statements are true or false?

   a. Our brains are completely at rest (they "turn off") when we sleep.   T   F

   b. We spend only 2–4% of our sleep time dreaming.   T   F

   c. When we are dreaming, we are most completely asleep. It is hardest to wake us up then.   T   F

Look for the answers to 3. a–c in the reading.

READING

Look at the words and picture next to the reading. Then read without stopping.

Sleep and the Brain

1   Human beings, like all mammals,[1] need sleep. People need an **average** of 7.5 hours a night. However, the average amount may not be right for you, just as the average-size shoe might not be right for your foot.

2   People may not need the same amount of sleep, but everyone needs the same two types of sleep. Your sleep is **divided** between REM sleep (*REM* is **pronounced** "rem") and NREM sleep (pronounced "en-rem" or "non-rem"):

- *REM* comes from the words "rapid[2] eye movement." During this type of sleep, your eyes move quickly. This movement shows that you are dreaming.

- *NREM* means "non-REM," or no eye movement. This is dreamless sleep, and it has four stages.

3   During the night, you go through several sleep cycles. A cycle is a **set**, or group, of events. Events in cycles happen again and again, like the cycle of seasons that happens every year. In each sleep cycle, you go from a light sleep to a deeper sleep and back again. You enter your first cycle when you fall asleep, and it lasts about 90 minutes. This cycle **includes** both REM sleep and the four stages of NREM sleep. It usually goes like this:

1. You begin with a **period** of light NREM sleep. This type of sleep is called Stage 1 sleep. During Stage 1 sleep, a noise could easily wake you up. This first period of Stage 1 sleep lasts less than 15 minutes.

2. Next, you move into another kind of NREM sleep for about 15–20 minutes. It is not so easy to wake you up from this type of sleep. It is called Stage 2 sleep. During the night, you spend about half your sleep time in Stage 2.

3. A short period of Stage 3 sleep is next. This marks the beginning of deep sleep. Your brain becomes less

[1] *mammals* = animals that get milk from their mothers when young

[2] *rapid* = fast

continued

active, and you breathe more slowly. Your muscles[3] relax.

4. Stage 4 follows Stage 3 and lasts 20 to 30 minutes. These two stages are a lot **alike**, but Stage 4 is your deepest sleep. Adults usually get all their Stage 4 sleep during the first few hours of the night. During this stage, some people talk or walk in their sleep.

[3] *muscles*

5. Next, you return to the level of Stage 2 sleep for a short time. Your heart **rate** and your breathing get faster.

6. Then you enter REM sleep. Your brain becomes very active for 10 to 20 minutes, and you have dreams. Your body doesn't move, except for your eyes. **In fact**, your body seems to be paralyzed during REM sleep. That is, it seems unable to move.

7. You return to Stage 2 sleep. This marks the end of your first sleep cycle of the night.

4   In most cases, you will go through a **series** of four to six sleep cycles each night. During the night, the cycles change. The amount of deep sleep **decreases**. You start to spend more time dreaming. **In general**, you spend about 20% of the night in REM sleep.

5   Why do people need sleep? Is it more for our bodies or for our brains? No one really knows. However, it is clear that sleep is important. What happens if people don't get enough? **Research** shows that we forget words, we are less **creative**, and we react[4] more slowly. You can probably think of other **effects** of not getting enough sleep. We all know we need it. Maybe future research will tell us why.

[4] *react* = feel or do something because of something that just happened

Quick Comprehension Check

Read these sentences. Circle T (true) or F (false).

1. All adults need the same amount of sleep each night. T   F

2. We experience two basic types of sleep. T   F

3. Your eyes move when you dream. T   F

4. REM sleep is deep and dreamless. T   F

5. During NREM sleep, we go through several stages. T   F

6. Scientists still can't explain why we need sleep. T   F

EXPLORING VOCABULARY

Thinking about the Vocabulary

Look at the target words and phrases. Which ones are new to you? Circle them here and in the reading. Then read "Sleep and the Brain" again. Look at the context of each new word and phrase. Can you guess the meaning?

Target Words and Phrases			
average (1)	includes (3)	rate (3)	in general (4)
divided (2)	period (3)	in fact (3)	research (5)
pronounced (2)	active (3)	series (4)	creative (5)
set (3)	alike (3)	decreases (4)	effects (5)

Using the Vocabulary

A These sentences are **about the reading**. Complete them with the words in the box.

active	average	creative	decreases	divided	effects
includes	rate	research	series	set	

1. People need an _____ of 7.5 hours of sleep. This is the usual amount, but some people need more and others need less.

2. Our sleep is _____ between two types of sleep. We spend part of the night in REM sleep and part in NREM sleep.

3. A _____ is a group of things that belong together or a group of events that have a connection, like the different types of sleep in a sleep cycle.

4. REM sleep and NREM sleep are both part of your first sleep cycle. This cycle _____ both types of sleep.

5. During Stages 3 and 4, your brain is less _____ than usual. Your brain doesn't do so much.

6. Your heart _____ tells how fast your heart is working (for example, 60 or 70 times a minute).

7. During the night, you go through a _____ of four to six sleep cycles. This means the cycles happen one after another, in order: the first cycle, then the second, the third, and so on.

8. During the night, the type of sleep you get changes. Your dream time increases and your deep sleep time _____.

9. Scientists do _____ on sleep. They study it to learn new things about it.

10. When we don't get enough sleep, it is harder to think of new ideas or different ways to do things. We are less _____.

11. Forgetting words, thinking more slowly, getting angry more easily—these are some of the _____, or results, of not getting enough sleep.

B These sentences use the target words **in new contexts. Complete them with the words in the box.**

active	average	creative	decrease	divided	effect
included	rates	research	series	sets	

1. One hundred _____ by two is fifty.

2. Some animals sleep during the day and are _____ at night.

3. They own two _____ of dishes, one for everyday use and one for special meals.

4. *Superman—The Movie* was the first in a long _____ of Superman movies.

5. Artists are _____ people. They are always thinking of new ideas.

6. This is a very smart class. Everyone's grades are far above the _____.

7. Marie and Bill plan to save more money, so they will _____ their spending.

8. All her English practice had a great _____ on her skills.

9. These scientists do _____ on the brain and how different foods affect it.

10. Children learn at different _____. Some learn quickly, others more slowly.

11. My class _____ students from South America. Two of my classmates were Colombian.

C Read these sentences. Write the **boldfaced** words or phrases next to their definitions.

  a. How do you **pronounce** your last name?

  b. Each **period** at the high school is 50 minutes long.

  c. She and her sister look **alike**, but they are very different.

  d. **In general**, I take good notes, but sometimes I don't understand them later!

  e. Their school term is almost over. **In fact**, Friday is the last day of classes.

Target Words/Phrases   Definitions

  1. _____ = almost exactly the same

  2. _____ = an amount of time

  3. _____ = usually, in most cases

  4. _____ = say the sound of a letter or word the correct way

  5. _____ = This is a phrase used to add more information, often
          surprising information.

Building on the Vocabulary

Studying Word Grammar

The verb *affect* and the noun *effect* are different.

  • Use *affect* to mean "make changes in": *Will missing class **affect** my grade?*

  • Use *effect* to refer to a result: *All that candy had a bad **effect** on her teeth.*

A Complete the sentences with *affects* or *effects*.

  1. The weather often _____ my plans for the weekend.

  2. I'm feeling the _____ of too little sleep.

  3. A cold usually _____ your ability to smell things.

  4. The new drug is not yet for sale. Researchers are still studying its

      _____.

B Write your own sentences with *affect* and *effect*.

  1. _____

  2. _____

DEVELOPING YOUR SKILLS

Reading for Details

**Read these sentences. Then reread "Sleep and the Brain" for the answers.
If the reading doesn't give the information, check (✓) *It doesn't say.***

	True	False	It doesn't say.
1. The average person needs 7.5 hours of sleep a night.			
2. The two basic types of sleep are REM and NREM sleep.			
3. People's eyes move quickly during NREM sleep.			
4. Most people never remember any dreams.			
5. Stage 1 sleep is very light.			
6. People spend about half the night in Stage 2 sleep.			
7. People start dreaming during Stage 3 sleep.			
8. Some people walk in their sleep while they dream.			
9. About 20% of people talk in their sleep.			
10. Too little sleep has bad effects on people.			

Summarizing

**Complete this summary of "Sleep and the Brain." Write one or more
words on each line.**

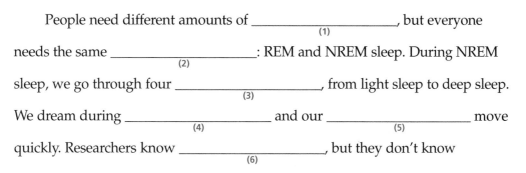

People need different amounts of _____, but everyone
(1)

needs the same _____: REM and NREM sleep. During NREM
(2)

sleep, we go through four _____, from light sleep to deep sleep.
(3)

We dream during _____ and our _____ move
(4)   (5)

quickly. Researchers know _____, but they don't know
(6)

_____.
(7)

Interviewing

How sleepy are you? Work with a partner, and take turns asking the questions below.* Write your partner's answers. Use numbers:

0 = No   1 = Probably not   2 = Maybe   3 = Probably

WOULD YOU FALL ASLEEP WHILE YOU WERE . . .	
1. sitting and reading?	
2. watching TV?	
3. riding in a car for an hour?	
4. lying down in the afternoon?	
5. sitting and talking to someone?	
6. sitting quietly after lunch?	
7. sitting in a car that is stopped in traffic for a few minutes?	
Total:	

Add up the numbers, and tell your partner the total.
0–6: That's great! You're getting enough sleep.
7–8: You're average.
9 and up: Get more sleep!

*Based on the Epworth Sleepiness Scale designed by Murray W. Johns, M.D.

Using New Words

Ask and answer these questions with a partner. Use one of the words or phrases in parentheses. Then tell the class something about your partner.

1. What is the **average** number of hours you (sleep/spend on homework) a night?
2. How much is 100 **divided** by (10/25)?
3. **In general**, do you like (sweet/salty) foods?
4. Do you and anyone in your family (look/think) **alike**?
5. What is a good job for someone who is very (**creative/active**)?

Writing

Are you a light sleeper (everything wakes you up) or a heavy sleeper (nothing wakes you up)? Do you get enough sleep in general? What happens when you don't get enough? Write a paragraph about yourself as a sleeper.

CHAPTER 8

In Your Dreams

The idea for the story of Frankenstein came to writer Mary Shelley in a dream.

GETTING READY TO READ

Talk in a small group or with the whole class.

1. What's happening in the picture above?
2. How often do you remember your dreams?
3. What do you remember about your dreams?
4. Do you think people can get creative ideas while they're sleeping?
5. Do you think people can find the answers to problems in their sleep?
6. Do you think animals dream?

READING

Look at the words and pictures next to the reading. Then read without stopping.

In Your Dreams

1   Bruno Beckham has a good job. He also has a new job offer. He has to make a decision **right away**, but he isn't sure **whether or not** he should accept the offer. What will he do? He's not going to make up his mind tonight. "I'll know in the morning," he says. Why? Will the right answer come to Bruno in his dreams? "I don't know," he says, "but **whenever** I have a big decision to make, I have to sleep on it."

2   When you face a big decision, do your friends say, "Sleep on it!"? People in Italy say, "Dormici su." It means exactly the same thing. In France, they say, "La nuit porte conseil." This means "The night brings advice." People in many **cultures** believe that something **useful** happens during sleep. But what happens, and why?

3   Maybe the answer can be found in our dreams. Many people believe that dreams help us in our **daily** lives. The famous German composer[1] Beethoven believed this. He said that he wrote music that came to him in dreams. The American boxer[2] Floyd Patterson believed it, too. He used to dream of new ways to move in a fight. He **claimed** that these moves helped him surprise other fighters. Srinivasa Ramanujan, an important mathematician[3] from India, was a great believer in dreams. He said all his **discoveries** came to him that way. Scientists and writers report getting ideas from dreams, too. The English writer Mary Shelley did. She said that the story of Frankenstein came to her in a dream.

4   Scientists don't agree on what dreams mean or why people dream. Some say that dreams have no meaning and no **purpose**. They say dreams show **activity** in the brain, but it's like the activity of a car going in circles with no driver. It doesn't do anything useful. **On the other hand**, some scientists claim that dreams are **helpful**. They say

continued

[1] a *composer* = a writer of music

[2] a *boxer*

[3] a *mathematician* = someone who does research in math

dreams are good for learning new skills and developing strong memories.

5   Some researchers hope to learn more about people's dreams by studying the dreams of animals. At the Massachusetts Institute of Technology (MIT), scientists have studied the dreams of rats. During the day, the rats were learning to run through a maze.[4] The scientists made pictures of the activity in the rats' brains. Then, during REM sleep, the rats' brains showed exactly the same activity. The rats were going through the maze again in their dreams. Researchers could tell if the dreaming rats were running or standing **still**. In fact, MIT researcher Matthew Wilson reported, "We can pinpoint[5] where they would be in the maze if they were awake."

6   Were the rats practicing for the next day? Does dreaming **somehow** help them learn and remember? Do human brains work this way? Wilson and his team **are searching** for the answers to these questions. Right now, we have no good **explanation** for dreams. There is a lot we don't know about the sleeping brain. Maybe one day we will know all its secrets.

Matthew Wilson's words come from an article by Sarah Smith, "Caught in a Maze," *Psychology Today* 34, no. 3 (May 2001), 20.

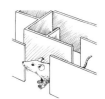

[4] a rat in a *maze*

[5] *pinpoint* = show exactly where something is without any mistake

QUICK COMPREHENSION CHECK

Read these sentences. Circle T (true) or F (false).

1. Bruno Beckham says sleep helps him make decisions.   T   F

2. Many people think dreams help us.   T   F

3. According to some famous people, good ideas come in dreams. T   F

4. Scientists all agree: There are two basic reasons why we dream. T   F

5. Scientists say dreams are bad for your brain.   T   F

6. Only human beings dream.   T   F

EXPLORING VOCABULARY

Thinking about the Vocabulary

Look at the target words and phrases. Which ones are new to you? Circle them here and in the reading. Then read "In Your Dreams" again. Look at the context of each new word and phrase. Can you guess the meaning?

Target Words and Phrases			
right away (1)	useful (2)	purpose (4)	still (5)
whether or not (1)	daily (3)	activity (4)	somehow (6)
whenever (1)	claimed (3)	on the other hand (4)	are searching (6)
cultures (2)	discoveries (3)	helpful (4)	explanation (6)

Using the Vocabulary

A These sentences are **about the reading**. Complete them with the words and phrases in the box.

activity	are searching	claimed	cultures	explanation
on the other hand	somehow	still	useful	whenever
whether or not				

1. Bruno doesn't know _____ to accept his new job offer. He can choose to accept it or not.

2. Every time that he faces a big decision, Bruno sleeps on it. This means, _____ Bruno has a big decision to make, he waits until morning.

3. People in different countries have different _____. They have their own ways of doing things—their own art, music, religious beliefs, etc.

4. Many people believe something _____ happens while we sleep, something that helps us.

5. The boxer Floyd Patterson _____ that his dreams helped him win fights. Was it true? No one knows for sure. However, this is what he said.

6. Dreams show _____ in the brain. Something is happening there.

7. Some scientists say that dreams have no effect on us. _____, there is research showing that dreams help us learn and remember.

8. Sometimes the rats moved through the maze. At other times, they stood _____.

9. Did dreaming help the rats in some way? Did it _____ help them remember where to go in the maze?

10. The researchers at MIT _____ for answers to the question "Why do we dream?" They are trying to find answers.

11. Right now, no one can really explain dreams. We have no good _____ for them.

B These sentences use the target words and phrases **in new contexts**. Complete them with the words and phrases in the box.

activity	claimed	culture	explanation	on the other hand
searched for	somehow	still	useful	whenever
whether or not				

1. The police _____ the missing child.

2. You must sit _____ when I take your picture.

3. She couldn't decide _____ to cut her hair.

4. In general, the stores are busier _____ it rains.

5. I don't know how he did it, but _____, he managed to win.

6. He's so busy that he never seems to sit down! His days are full of _____.

7. I don't understand why she was so upset. Did she give you any _____?

8. You want to store _____ facts in long-term memory so that you'll remember them later.

9. Their _____ teaches them not to show their emotions in public.

10. Bob _____ that his dog could read his mind, but I think he was imagining things.

11. Chris has two job offers. The first one pays better; _____ the second one sounds more secure. A secure job **vs.** a better-paying one— which is more important?

> **Common Abbreviations**
> The abbreviation *vs.* is short for the Latin word *versus.* It means "as opposed to or against." This abbreviation is often used for two things being compared, two sports teams going against each other, or the two sides in a court case.

C Read each definition and look at the paragraph number in parentheses ( ). Look back at the reading to **find the target word or phrase** for each definition. Write it in the chart.

Definition	Target Word or Phrase
1. happening very soon, immediately (1)	
2. happening every day (3)	
3. new facts, or answers to questions, that someone learns (3)	
4. a reason for happening or for doing something (4)	
5. useful, good for something (4)	

Building on the Vocabulary

Studying Collocations

The word **right** means "immediately" or "very soon" when it is used with certain other words. Look at these examples of phrases with *right:*

- I need the money **right away.**
- I'm coming **right back.** / I'll be **right back.**
- We're leaving **right now.**

Write three sentences using the three phrases above with *right.*

1. _____

2. _____

3. _____

DEVELOPING YOUR SKILLS

Fact vs. Opinion

Ⓐ **Decide if each statement is a fact or an opinion. Base your answers on information from the reading. Circle *Fact* when it is possible to show that the statement is true. Circle *Opinion* when people may believe it, but they can't show that it is true.**

1. There is activity in the brain while we sleep.   (Fact)/Opinion
2. Our dreams are useful.   Fact/Opinion
3. Some famous people have believed in the power of dreams.   Fact/Opinion
4. Dreams help us learn new skills.   Fact/Opinion
5. MIT scientists have studied the dreams of rats.   Fact/Opinion
6. In the future, scientists will discover why we dream.   Fact/Opinion

Ⓑ **Write two sentences.**

1. Write a fact about dreams from "In Your Dreams."

   _____

   _____

2. Write an opinion of your own about dreams.

   _____

   _____

Summarizing

Write answers to these questions on a piece of paper. Then use your answers to write a summary of the reading. Write your summary as a paragraph.

1. When do people say, "Sleep on it"?
2. Why do they say it?
3. What do some people say dreams can do?
4. What example can you give of dreams being useful to someone?
5. What do scientists say about the meaning and purpose of dreams?
6. Why do scientists study the dreams of animals?
7. What is one possible reason for dreaming?

Sharing Opinions

Talk about these questions in a small group.

1. Is it important to remember and think about your dreams? Why or why not?

2. Would you like someone to tell you the meaning of your dreams? Why or why not?

3. Do you believe people can learn while they sleep? Why or why not?

Using New Words

Work with a partner. Choose five target words or phrases from the list on page 66. On a piece of paper, use each word or phrase in a sentence.

Writing

Choose a topic. Write a paragraph.

1. Whenever Bruno Beckham faces a big decision, he sleeps on it. What do you do? What, or who, helps you make decisions? How?

2. Think about a time when you had to make a choice. What did you decide? How did you make your decision? Do you think it was the right one? Why or why not?

Wrap-up

REVIEWING VOCABULARY

(A) Which of the words below can describe a person? There are five correct answers. The first one has been marked for you. Check four more boxes.

A person can be . . .

- ☑ awake.
- ☐ feed.
- ☐ upset.
- ☐ creative.
- ☐ luckily.
- ☐ weak.
- ☐ daily.
- ☐ smart.
- ☐ weight.

(B) Think about the type of words in each of these groups. Are they nouns, verbs, or adjectives? Cross out the word that does not belong in each group.

1. helpful   ~~somehow~~   deep   active
2. region   period   purpose   alike
3. closet   realize   create   look up
4. emotion   activity   anymore   culture

(C) Complete the sentences below. There is one extra word or phrase.

according to	concerns	contain	in fact	meant
on the other hand	rate	right away	set	whether or not

1. I don't know _____ I'll go. I have to decide.
2. There is a complete _____ of tools in that box.
3. The doctor listened to the patient's heart _____.
4. Call if you need help, and I'll come _____.
5. Tea doesn't _____ as much caffeine as coffee.
6. I'm a little tired. _____, I think I'll go to bed.
7. _____ the weather report, the rain should end soon.
8. He had a lot of homework. That _____ he couldn't go out.
9. His research _____ the connections between sleep and memory.

EXPANDING VOCABULARY

A A **prefix** is a word part added to the beginning of a word. It changes the word's meaning. Study the chart below.

Prefix	Meaning	Examples
dis-	not or opposite of	**dis**agree, **dis**appear, **dis**connect
ex-	was in the past, but not now	**ex**-boss, **ex**-boyfriend, **ex**-wife
re-	again or back	**re**create, **re**supply, **re**train

Add the correct prefix to the word in parentheses, and use the new word.

1. (agree) Researchers _____*disagree*_____ about the purpose of dreams. They have different ideas about why we dream.

2. (wife) He and his _____ never speak to each other.

3. (supply) The truck carried water to _____ the firefighters.

4. (connect) The phone isn't working. Did someone _____ it?

5. (create) The artist is trying to _____ the work that was destroyed in the fire.

6. (appear) When you visit, my cats _____. They're afraid of you.

B A **suffix** is a word part added to the end of a word to make a new word. The new word is often a different part of speech. For example, the suffix -*tion* (also -*sion* or -*ion*) added to a verb often creates a noun. Sometimes the noun has a change in the spelling of the **stem** or **root** (the main part of the word).

Choose the word that completes the sentence correctly.

1. (connect, connection) Two bridges across the river _____ the towns on either side.

2. (create, creation) Which plan will _____ more jobs?

3. (divide, division) It is easy to _____ an orange into pieces.

4. (explain, explanation) Did he give any _____ for his actions?

5. (invent, invention) The telephone was a great _____.

6. (pronounce, pronunciation) I know the meaning of the word but I'm not sure of its _____.

PLAYING WITH WORDS

There are 12 target words from Unit 2 in this puzzle. The words go across (→) and down (↓). Find the words and circle them. Then use them to complete the sentences below.

```
A  X  Z  P  U  R  P  O  S  E
M  I  N  C  L  U  D  E  T  T
O  S  T  I  L  L  A  X  O  Q
U  D  I  S  C  O  V  E  R  Y
N  D  K  W  T  W  E  K  E  S
T  X  V  M  E  K  R  M  Z  E
S  I  N  C  R  E  A  S  E  R
X  Z  H  B  M  Z  G  X  H  I
S  U  P  P  L  Y  E  Z  R  E
W  W  H  E  N  E  V  E  R  S
```

1. They have a big family, so they buy food in large _____amounts_____.

2. Why do we have to do this work? What's the _____ of it?

3. In the summer, I _____ my winter clothes in the back of my closet.

4. Does the price _____ the tax, or do we have to add that?

5. Stand _____ so that I can take your picture.

6. There is an _____ of two children in each family.

7. The scientist explained her _____ to reporters.

8. They worry about the long-_____ effects of this change.

9. After a long _____ of meetings, they came to an agreement.

10. The boss promised us an _____ in pay.

11. Parents try to _____ their children with everything they need.

12. Come _____ you want. We'll be home all day.

BUILDING DICTIONARY SKILLS

Finding Words in the Dictionary, Part 2

Sometimes it is easy to find the word you are looking for in the dictionary. For example, look at *immediately* below. It follows *immediate*. Each word has its own entry in the dictionary. Sometimes a word does not have its own entry. For example, look for *emotionally* below.

---

im·me·di·ate /ɪˈmidiɪt/ *adj* **1** happening or done at once with no delay: *Police demanded the immediate release of the hostages*. **2** existing now, and needing to be dealt with quickly: *Our immediate concern was to stop the fire from spreading*. **3** near something or someone in time or place: *We have no plans to expand the business in the immediate future*. **4** **immediate family** your parents, children, brothers, and sisters
im·me·di·ate·ly /ɪˈmidiɪtli/ *adv* **1** at once and with no delay: *Mandy answered the phone immediately*. **2** very near to something in time or place: *We left immediately afterwards*. | *They live immediately above us*.

---

e·mo·tion·al /ɪˈmoʊʃənəl/ *adj* **1** making people have strong feelings: *The end of the movie was really emotional*. **2** showing your emotions to other people, especially by crying: *Please don't get all emotional*. **3** relating to your feelings or how they are controlled: *the emotional development of children* **4** influenced by what you feel rather than what you know: *an emotional response to the problem* —**emotionally** *adv*
e·mo·tive /ɪˈmoʊtɪv/ *adj* making people have strong feelings: *an emotive speech about the effects of war*

The adverb *emotionally* does not have its own entry. Adverbs ending in *-ly* are often at the end of adjective entries. Other kinds of words also can come at the end of entries.

1. Circle the adverb form of *lucky* below.
2. Circle words related to *useful* at the end of the entry below.

---

luck·y /ˈlʌki/ *adj* **1** having good luck; fortunate: *He's lucky to still be alive*. | *"I just got the last bus." "That was lucky!"* **2** **I'll be lucky if** SPOKEN said when you think something is very unlikely: *I'll be lucky if I can pay my bills this month*. —**luckily** *adv*: *Luckily, no one was hurt*.
—opposite UNLUCKY —see usage note at LUCK[1]

---

use·ful /ˈyusfəl/ *adj* helping you to do or to get what you want: *useful information* | *a useful book for travelers* —**usefully** *adv*
—**usefulness** *n* [U]

---

3. Fill in the word family chart for *useful*. Then write two sentences with members of this word family.

Noun	Verb	Adjective	Adverb
	use		

a. _____

b. _____

UNIT 3

COMMUNICATION

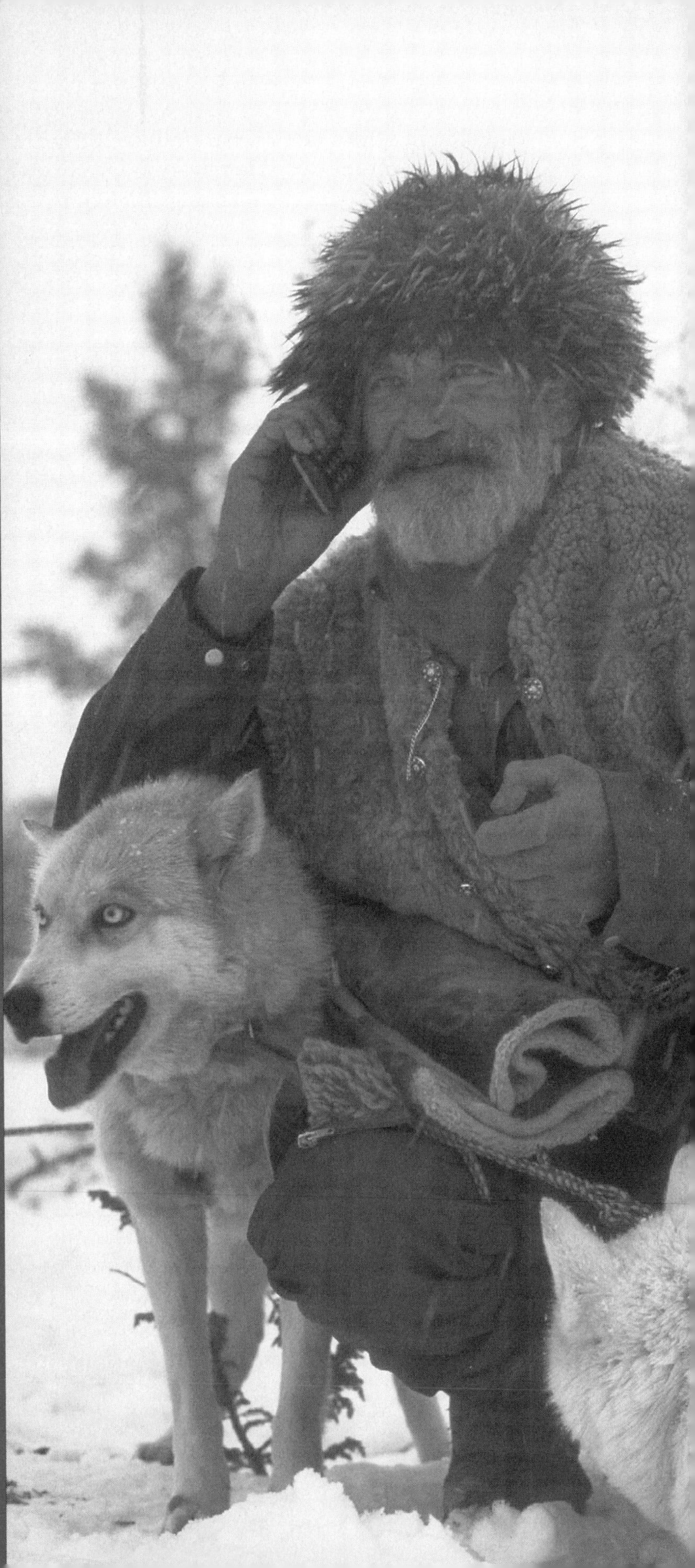

CHAPTER 9

Who Does It Better?

African elephants—in conversation?

GETTING READY TO READ

Talk with a partner or in a small group.

Do human beings and animals communicate in each of the ways listed below? Circle *Yes* or *No*. For each *yes* answer, give an example.

	Words	Sounds	Movements	Smells
Humans	(Yes) *Hello* No	Yes No	Yes No	Yes No
Animals	Yes No	Yes No	Yes No	Yes No

Share your answers with the rest of the class.

READING

Look at the words and pictures next to the reading. Then read without stopping. Don't worry about new words. Don't stop to use a dictionary. Just keep reading!

Who Does It Better?

1   Who is better at communicating, people or animals? If you think about human inventions such as the telephone, the radio, and the Internet, then the answer to this question seems clear. Human beings are "The Great Communicators." However, think about your own **personal** communication skills. If you compare what you can do with the abilities of certain animals, then the answer is not so simple. Animals can do some things that people cannot.

2   We humans depend on our **voices** for much of our communication. We use words and sounds to pass information to the people around us. But the sound of our voices cannot travel very far. Even the voice of an opera singer[1] with years of training cannot be heard as well as many animal voices. Think of the elephant, for example. Its voice has great **strength** because of the elephant's great size, so it can be heard for miles. Elephants can also make very **low** sounds, sounds that are too deep for any human to hear. These low sounds let elephants communicate over even longer distances. The sounds travel in sound **waves** through the air and through the **ground**. How do elephants receive messages like these? No one knows. Maybe they hear them with their ears, or maybe they **sense** them in some other way. It is possible that these sound waves pass from the ground through the elephants' toenails[2] into their bones and then to their brains!

3   Let's also consider communication **through** movement. For example, some people use dance to share ideas or emotions. When we watch these dancers, we may understand what they are thinking or feeling. But even a great dancer's ability to speak through movement can't match the average honeybee's.[3] Bees do a very special dance to tell other bees where to find food. The dance tells the other bees which way to go so that they can fly in a **straight** line to the food. It also tells them exactly how far to go. It gives clear

continued

[1] an *opera singer*

[2] an elephant's *toenails*

[3] a *honeybee*

information about both the **direction** and the distance to a **specific** place.

4   Many animals communicate through smells. A smell can carry a lot of information. For example, a smell can say, "This is my place—get out!" or a smell can give an **invitation**. Often a **female** animal who wants a **male** to come to her will produce a smell to **attract** him. It says to the male, "Here I am—come and find me." Many animals receive messages through their noses just as humans do. For example, your nose might tell you, "There's fresh coffee in the kitchen. It's time to get out of bed." But people don't usually use smells to communicate, and our noses don't receive messages very well. We certainly can't **compete** with the Great White Shark.[4] A large part of its brain—14% of it—is just for "reading" smells in the ocean.

[4] a *Great White Shark*

5   Our noses are not the best, our voices are not the strongest, and our dancing may not say anything at all. But people are the only ones with words and written languages. So, maybe we can still say we are "The Great Communicators."

Quick Comprehension Check

Read these sentences. Circle T (true) or F (false).

1. Humans communicate better than animals in every way.   T   F

2. Elephants can make sounds that travel far.   T   F

3. Bees can communicate with other bees through movement.   T   F

4. A honeybee dances to tell other bees about danger.   T   F

5. Both animals and people use their noses to get information.   T   F

6. The Great White Shark is good at "reading" smells in the ocean.   T   F

EXPLORING VOCABULARY

Thinking about the Vocabulary

Which target words are new to you? Circle them here and in the reading. Then read "Who Does It Better?" again. Look at the context of each new word. Can you guess the meaning?

Target Words			
personal (1)	**waves** (2)	**straight** (3)	**female** (4)
voices (2)	**ground** (2)	**direction** (3)	**male** (4)
strength (2)	**sense** (2)	**specific** (3)	**attract** (4)
low (2)	**through** (3)	**invitation** (4)	**compete** (4)

Using the Vocabulary

A Complete the sentences. Write *female*, *ground*, *straight*, and *waves*.

1. She's sitting on the _____.

2. _____ birds lay eggs.

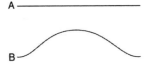

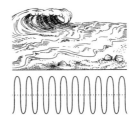

3. Only line A is _____.

4. Here are ocean _____ and sound waves.

B These sentences are **about the reading**. Complete them with the words in the box.

attract	compete	direction	invitation	low	male
personal	sense	specific	strength	through	voice

1. Each person has his or her own _____ communication skills. These are the skills that belong to that one person.

2. When you speak or sing, you use your _____. Other people hear it.

3. An elephant has great _____. This means an elephant is very strong.

4. Elephants sometimes make sounds that are not high enough for the human ear to hear. These are very _____ sounds. (Other animals, such as dogs, can hear sounds that are too high for human ears.)

5. Elephants hear with their ears. Maybe they also _____ sounds through their toenails. It is not clear how they receive some very low sounds.

6. Some animals, like bees, communicate _____ movement. They use movement.

7. The bee's dance tells other bees the _____ to fly in (which way to go) and also how far to go to find food.

8. A bee can tell other bees how to get to a _____ place—that is, one certain place.

9. A smell can mean "Go away!" or it can give an _____, a friendly offer like, "Come and be with me!"

10. A female animal may produce a smell to get the attention of a _____ animal. She wants him to know she is there.

11. When a female wants a male to come to her, she tries to _____ him, or make him interested in her.

12. Humans should not try to _____ with the Great White Shark as far as the ability to smell is concerned. The shark would always win.

C These sentences use the target words **in new contexts**. Complete them with the words in the box.

attracted	compete	direction	invitation	low	male
personal	sensed	specific	strength	through	voices

1. I was upset about not getting an _____ to the party.

2. "Put it in *a* closet" means in any closet, but "Put it in *the* closet" means in one _____ closet.

3. The scientist made his discoveries _____ years of hard work.

4. At night, the light _____ insects, so we turned it off.

5. She turned the car around and drove off in the opposite _____.

6. She didn't say anything, but I _____ that something was wrong.

7. Men usually have lower _____ than women do.

8. He has learned about the business world both in school and through his own _____ experience.

9. Athletes from many countries _____ at the Olympic games. Each person tries to win.

10. He was so sick he didn't have the _____ to get out of bed.

11. _____ animals are often larger than female animals of the same kind.

12. A piano makes _____ sounds when you play the keys on the left end.

Building on the Vocabulary

Studying Word Grammar

The word *low* is usually an adjective. It can describe:

- a quiet or deep sound: *a low whisper, a low voice*
- something that isn't high or tall: *a low wall, a low building*
- a small amount or number: *low-fat food, low grades*
- the bad nature of something: *a low opinion, a low trick*

Low can also be:

- an adverb (*The plane was flying low.*)
- a noun (*Prices fell to a new low.*)

A **Is *low* a noun, an adjective, or an adverb in each sentence? Circle your answers.**

1. The TV sits on a low table.   *n. / adj. / adv.*
2. Everybody's life has its highs and lows. *n. / adj. / adv.*
3. Shoppers like low prices.   *n. / adj. / adv.*
4. He threw the ball low.   *n. / adj. / adv.*
5. I got a low score on the test.   *n. / adj. / adv.*

B **Write four sentences using *low* in four different ways.**

1. _____

   _____

2. _____

   _____

3. _____

   _____

4. _____

   _____

DEVELOPING YOUR SKILLS

Reading for Details

Read these sentences. Then reread "Who Does It Better?" for the answers. If the reading doesn't give the information, check (✓) It doesn't say.

	True	False	It doesn't say.
1. We depend on our voices for much of our communication with other people.			
2. Elephants have the best hearing of any animals.			
3. Sound waves can travel only through the air.			
4. The dance of the honeybee tells other bees which way to go to find food.			
5. The dance of the honeybee tells other bees what kind of food they will find.			
6. All living things use smells to communicate.			
7. Most of a Great White Shark's brain is used for reading smells in the ocean.			
8. Words give human beings a very special way to communicate.			

Understanding Main Ideas and Supporting Details

Ⓐ Match the main ideas and the details that support them. Write the letters.

Main Ideas	Supporting Details
_c_ 1. Certain inventions help people communicate.	a. Bees do a dance to tell other bees where food is.
___ 2. The human voice can't travel as far as some animal voices.	b. A female animal may produce a smell to attract a male.
___ 3. Some animals communicate through movement.	c. Think of the telephone, the radio, and the Internet.
___ 4. Animals sometimes use smells to communicate with other animals.	d. The Great White Shark has a much better sense of smell than we do.
___ 5. People can't compete with animals in some ways.	e. An elephant's voice can be heard for miles.

B Think of another example to support each general statement in Part A. Write complete sentences.

1. <u>Inventions like pens and paper let people write to each other.</u>

2. _____

3. _____

4. _____

5. _____

Discussion

Talk about these questions in a small group.

1. According to the reading, people don't usually communicate through smell. But what are people saying when they put on something that smells good, such as perfume, cologne, or aftershave?

2. In what ways do people and animals communicate with each other? Think of at least three examples.

Using New Words

Work with a partner. Take turns asking and answering these questions. Then tell the class something your partner said.

1. Who has **straight** hair?
2. What singer's **voice** do you like?
3. What are three ways to build up your **strength**?
4. When or where do you sit on the **ground**?
5. How would you complete this sentence? *I would like an **invitation** to . . .*

Writing

Choose a topic. Write a paragraph.

1. Pets sometimes play an important part in people's lives. People communicate with their pets in several ways. Have you ever had a pet? How do or did you communicate?

2. What kind of animal would you like to be? Why? Tell both the good and the bad things about being this kind of animal.

3. Imagine that you are an animal. Describe a day in your life.

CHAPTER 10

When and Why We Laugh

A room full of laughter

GETTING READY TO READ

Talk in a small group or with the whole class.

1. Look at the picture. Which person is laughing "in English"? What about the others? Do you see a word that is used in your first language to show laughter?

2. Ask one person in your group to make himself or herself laugh. Then talk about what happened in your group when this person laughed, or tried to.

3. How many people in your group are ticklish?[1]

[1] *ticklish* = easily made to laugh when someone touches certain parts of your body

READING

Look at the words and picture next to the reading. Then read without stopping.

When and Why We Laugh

1　　People have many ways to **express** themselves—to show how they feel or what they think. One way that feels especially good is **laughter**. We laugh when we see or hear something funny, and we laugh sometimes just because other people are laughing. Some people laugh when someone tickles[1] them. Laughter has an important place in human communication. The question is, what are we saying when we laugh?

2　　A team of psychologists[2] studied the laughter of 120 students at an American university. They had the students watch funny movies. Sometimes the students were alone, and sometimes they were in pairs. The psychologists **recorded** the students' laughter, and they **noticed** that the students made a wide **variety** of laughing sounds. They found that there were differences both in how a student laughed and in how many times the student laughed. Both these things depended on his or her partner. Was the other person the same sex or the opposite sex? And what was the **relationship** between the two? Was the person a friend or a **stranger**? Here are some of the researchers' findings:[3]

- Men laughed much more during the movies when they were with a friend. The friend could be male or female. They laughed much less when their partner was a stranger or when they were alone.

- Women laughed most with men friends.

- Women laughed in a higher voice with male strangers.

- There were three basic types of laughs: high song-like laughs, laughs with the sounds coming mostly through the nose, and low grunting[4] laughs like the sounds a pig makes.

3　　In another **study**, the researchers asked people to listen to these three types of laughter. They wanted to know which kind people liked best. They asked questions like: Does the person laughing sound friendly? Do you think he or she

continued

[1] *tickle* = touch certain parts of someone's body to make him or her laugh

[2] a *psychologist* = someone trained in the study of the mind and how it works

[3] *findings* = the information that someone learns as a result of research

[4] A pig makes low *grunting* sounds.

sounds **attractive**? Would you like to meet this person? Most people **preferred** the high song-like sounds. They were attracted to people who laughed this way.

4   The researchers believe that laughter is a tool we use, usually without thinking about it. They say we use it to influence the emotions and **behavior** of other people. We often use it to show that we want to be friends. In fact, most laughter during conversation is *not* because we are listening to something funny. Researcher Robert Provine says that in conversation, listeners **actually** laugh less than speakers do. The speakers' laughter has a social[5] purpose. Provine calls laughter "the **oil** in the social machine." **In other words**, it helps relationships between people work **smoothly**.

5   Did you know that humans are not the only ones who laugh? Dogs do, too. Dog laughter sounds something like "Huh, huh, huh." It seems to express the idea "Let's play!" Another university researcher, Jaak Panksepp, reports that rats laugh, too. They laugh when he tickles them. But please don't go out and try this. Panksepp **warns**, "You have to know the rat."

Robert Provine's words come from "He Who Laughs Less?" *PBS—Scientific American Frontiers: Life's Little Questions II,* <www.pbs.org/saf>. Jaak Panksepp was quoted in "Don't Look Now, But Is That Dog Laughing?" *Science News* 160, no. 4 (July 28, 2001), 55.

[5] *social* = relating to living together in groups

Quick Comprehension Check

Read these sentences. Circle T (true) or F (false).

1. Laughter is part of human communication. T F
2. Researchers study why and how people laugh. T F
3. The people who are with us affect how we laugh. T F
4. The college students in the study laughed only with their friends. T F
5. Researchers say that we laugh to influence other people. T F
6. Only human beings laugh. T F

EXPLORING VOCABULARY

Thinking about the Vocabulary

Which target words and phrases are new to you? Circle them here and in the reading. Then read "When and Why We Laugh" again. Look at the context of each new word and phrase. Can you guess the meaning?

Target Words and Phrases			
express (1)	variety (2)	attractive (3)	oil (4)
laughter (1)	relationship (2)	preferred (3)	in other words (4)
recorded (2)	stranger (2)	behavior (4)	smoothly (4)
noticed (2)	study (3)	actually (4)	warns (5)

Using the Vocabulary

 These sentences are about the reading. Complete them with the words and phrases in the box.

actually	behavior	express	in other words	laughter	noticed
preferred	relationship	studies	variety	warned	

1. People communicate ideas and emotions with words. We can also
   _____ ourselves with sounds.
2. The sound of _____ sometimes makes other people laugh,
   too.
3. The researchers _____, or realized, that the students laughed
   differently.
4. Not everyone laughs the same way. People make a _____ of
   sounds.
5. Researchers studied the laughter of pairs of students. It was important to
   consider the _____, or connection, between the two
   students—that is, how well they knew each other.
6. Scientists do _____ to find the answers to research questions.
   Then they write reports on their results.

7. In one study, people listened to three types of laughter and chose the one they liked best. Most people _____ the same type.

8. Researchers say we use laughter to influence the _____ of other people—that is, to influence what they do and say.

9. Who laughs more in conversation, the speaker or the listener? Most people would guess "the listener," but _____, it is the speaker.

10. You can use the phrase "_____" to mean "Here is another way to say the same thing." Often the second way is easier to understand.

11. One researcher said to be careful about tickling rats. He _____ people to be careful.

B These sentences use the target words and phrases **in new contexts.** Complete them with the words and phrases in the box.

actually	behavior	expresses	in other words	laughter	notice
prefer	relationship	study	variety	warns	

1. The room was full of the sounds of music, conversation, and

    _____.

2. The teacher called the boy's parents to talk about his bad

    _____.

3. The sign _____ drivers that the road is bad, so they should be careful.

4. He likes his boss. They have a friendly _____.

5. What would you _____ to do, go to a movie or go out to eat?

6. She claimed to be 21, but she was _____ 19.

7. He almost never _____ his feelings or talks about anything personal.

8. I walked past the car, but I didn't _____ if anyone was in it.

9. The college offers a wide _____ of courses. There are a lot of choices for students.

10. The scientists were interested in the effects of sleep on memory, so they did a _____.

11. This street is a dead end. _____, it doesn't connect with another street, so you can't drive through.

C Read each definition and look at the paragraph number in parentheses ( ). Look back at the reading to **find the target word** for each definition. Write it in the chart.

Definition	Target Word
1. a person you do not know (2)	
2. stored music or other sound so as to be able to hear it again (2)	
3. nice or pleasing to look at, interesting (3)	
4. a liquid used to help machine parts move easily (4)	
5. happening without problems or difficulties (4)	

Building on the Vocabulary

Studying Collocations

Prepositions, such as *at, in,* and *to,* help show relationships between people, places, and things. Certain prepositions follow certain adjectives. Use:

> *attractive + to*   *upset + about*
> *excited + about*   *useful + for/to*
> *interested + in*

Example: *I am excited about our trip.*

A Complete each sentence with the correct preposition.

1. He wrote a book that's useful _____ travelers visiting Japan.
2. The children were excited _____ getting your invitation.
3. Chris is very attractive _____ the opposite sex.
4. Everyone was upset _____ the accident.
5. I'm interested _____ learning about other cultures.

B Write five sentences. Use each adjective + preposition in Part A.

1. _____
2. _____
3. _____
4. _____
5. _____

DEVELOPING YOUR SKILLS

Finding Clues to Meaning

Writers use a variety of ways to supply the meaning of a word or phrase in a reading.

- Sometimes a writer follows the word or phrase with a comma (,) or a dash (—) and then a definition or explanation. For example, "Mahmoud was born near Tehran, the largest city in Iran." or "This body part is small—only 2–3% of your total body weight—but it uses . . ."
- Sometimes a phrase like *that is* or *in other words* introduces a definition or explanation. For example, "Does the information affect our emotions? That is, does it make us happy, sad, excited, or upset?"

Look at "When and Why We Laugh." Find the definitions or explanations given for the boldfaced phrases below and copy them here.

1. "People have many ways to **express themselves** _____
   _____"

2. "Provine calls laughter '**the oil in the social machine**.' _____
   _____"

Reading for Details

Read these questions about "When and Why We Laugh." Refer back to the reading and write short answers or complete sentences.

1. What are three reasons for laughter?
   a. _____
   b. _____
   c. _____
2. Who did a study on laughter? _____
3. Who was in the study? _____
4. What did the students have to do? _____
   _____
5. What did changes in the students' laughter depend on? _____
   _____
6. When did the female students in the study laugh most? _____
7. When did the male students laugh most? _____

8. According to researcher Robert Provine, who laughs more during a conversation, the person speaking or the one listening? _____

9. a. What does Provine call laughter? (Use Provine's exact words to answer this question.) _____

   b. What does this mean? _____

Discussion

Work with a partner. Talk about your answers to these questions.

1. Research on laughter shows that the average adult laughs about 17 times a day. How many times do you think you laugh during the day? What kinds of things make you laugh?

2. What do you think is the difference between "laughing at someone" and "laughing with someone"?

3. According to the reading, the female college students in the study

   a. laughed most with male friends and

   b. laughed in a higher voice with male strangers.

   Why do you think they laughed like this?

Using New Words

Work with a partner. Choose five target words or phrases from the list on page 89. On a piece of paper, use each word or phrase in a sentence.

Writing

Choose a topic. Write a paragraph.

1. Some people say, "Laughter is the best medicine." Do you agree? Why or why not?

2. "Laughter is the best medicine" is a common saying in English. Think of a common saying about laughter in your first language. Tell what it is, what it means, and why you do or don't agree with it.

CHAPTER 11

The Inventor of the Telephone

The inventor of the telephone

GETTING READY TO READ

Mark your answers to the following questions. Then discuss your answers in a small group or with the whole class.

1. Who invented the telephone?

   ❏ Thomas Edison   ❏ Guglielmo Marconi   ❏ Alexander Graham Bell

2. How many times a day do you usually use a telephone?

   ❏ 0–2 times   ❏ 3–10 times   ❏ more than 10 times

3. Which of the following communication tools do you use regularly?

   At home: Away from home:

   ❏ a telephone   ❏ a cell phone

   ❏ an answering machine   ❏ pay phones

   ❏ other: _____   ❏ other: _____

READING

Look at the words and pictures next to the reading. Then read without stopping.

The Inventor of the Telephone

1   We can thank Alexander Graham Bell for the telephone. This great inventor was born in 1847 in Scotland. All through his life, Bell had an interest in communication. This interest came **partly** from the influence of his family. His grandfather was an actor and became famous as a **speech** teacher. His father developed the first international phonetic alphabet.[1] For his mother, communication was never easy. It took a great **effort** because she was almost completely **deaf**. She usually held a tube[2] to her ear **in order to** hear people. Her son Alexander discovered another way to communicate with her when he was a little boy. He used to **press** his mouth against her forehead[3] and speak in a low voice. The sound waves traveled to her ears through the bones of her head. This was among the first of his many discoveries about sound.

2   As a teenager, Bell taught music and public speaking at a boys' school. In his free time, he had fun working on **various** inventions with an older brother. These included a useful machine for farmwork. Then both of Bell's brothers got sick and died. He got the same terrible **sickness**—tuberculosis[4]—so the family moved to Canada. There his health returned.

3   Bell moved to the United States when he was 24. He went to Boston to teach at a school for deaf children. In Boston, he fell in love with Mabel Hubbard, a student of his who later became his wife. During this period of his life, Bell was a very busy man. **In addition to** teaching, he was working on several inventions.

4   Bell's main goal was to make machines to help deaf people hear. He was also trying to build a better telegraph.[5] In those days, the telegraph was the only way to send information quickly over a long distance. Telegraph messages traveled over **wires**. They were sent in Morse code,[6] which used specific long and short sounds for the letters of the

continued

[1] a *phonetic alphabet* = a way to show the sounds of words, for example *laugh* = /læf/ or (läf)

[2] a hearing *tube*

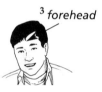

[3] *forehead*

[4] *tuberculosis* = a serious sickness that affects a person's ability to breathe

[5] a *telegraph* operator sending a message

[6] *Morse code* for SOS, a call for help

· · · — — — · · ·

alphabet. Bell was trying to find a way to send the human voice along a wire. However, almost no one believed in this idea, and people told him, "You're **wasting** your time. You should try to invent a better telegraph—that's where the money is."

5   Bell understood a lot about sound and **electricity**, but he wasn't really very **good at** building things. Luckily, he met someone who was. The man's name was Thomas Watson, and he was a great help to Bell. One day—it was March 10, 1876—the two men were working in **separate** rooms. They were getting ready to test a new invention, which had a wire going from one room to the other. Something **went wrong** and Bell **shouted**, "Mr. Watson, come here. I want you!" His voice traveled along the wire, and Watson heard it coming from the new machine. It was the world's first telephone call. Bell was on his way to becoming a very rich man.

6   Soon afterward, Bell wrote to his father:

> The day is coming when telegraph wires will [go] to houses just like water or gas—and friends will converse with each other without leaving home.

Maybe his father laughed to hear this idea. At the time, most people expected the phone to be just a tool for business, not something that anyone would have at home. Bell could see a greater future for it. However, even he could probably never imagine what telephones are like today.

The quotation from Alexander Graham Bell's letter to his father comes from "Alexander Graham Bell—The Inventor," <http://www.fitzgeraldstudio.com/html/bell/inventor.html>.

Quick Comprehension Check

Read these sentences. Circle T (true) or F (false).

1. Alexander Graham Bell's family influenced his career.   T   F

2. Bell started inventing things while he was growing up.   T   F

3. He was born and grew up in the United States.   T   F

4. He never married.   T   F

5. He invented the telephone working all alone.   T   F

6. He believed that in the future, people would have phones at home.   T   F

EXPLORING VOCABULARY

Thinking about the Vocabulary

Which target words and phrases are new to you? Circle them here and in the reading. Then read "The Inventor of the Telephone" again. Look at the context of each new word and phrase. Can you guess the meaning?

Target Words and Phrases			
partly (1)	**in order to** (1)	**in addition to** (3)	**good at** (5)
speech (1)	**press** (1)	**wires** (4)	**separate** (5)
effort (1)	**various** (2)	**wasting** (4)	**went wrong** (5)
deaf (1)	**sickness** (2)	**electricity** (5)	**shouted** (5)

Using the Vocabulary

Ⓐ **Complete these sentences. Write *a great effort*, *pressing*, *shouting*, and *wires*.**

1. He's _____.

2. It's taking _____.

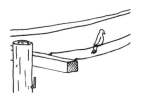

3. These are telephone _____.

4. He's _____ a button.

B These sentences are **about the reading**. Complete them with the words and phrases in the box.

deaf	electricity	good at	in addition to	in order to	partly
separate	sickness	speech	various	waste	went wrong

1. Some, but not all, of Bell's interest in communication was because of his family. It came _____ from their influence on him.

2. Bell's grandfather taught people to speak clearly. He was a _____ teacher.

3. Bell's mother could hear only a little. She was almost completely _____.

4. She used a tube _____ hear people. She used it for this purpose.

5. As a teenager, Bell worked with his brother on _____ inventions. They built a variety of things together.

6. Bell's two brothers got sick and died. Then he got the same _____.

7. Bell had a teaching job in Boston. He also had more to do: _____ his job, he worked on several inventions.

8. People told Bell to use his time carefully. They told him not to _____ his time.

9. Bell understood a lot about _____. For example, he knew how it could supply power to lights.

10. Bell was a great thinker, but he wasn't so _____ building things.

11. On March 10, 1876, Bell and his partner were not working in the same room. They were in _____ rooms.

12. While he was working, Bell had an accident of some kind. Something _____.

C These sentences use the target words and phrases **in new contexts**. Complete them with the words and phrases in the box.

deaf	electricity	good at	go wrong	in addition to	in order to
partly	separate	sickness	speech	various	waste

1. The sky was only _____ cloudy in the morning but completely cloudy later on.
2. He's going _____. I have to shout so that he can hear me.
3. This type of car is available in _____ colors.
4. Michael plays basketball and golf very well. He is _____ both sports.
5. We depend on _____ for lights, radios, TVs, refrigerators, etc.
6. The company wants a study on how many work days are lost because of _____.
7. Relax! I'm sure everything will go smoothly. Nothing will _____.
8. Don't _____ your money on that movie. We saw it, and it was very disappointing.
9. He took science courses _____ prepare for a career in medicine.
10. I keep my notes for each of my courses in _____ parts of my notebook.
11. Only humans can express themselves through _____.
12. We use laughter to communicate, _____ words, sounds, and body language.

Building on the Vocabulary

Studying Collocations

Remember: Certain verbs go with certain nouns. Use the verbs *make, take,* and *put* with the noun **effort.** Also note that *effort* is sometimes a count noun and sometimes a noncount noun. Study these examples:

- make an effort to do something
- it takes (an/some) effort to do something
- put (some/a lot of) effort into something

A Complete the sentences. Use *make, put,* or *take.*

1. Does it _____ a lot of effort to learn a language?

2. Please _____ an effort to be on time.

3. He won't _____ any effort into his homework.

B Write three sentences with *make, put,* and *take + effort.*

1. _____

2. _____

3. _____

DEVELOPING YOUR SKILLS

Reading Between the Lines

Are the following statements true or false? You cannot skim the reading for the answers. You must think about what the reading says and decide. Circle T or F, and give one or more reasons for your answer. Write complete sentences.

1. Alexander Graham Bell was probably close to his family.   (T)   F

   His family influenced his career, and he and his brother invented things
   together.

2. Bell had a fear of speaking in front of groups of people.   T   F

   _____

   _____

3. Tuberculosis was a serious sickness in the 1800s.   T   F

   _____

   _____

4. Bell's wife was deaf.   T   F

   _____

   _____

5. What Bell wanted most in life was to become rich and famous.   T   F

   _____

   _____

6. Thomas Watson believed in Bell's ideas when others did not.   T   F

   _____

   _____

Summarizing

On a piece of paper, write a summary of "The Inventor of the Telephone." Use no more than ten sentences. Use your own words. That is, do not copy sentences from the reading. Include:

- the inventor's name
- why he is famous
- when and where he was born
- where he spent his life
- his main goal as an inventor
- the date of the first phone call

Discussion

Talk about these questions in a small group.

1. How did Alexander Graham Bell's family influence his career?
2. Have you ever spent one or more days in a place where you had no phone nearby? If so, where were you? Describe your feelings about being far from a phone.
3. Imagine the perfect telephone of the future. What will it be like? What will it be able to do?

Using New Words

Work with a partner. Take turns asking for and giving information. Use one of the words in parentheses. Then tell the class something your partner said.

1. Name a machine (with/without) buttons you **press** to make it work.
2. Name a machine that (uses/doesn't use) **electricity**.
3. Name a machine (with/without) **wires**.
4. Name a place where you can see **various** kinds of (fish/birds).
5. Name a time and place where it is (OK/not OK) to **shout**.

Writing

Choose a topic. Write a paragraph.

1. How important are telephones in your life? Why and how often do you make or get phone calls? Write about your relationship with the telephone.
2. Complete this sentence: *I wish somebody would invent. . .* Explain why this invention would be a good thing.

CHAPTER 12

Going Online

Online at home

GETTING READY TO READ

Answer the questions. Then talk about your answers with the class.

1. Do you use the Internet?

   ☐ No, I don't.   ☐ Yes, I use it for:

   ____ e-mail   ____ meeting people

   ____ shopping   ____ music

   ____ getting information   ____ other: _____

2. Circle one: (Many/Some/Only a few) people in my country use the Internet.

3. Do you believe the following statement is true or false?
   People who use the Internet a lot don't like to spend time with other people.

READING

Look at the words next to the reading. Then read without stopping.

Going Online

1   All over the world, people are **gaining** access[1] to the Internet. More and more people are using computers to go **online**. This change has happened quickly. For example, in 1997, there were fewer than eight million Internet users in Japan. Just five years later, there were almost 65 million. During that same period, Internet use around the world grew by 600%. Clearly, the Internet is affecting many, many lives, and it is changing how we communicate. But are these changes good or bad?

2   The Internet can be a great tool for communication. Everyone agrees on that. People can use e-mail to keep **in touch** with family and friends whether they are far away or just across town. Sending an e-mail message is quick, easy, and **cheap**. People can also use the Internet to find new friends. Do you want to talk about politics[2] or sports or how to find true love? Go online! You will find people who share your interests. Maybe you will make friends in **distant** places and learn about other cultures. In many ways, the Internet can bring people together.

3   However, some people say that the Internet has the opposite effect. They claim that it is leading to *less* communication, not more. These people believe that time online means time alone. "The Internet is taking people away from their families and friends," they say. "It **draws** people away from their **communities**, and that is not good."

4   So, what is actually happening? Researchers are trying to find out. They are studying the effects of the Internet on our lives. They are looking at the behavior of people who use it and people who do not. At this **point**, there are two basic ideas about what is happening:

- Some researchers who have done studies in the United States have bad news for people who often go online. They report that people who use the Internet **on a regular basis** are more often lonely and unhappy. They say that these people are spending time at their

continued

[1] *access* = the ability, chance, or right to use something

[2] *politics* = activities and ideas concerned with getting and using power in a country, city, etc.

computers instead of with other people, so they have less active **social** lives.

• Other researchers disagree. They describe other studies from the United States and some from England. These show that people who often go online make *more* connections with other people because they use the Internet to communicate. And here is a surprise: According to these studies, **frequent** Internet users get in touch more not just online but by phone and in person,[3] too. They have busier social lives, and they are usually happier. They also watch less TV.

5   Does going online affect everyone in the same way? Perhaps not. Perhaps the effects of Internet use depend on a person's **character**. Psychologist[4] Robert Kraut thinks this is so. According to Kraut, the Internet **allows** social people to become even more social. It lets them get in touch with friends more easily, and they go out more often. And people who are not social? They may use the Internet to **avoid** others. They may like going online so that they don't have to talk to anyone. However, this does not mean that the Internet is unhealthy for shy people. In fact, the Internet can help **shy** people make friends. Researchers find that shy people frequently communicate more easily online than face-to-face.

6   The Internet is changing how we communicate. Maybe you can see its effects on your own life. It is less easy to see larger changes in our communities or around the **entire** world, but changes are happening. It is something to think about.

[3] *in person* = by going and meeting someone, not by phone, letter, or computer

[4] a *psychologist* = someone trained in the study of the mind and how it works

Quick Comprehension Check

Read these sentences. Circle T (true) or F (false).

1. Use of the Internet is growing around the world.   T   F

2. Everyone agrees that the Internet is great for families.   T   F

3. There is no research yet on Internet use in people's homes.   T   F

4. Researchers are studying the behavior of people who often go online.   T   F

5. The Internet is changing how people communicate.   T   F

6. The effects of these changes are clear.   T   F

EXPLORING VOCABULARY

Thinking about the Vocabulary

Which target words and phrases are new to you? Circle them here and in the reading. Then read "Going Online" again. Look at the context of each new word and phrase. Can you guess the meaning?

Target Words and Phrases			
gaining (1)	distant (2)	on a regular basis (4)	allows (5)
online (1)	draws (3)	social (4)	avoid (5)
in touch (2)	communities (3)	frequent (4)	shy (5)
cheap (2)	point (4)	character (5)	entire (6)

Using the Vocabulary

A These sentences are about the reading. What is the meaning of each **boldfaced** word? Circle a, b, or c.

1. More and more people are **gaining** experience with the Internet. *Gain* means:

   a. decrease
   b. imagine
   c. get

2. Not every computer has a connection to the Internet, but many computers do. People can use those computers to spend time **online**. *Online* means:

   a. in communication with other computers
   b. using computer hardware
   c. developing computer games

3. Both e-mail and the telephone let people get **in touch** with friends. *In touch* means:

   a. putting hands on
   b. in communication
   c. competing

4. Phone calls can be expensive, but e-mail is **cheap**. *Cheap* means:

   a. a waste of time
   b. low in cost
   c. not useful

5. You can send e-mail to people in the same building or in **distant** places. *Distant* means:

   a. far away
   b. attractive
   c. specific

6. Some people think time online **draws** people away from others. *Draws* means:

   a. pulls
   b. rushes
   c. supplies

7. At this **point**, the effects of the Internet are not yet clear. Here, *point* means:

   a. an idea or belief   **b.** a specific moment   **c.** a reason or
                                      or time   purpose

8. Some people never go online; others use the Internet **on a regular basis**.
   On a regular basis means:

   a. being awake   **b.** moving smoothly   **c.** happening
                                                          often

9. Some Internet users prefer to be alone. Others have busy **social** lives.
   Social means:

   a. relating to other   **b.** relating to research   **c.** relating to
      people   power

10. Some people use the Internet to **avoid** other people because they prefer to
    be alone. *Avoid* means:

    a. make friends with   **b.** keep away from   **c.** spend time
                                                                with

B These sentences use the target words and phrases **in new contexts**.
Complete them with the words and phrases in the box.

avoid	cheap	distant	draw	gain
in touch	on a regular basis	online	point	social

1. They don't have much money, so they want a _____ used car.

2. He's so thin! He needs to _____ some weight.

3. That child spends too much time alone. He's not developing
   _____ skills.

4. He disappeared at some _____ during the party, but no one
   noticed when.

5. The doctor warned me to _____ high-fat foods.

6. I go _____ for a variety of reasons. For example, I get news
   and weather reports off the Internet.

7. He practices every day. He says, "You need to practice _____
   in order to get better at anything."

8. She dreams of having the money to travel to _____ places.

9. I'd like to _____ your attention to a report in today's
   newspaper.

10. Both *keep* and *stay* _____ *with someone* mean to continue
    communication with the person, usually by phone or by writing.

C **Read these sentences. Write the boldfaced target words next to their definitions.**

a. They lead active social lives. They seem to know everyone in the **community**.

b. He may seem unfriendly at first, but he's actually just **shy**.

c. She used to get headaches every day, but they are becoming less **frequent**.

d. We spent the **entire** day getting ready for the party.

e. The city doesn't **allow** people to smoke in restaurants.

f. He's a stranger to me, so I can't tell you anything about his **character**.

Target Words	Definitions
1. _____	= what a person is like
2. _____	= nervous or uncomfortable about meeting and talking to people
3. _____	= all the people living in a place, or a group that shares an interest
4. _____	= whole, complete
5. _____	= happening very often
6. _____	= let (someone do something)

Building on the Vocabulary

Studying Collocations

Certain verbs are used with certain nouns. For example, the verb *gain* is often used with the nouns *experience, strength,* and *weight. Gain* usually means to get more and more of something over a period of time. Similar verbs are *earn* (*money, points*) and *win* (*a game, a prize*).

Complete these sentences with *gain, earn,* or *win.* Use the verb that goes with the noun.

1. The job doesn't pay much, but he'll _____ useful experience.

2. I have to watch what I eat. I _____ weight easily.

3. I hope they'll _____ their next game.

4. You can't _____ much money at most part-time jobs.

5. He's doing exercises to _____ strength in his arms.

DEVELOPING YOUR SKILLS

Pronoun Reference

Pronouns are words like *he, she, it,* or *them. This, that, these,* and *those* can also be pronouns. We often use pronouns to avoid repeating words. A pronoun takes the place of a noun or a noun phrase (a noun phrase = a group of words for a person, place, or thing: *Internet users, the opposite effect*). A pronoun can also refer back to a whole sentence or an idea.

What do the boldfaced pronouns refer to in these sentences? Look back at the reading.

1. Paragraph 2: Everyone agrees on **that**. <u>the idea that the Internet is a</u>
   <u>great tool for communication</u>

2. Paragraph 3: **It** draws people away from their communities . . . _____
   _____

3. Paragraph 4: **They** are studying the effects of the Internet on . . . _____
   _____

4. Paragraph 4: **These** show that people who often go online make *more*
   connections . . . _____

5. Paragraph 4: **They** have busier social lives, and . . . _____

6. Paragraph 5: Psychologist Robert Kraut thinks **this** is so. _____
   _____

Fact vs. Opinion

Ⓐ Decide if each statement expresses a fact or an opinion. Base your answers on information from the reading. Circle *Fact* when it is possible to show that the statement is true. Circle *Opinion* when people may believe it, but they can't show that it is true.

1. The Internet has changed how people communicate.   Fact/Opinion

2. Use of the Internet has increased in many countries.   Fact/Opinion

3. Time spent online makes people less connected to   Fact/Opinion
   their communities.

4. Researchers are studying the behavior of Internet users.   Fact/Opinion

5. Going online is good for social people.   Fact/Opinion

6. Going online is good for shy people.   Fact/Opinion

B **Write two sentences.**

1. Write a fact about the Internet from "Going Online."

   _____

2. Write an opinion of your own about Internet use.

   _____

Discussion

Talk about these questions in a small group.

1. When did you, or will you, learn to use the Internet? How did you, or will you, learn about it?

2. Celine Adams is a grandmother in Canada. Her children just got her a computer. They live far away, and she is excited about getting e-mail from them. But she worries, "Will they stop calling me? I still want to hear their voices." After reading "Going Online," what would you tell Celine? Why?

Using New Words

Work with a partner. Choose five target words or phrases from the list on page 105. On a piece of paper, use each word or phrase in a sentence.

Writing

Choose a topic. Write a paragraph.

1. Do you feel that you are part of a community at school, at work, or where you live? If so, how would you describe this community? How does it feel to be a part of it?

2. Do you keep in touch with friends or family in distant places? Tell why or why not. Explain how you stay in touch or what keeps you from staying in touch.

Wrap-up

REVIEWING VOCABULARY

A Match the words in the box with their definitions. There is one extra word.

cheap	compete	deaf	distant	draw	effort
frequent	online	prefer	sense	study	wire

1. _____ = unable to hear
2. _____ = try to win or gain something
3. _____ = low-cost, not expensive
4. _____ = know or feel something without seeing or being told about it
5. _____ = a piece of work that is done to answer a research question
6. _____ = like (some person or thing) more than another
7. _____ = attract or pull (someone in a certain direction)
8. _____ = energy or work needed to do something
9. _____ = a long, thin piece of metal, often used to carry electricity
10. _____ = happening often
11. _____ = far away

B Complete the sentences below.

actually	allow	entire	in addition to	in order to	in other words
in touch	notice	partly	smoothly	straight	through

1. I keep _____ with her by phone.
2. She said, "Hi," but he didn't _____. He walked on by.
3. He finds it hard to meet new people and talk to them. _____, he's shy.
4. I had to take two buses _____ get there.
5. Somehow he manages to do a weekend job _____ his regular job.

110

6. He got the job _____ his own efforts, not because of family connections.

7. We had no problems with the training. Everything went very _____.

8. She looks younger than her husband does, but she's _____ older than he is.

9. You seemed only _____ awake when you answered the phone this morning.

10. The shortest distance between two points is a _____ line.

11. She will not _____ her children to stay up late on school nights.

12. My _____ family—all twenty of us—got together for the holidays.

EXPANDING VOCABULARY

	Nouns	Verbs	Adjectives
1.	attraction	attract	attractive
2.			
3.			
4.			
5.			

Ⓐ **Complete the chart of word families with words from the sentences below.**

1. a. Flowers attract certain insects, like bees.

   b. She is an attractive young woman.

   c. It was easy to see the attraction between Jack and Diana.

2. a. His bad behavior often got him into trouble.

   b. Parents teach their children how to behave.

3. a. Do boys and girls go to separate schools in your country?

   b. Separate the light-colored clothes from the dark ones before washing them.

   c. They were married for five years before their separation.

4. a. We warned them to be careful after dark.

   b. There is a warning on every cigarette package.

5. a. She is too shy to talk to the boys in her class.

   b. His shyness keeps him from going to parties.

B *Gain, sense, shout,* and *waste* can be nouns or verbs. Use each word as a noun to complete one of the following sentences. Then use it as a verb in a new sentence.

1. a. We didn't do anything useful at the meeting. It was a _____ of time.

   b. _____

   _____

2. a. You can be proud of the _____s you have made in learning English.

   b. _____

   _____

3. a. I heard a _____, so I turned around to look.

   b. _____

   _____

4. a. I don't have a very good _____ of smell.

   b. _____

   _____

PLAYING WITH WORDS

Complete the sentences with words you studied in Chapters 9–12. Write the words in the puzzle.

Across

1. Before you leave the plane, check for your personal_____ belongings.

4. The child's parents warned her not to talk to s_____.

10. You can trust him. He's a man of good c_____.

11. I have socks in v_____ colors.

12. She is a leader in her c_____. Everyone in town respects her.

13. Let's leave early and a_____ the traffic.

Down

2. Our TV uses e_____.

3. He said to call tomorrow. He didn't give a s_____ time.

5. I have a good r_____ with my brother. He's my best friend.

6. A supermarket has a wide v_____ of products.

7. He does exercises to gain s_____.

8. After the rain, the g_____ was very wet.

9. They have busy s_____ lives on weekends. They're always out with friends.

BUILDING DICTIONARY SKILLS

A Look at these dictionary entries.

> **ex·press**[1] /ɪk'sprɛs/ v [T] **1** to use words or actions in order to let people know what you are thinking or feeling: *A number of people expressed the fear that they would never get another job.* | *It's hard sometimes for children to* **express themselves**. **2 express an interest in something** to say that you are interested in something: *She expressed an interest in seeing the old map.*
>
> **express**[2] *adj* **1** specific, deliberate, or exact: *It was her* **express wish** *that you inherit her house.* **2 express train/bus** a train or bus that travels quickly and does not stop in many places

Do you see **express**[1] and **express**[2]? The small raised numbers [1] and [2] are superscripts. They tell you that *express* can be more than one part of speech. One entry for *express* explains the meanings of the verb; the other explains the adjective.

Which meaning of *express* is used in each sentence? Circle *express*[1] or *express*[2].

1. Is there an express bus this afternoon? (express[1] / express[2])

2. She doesn't often express her opinions. (express[1] / express[2])

B Words often have more than one meaning. Dictionaries number the meanings.

Look at this entry for *regular*. Write the number of the meaning used in each sentence below.

> **reg·u·lar**[1] /'rɛgyələ/ *adj*
> **1 ▸ REPEATED ◂** repeated, with the same amount of time or space between each thing and the next: *His heartbeat is strong and regular.* | *Planes were taking off at regular intervals.*
> **2 ▸ NORMAL SIZE ◂** of standard size: *fries and a regular coke*
> **3 ▸ SAME TIME ◂** happening or planned for the same time every day, month, year etc.: *regular meetings* | *Once I start working regular hours, things should get better.*
> **4 ▸ HAPPENING OFTEN ◂** happening or doing something very often: *He's one of our regular customers.*
> **5 ▸ USUAL ◂** normal or usual: *She's not our regular babysitter.*
> **6 ▸ ORDINARY ◂** ordinary: *I'm just a regular doctor, not a specialist.*
> **7 ▸ EVENLY SHAPED ◂** evenly shaped with parts or sides of equal size: *regular features* (= an evenly shaped face)
> **8 ▸ GRAMMAR ◂** TECHNICAL a regular verb or noun changes its forms in the same way as most verbs or nouns. The verb "walk" is regular, but "be" is not: **–regularity** /ˌrɛgyə'lærəti/ *n* [U]

__4__ 1. He is a regular user of the Internet.

_____ 2. I don't work regular hours. They're always changing.

_____ 3. *Talk* and *look* are regular verbs; *go* and *have* are irregular.

_____ 4. The patient's breathing was slow and regular.

_____ 5. I'll have a regular orange juice—no, wait, a large one, please.

_____ 6. I didn't see my regular dentist because he's away.

_____ 7. He's a famous actor, but he's easy to talk to. He seems like a regular guy.

_____ 8. She has nice, regular teeth.

Vocabulary Self-Test 1

**Circle the letter of the word or phrase that best completes each sentence.
Example:**

I like working for her. She is a good _____.

a. software   c. boss

b. needle   d. speech

1. Listen to this singer—she has a beautiful _____.

   a. oil   c. leather

   b. ground   d. voice

2. Please, pay _____ to your driving.

   a. agreement   c. professor

   b. attention   d. medicine

3. Changes in class size will _____ all students and teachers.

   a. cause   c. record

   b. disappear   d. affect

4. The cost of some hotel rooms _____ breakfast.

   a. invents   c. includes

   b. competes   d. develops

5. I thought her name was Joan, but it is _____ JoAnne.

   a. partly   c. by accident

   b. right away   d. actually

6. She has a big _____ on her little sister.

   a. stage   c. research

   b. point   d. influence

7. I don't know all the _____ of the plan.

   a. details   c. wires

   b. insects   d. scores

8. After college, they will _____ for jobs.

   a. imagine   c. decrease

   b. apply   d. warn

115

9. Before you start your new job, you will need some _____.

    a. forest   **c.** training

    b. bomb   **d.** field

10. I read only part of the report, not the _____ thing.

    a. weak   **c.** distant

    b. gentle   **d.** entire

11. We couldn't find two seats together on the train, so we sat in _____ places.

    a. still   **c.** separate

    b. medical   **d.** daily

12. The two brothers spend a lot of time together. They have a close _____.

    a. laughter   **c.** case

    b. movement   **d.** relationship

13. People usually drive faster on _____ roads.

    a. social   **c.** male

    b. straight   **d.** immediate

14. I didn't _____ myself well. Let me try to explain my idea again.

    a. express   **c.** gain

    b. draw   **d.** create

15. We gain _____ when we eat too much.

    a. points   **c.** sickness

    b. weight   **d.** skills

16. I drove slowly, trying to _____ the bad places in the road.

    a. avoid   **c.** get into

    b. increase   **d.** support

17. The _____ of all the grades in the class was 85%.

    a. study   **c.** closet

    b. average   **d.** report

18. Most stores close at 9:00, but _____ ones stay open later.

    a. certain   **c.** calm

    b. shy   **d.** upset

19. He likes doing things _____, like bicycling and fishing.

    a. outdoors   **c.** anymore

    b. however   **d.** whenever

20. We _____ for the information online, but we couldn't find it.

    a. searched   **c.** referred

    b. wasted   **d.** meant

21. The store will be closed for a short _____—a week at most.

    a. behavior   **c.** supply

    b. period   **d.** rate

22. There were no tables _____ at the first restaurant, so we went to another.

    a. relaxed   **c.** disappointed

    b. available   **d.** creative

23. Let's make an _____ to be there early.

    a. effort   **c.** activity

    b. electricity   **d.** amount

24. It's 11:00? Oh, no! I didn't _____ that it was so late.

    a. contain   **c.** claim

    b. store   **d.** realize

25. The letter from the school _____ classes that the student had missed.

    a. sensed   **c.** concerned

    b. fed   **d.** preferred

26. We expect rain across the whole _____ tomorrow.

    a. set   **c.** region

    b. culture   **d.** explanation

27. Her _____ show clearly on her face.

    a. notes   **c.** emotions

    b. tools   **d.** strangers

28. I'm not shopping for anything _____. I'm looking at all kinds of things.

    a. specific   **c.** somehow

    b. advanced   **d.** ahead

29. The bus makes _____ stops, so it takes a long time to get there.
    a. active
    b. low
    c. frequent
    d. sharp

30. They had a long _____ of meetings to plan for the new school.
    a. goal
    b. series
    c. character
    d. direction

31. The hospital won't _____ visitors to stay after 9:00 P.M.
    a. practice
    b. pronounce
    c. shout
    d. allow

32. He had enough money for only a pair of _____ shoes.
    a. personal
    b. alike
    c. awake
    d. cheap

33. The _____ of his letter was to tell us of the change in plans.
    a. purpose
    b. connection
    c. variety
    d. season

34. The clothes in the store window _____ a lot of attention.
    a. divided
    b. attracted
    c. pressed
    d. noticed

35. I just moved here, so I don't yet know many members of the
    _____.
    a. discovery
    b. invitation
    c. community
    d. strength

36. We said good-bye and promised to keep _____ with each other.
    a. in fact
    b. in general
    c. in touch
    d. on the other hand

See the Answer Key on page 239.

UNIT 4

INTO THE
WORLD OF
BUSINESS

CHAPTER 13

A Family Business

Bruce Yang with his father

GETTING READY TO READ

Answer the question below. Then talk in a small group about the reasons for your answers.

Which of the following sounds best to you? Number your choices from 1 (the best) to 5.

_____ **a.** start my own business

_____ **b.** start a business with a partner or partners

_____ **c.** join a business owned by someone in my family

_____ **d.** go to work for a small local company

_____ **e.** go to work for a large international company

READING

Look at the words and picture next to the reading. Then read without stopping. Don't worry about new words. Don't stop to use a dictionary. Just keep reading!

A Family Business

1   Bruce Yang is a **director** of Taipan Supplies Limited. It is a family business, started by his grandfather. The company has its offices in Taiwan and Hong Kong. The author interviewed Bruce Yang in November of 2002.

2 *Interviewer:* Mr. Yang, what kind of business is Taipan Supplies?

3 *Bruce Yang:* Our company **deals in** three different types of business activity. First, we represent[1] **foreign** companies here in Taiwan. These companies want to sell their **goods** or **services** here, but they don't want to **set up** offices, find people to work for them, and so on. So our company **does business** for them. For example, we've represented some American airlines and companies that make earth-moving equipment.[2]

4   Second, we act as business consultants.[3] We have a lot of experience in construction[4] and in shipping—sending goods by air or sea. So companies sometimes want our advice on these **industries**. They come to us for information about doing business in Taiwan. We also work with Taiwanese companies who want to do business in other countries. And third, we put money into our own projects. For example, right now we have **investments** in a software **firm**, in oil, and in various other things.

5 *Interviewer:* How did your company get started?

6 *Bruce Yang:* My grandfather and his partners set it up back in the 1950s. At first, the company dealt in international **trade**, mostly between Taiwan and the U.S. Then in the '60s, my father joined the firm. He helped it grow in new directions.

continued

[1] *represent* = speak or do things for a person or group who can't be there

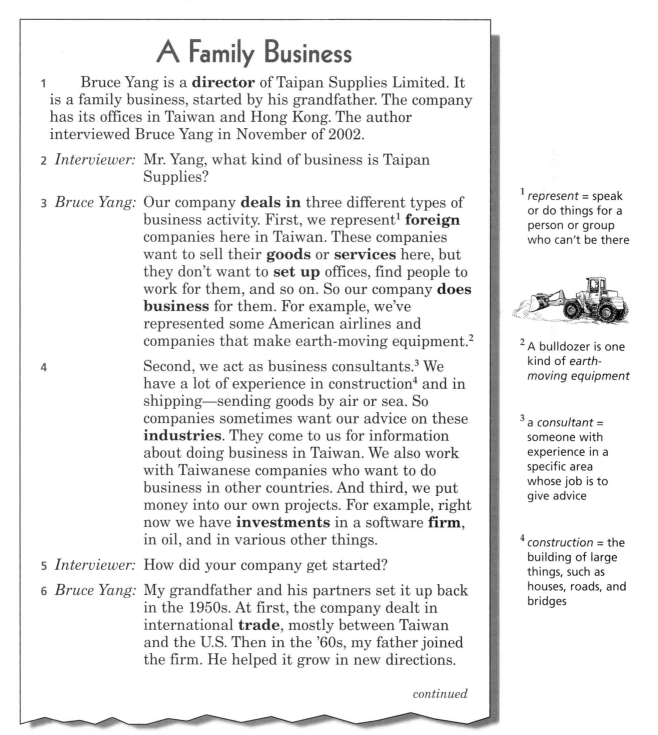

[2] A bulldozer is one kind of *earth-moving equipment*

[3] a *consultant* = someone with experience in a specific area whose job is to give advice

[4] *construction* = the building of large things, such as houses, roads, and bridges

7 *Interviewer:* And when did you join the business?

8 *Bruce Yang:* In 1985. At that time, I was working for a bank in Hong Kong. Now I **look after** the financial[5] health of Taipan Supplies.

[5] *financial* = concerned with money or money management

9 *Interviewer:* What's the best thing about working in your family business?

10 *Bruce Yang:* The best thing is to have the chance to work with my father. In my school years, my father was so busy working, I never had a chance to **get to know** him. In working with him in the company, I got to know him as a person, not just as my dad.

11 *Interviewer:* And what's the hardest part of working for your family business?

12 *Bruce Yang:* Working with my father! We are very different in character. We see the world differently. This means our discussions about business can be, shall I say, spirited![6] However, my father is the boss. After discussion and after a decision is made, I work to support that decision.

[6] *spirited* = full of energy and strong feeling

13 *Interviewer:* Do you think your children will follow you into the business?

14 *Bruce Yang:* My children—and my **nieces** and **nephews**— may not have the chance to. The company is doing very well, but the business world is changing at a great rate. So our future is **uncertain**.

Quick Comprehension Check

Read these sentences. Circle T (true) or F (false).

1.	Bruce Yang started his own company.	T	F
2.	Taipan Supplies Limited is a family business in Japan.	T	F
3.	The company has more than one kind of business activity.	T	F
4.	Bruce Yang enjoys working with his father.	T	F
5.	He and his father think very much alike.	T	F
6.	Bruce Yang expects his children to continue the family business.	T	F

EXPLORING VOCABULARY

Thinking about the Vocabulary

Which target words and phrases are new to you? Circle them here and in the reading. Then read "A Family Business" again. Look at the context of each new word and phrase. Can you guess the meaning?

Target Words and Phrases			
director (1)	services (3)	investments (4)	get to know (10)
deals in (3)	set up (3)	firm (4)	nieces (14)
foreign (3)	does business (3)	trade (6)	nephews (14)
goods (3)	industries (4)	look after (8)	uncertain (14)

Using the Vocabulary

A These sentences are **about the reading**. Complete them with the words and phrases in the box.

deals in	foreign	goods	industry	investments
look after	service	set up	trade	uncertain

1. Bruce Yang's company is active in three types of business. The firm _____ these three areas.

2. Bruce's firm works with companies from other countries. These are _____ companies.

3. Some companies make or sell a product you can touch. These products are sometimes called "_____." (This noun is always plural.)

4. Other companies do certain kinds of work for people. They sell a _____, such as cleaning things or giving medical advice.

5. When you start a business, you may have to _____ an office. This means you get an office ready to open.

6. Bruce's company gives advice based on its experience with certain areas of business activity. One of these areas is the construction _____.

7. The company puts money into projects in order to get more money back in the future. This is called making _____.

8. In the 1950s, the company dealt in international _____ —that is, the buying and selling of products between countries.

9. Bruce is in charge of the company's money. It is his job to

_____ the company's "financial health."

10. He cannot be sure what will happen to the company. Its future is

_____.

B These sentences use the target words and phrases **in new contexts**. Complete them with the words and phrases in the box.

deal in	foreign	goods	industry	investments
looks after	services	set up	trade	uncertain

1. Hollywood is important in the film _____. The American movie business was born there.

2. He made some smart _____, and they have made him rich.

3. Every student in the school has to study a _____ language.

4. Katya is their baby-sitter. She _____ the children while their parents are out.

5. The store sells men's clothing only. They don't _____ clothes for women or children.

6. A fire destroyed all the _____ in the store.

7. Our travel plans are _____ at this point. We're not sure when we're leaving or where we're going.

8. Most of Mexico's international _____ depends on selling products to the United States and buying U.S. goods.

9. An increase in the cost of oil led to an increase in the cost of many goods and _____.

10. Last year, the government _____ a new program to help workers who lose their jobs.

C Read these sentences. Write the **boldfaced** target words or phrases next to their definitions.

a. I see my **niece** and **nephew** when I visit my sister and brother-in-law.

b. I met her in college, but I didn't **get to know** her very well.

c. He's a film **director**. In other words, he makes movies.

d. Both banks **do business** with local farmers.

e. She is a lawyer in a large law **firm**.

Target Words/Phrases   Definitions

1. _____*niece*_____ = the daughter of someone's brother or sister

2. _____ = the son of someone's brother or sister

3. _____ = a business with two or more partners

4. _____ = gain an understanding of (a person or place)

5. _____ = a person who leads, controls, or manages a company or activity

6. _____ = be active in the making, buying, and selling of goods and services

Building on the Vocabulary

Studying Collocations

The verb *do* often goes with **business,** as in *The bank doesn't do business on Sundays.* Other useful phrases with *business* are:

- *go into business,* meaning "set up a company and start work"
- *go out of business,* meaning "stop working as a company"
- *on business,* meaning "for business purposes"
- *run a business,* meaning "be in charge of and control a business"

 A Complete the sentences with words from the box.

do business	on business	run the business
went into business	went out of business	

1. Are you going to London _____ or for the fun of it?

2. After college, he _____ with his father.

3. The company lost a lot of money and finally _____.

4. Big oil companies _____ with foreign governments.

5. My grandfather is the president of the company, but my parents really

   _____.

B Write three statements using phrases with *business.*

1. _____

2. _____

3. _____

DEVELOPING YOUR SKILLS

Understanding Cause and Effect

Complete the following sentences with *because* using information from "A Family Business." Try not to copy sentences from the reading. Use your own words.

1. Foreign companies sometimes ask Bruce Yang's company to represent them in Taiwan because _____.

2. Companies sometimes come to Taipan Supplies Limited for advice because

   _____.

3. Bruce likes working with his father because _____

   _____.

4. It is hard for Bruce to work with his father because _____

   _____.

5. Bruce doesn't know if his children will follow him into the family business because _____.

Summarizing

Ⓐ Use information from "A Family Business" to complete these notes about Taipan Supplies Limited. Write your additions in the chart.

Dates	Notes
1950s	Bruce Yang's grandfather & his partners set up the company to deal in international trade (U.S. & Taiwan)
1960s	
1985	
today	offices in Taiwan & Hong Kong the company deals in 3 areas: 1. 2. 3.

B On a piece of paper, write a paragraph summarizing the history of Taipan Supplies Limited. Use your notes from Part A and write the summary in **chronological order**. In other words, begin with the start of the company and continue to the present day.

Discussion

Talk with a partner about the questions below.

1. Some companies produce goods (they make things) and others deal in services (they do things). Where do the following belong in the chart?

   books, cars, cleaning, computers, education, job training, medical care, oil

Goods	Services
books	

2. What are two more examples you can add to each column?
3. How would you describe Bruce Yang's relationship with his father? Would you like to work for your father or mother? Tell why or why not.

Using New Words

Work with a partner. Take turns completing these statements. Then tell the class something about your partner.

1. I have _____ **niece(s)** and _____ **nephew(s)**.
2. I would like to **get to know** . . .
3. If I were a movie **director**, I would . . .
4. _____ asked me to **look after** . . .
5. I feel **uncertain** about . . .

Writing

Choose a topic. Write a paragraph.

1. How would you feel about being in business with members of your family? Explain.
2. No one can see into the future, but we can imagine the directions our lives may go in. Think about yourself ten years from now. Where do you think you will be? What will you be doing?

CHAPTER 14

When the Employees Own the Company

Jeffrey Hamelman, head baker and worker-owner, shows off bread made with King Arthur flour.

GETTING READY TO READ

Talk with a partner or in a small group.

1. Have you ever been the boss at work? Would you like a job where you were the boss? Explain why you would or would not.

2. Who works harder, the boss or the people who work for him or her? Tell how you would complete this statement and explain why:

   When you are the boss,

   a. you don't have to work so hard.

   b. you have to work harder.

READING

Look at the words and picture next to the reading. Then read without stopping.

When the Employees Own the Company

1   King Arthur Flour is the oldest **flour** company in the United States. Its flour is of very high **quality**. Just ask the people who **bake** with it. All across North America, people who care about making fine bread buy King Arthur flour. The company even has **customers** in Switzerland, Japan, China, and Saudi Arabia.

2   King Arthur Flour began in 1790 as the Sands, Taylor and Wood Company, and the Sands family has stayed with it all these years. Frank Sands started working there in 1963, when his father was in charge, and later his wife, Brinna, joined him there. Now Frank is the fifth member of the Sands family to lead the company. He will also be the last.

3   A few years ago, Frank and Brinna decided to retire.[1] However, **none** of their children wanted to **take over** the family business, which meant that the future of King Arthur was uncertain. Then one evening, Brinna asked Frank, "Who **besides** our kids is most like family?" The answer was clear: the people who worked at the company. Frank and Brinna trusted them to continue the family tradition. So, in 1996, they began to let the **employees** take over the business. Today, the 160 employees of King Arthur own and run the company.

4   Worker-owned businesses do not all start the same way. In some cases, a group of workers at a successful company find a way to buy it. In other cases, a company fails, but the employees start it up again. Often, a group of people decide to create a new business together. What makes them want to do this? Some want to be part of the decision making at their workplace. Others want a greater chance to share in a company's success. They know that when a company makes money, the owners do, too.

5   There are various types of worker-owned businesses. Some of them make a product, like flour, and others **provide** a service, such as cleaning or health care. There are various ways to **organize** worker-owned businesses, too. However, these businesses usually share certain ideas. One idea is that all the workers—not just the people in charge—should have the chance to be owners. Another is that the worker-owners

[1] *retire* = stop working at the end of a career (usually because of old age)

continued

should have the **right** to vote on business decisions. Then they have real control.

6   Here are the stories of how two more **such** companies began:

- Eight employees at a photocopy shop[2] in Massachusetts (United States) were unhappy with their jobs. "Working **conditions** were terrible and the pay was low," says Stephen Roy, one of the eight. "Plus,[3] we had no job **security**—the manager could **get rid of** any one of us at any time for any reason. We ran the shop for the owners, and we started to ask, 'Why can't we do it for ourselves?'" So they went into business together and started Collective Copies. Twenty years later, they have two shops. One afternoon a month, they close their doors to meet and make business decisions.

- In Coamo, Puerto Rico, there were not many jobs for young people. Miriam Rodriguez, who lived in Coamo, wanted to do something about it. She organized a committee[4] to work on the problem, and the result of their efforts was a furniture business, Las Flores Metalarte. The business now has 180 worker-owners producing tables, chairs, kitchen cabinets,[5] and so on. The success of the company has led to other new businesses in the town, including a sandwich shop and a child care center.

7   According to a study in Italy, worker-owned businesses are good for their communities. They lead to a higher quality of life. The researchers who did the study looked at things like health care, education, and social activities in many Italian towns. They also considered problems in the towns, such as **crime**. They found that towns with more worker-owned businesses were better places to live in almost every way.

Brinna Sands's words come from an article by Per Ola and Emily D'Aulaire, "Baking Up a Business," *Smithsonian* (November 2000): 114–115.

[2] a *photocopy shop* = a business that uses machines to make copies of print materials

[3] *plus* = and also

[4] a *committee* = a group of people asked to do a certain job, make decisions, etc.

[5] kitchen *cabinets*

Quick Comprehension Check

Read these sentences. Circle T (true) or F (false).

1. King Arthur Flour was a family business for many years.   T   F

2. All worker-owned companies start out as family businesses.   T   F

3. The workers at King Arthur bought the company after it failed.   T   F

4. Worker-owned businesses are not all the same.   T   F

5. Workers gain more control when they become worker-owners.   T   F

6. There are worker-owned businesses only in the United States.   T   F

EXPLORING VOCABULARY

Thinking about the Vocabulary

Which target words and phrases are new to you? Circle them here and in the reading. Then read "When the Employees Own the Company" again. Look at the context of each new word and phrase. Can you guess the meaning?

Target Words and Phrases			
flour (1)	none (3)	provide (5)	conditions (6)
quality (1)	take over (3)	organize (5)	security (6)
bake (1)	besides (3)	right (5)	get rid of (6)
customers (1)	employees (3)	such (6)	crime (7)

Using the Vocabulary

Ⓐ These sentences are about the reading. What is the meaning of each boldfaced word or phrase? Circle a, b, or c.

1. King Arthur Flour has over a million **customers**. *Customers* means:

   a. people who run a business   b. people who buy goods or services   c. people who sell a product

2. Frank and Brinna Sands hoped one of their children would continue the family business, but **none** of them wanted to. *None* means:

   a. all   b. most   c. not any

3. Frank and Brinna were ready to give up control of King Arthur. But their children didn't want to **take over** the company. *Take over* means:

   a. take control of   b. compete with   c. realize

4. Brinna asked who **besides** their children were most important to them. *Besides* means:

   a. because of   b. in addition to   c. in order to

5. Some businesses produce goods and others **provide** services. *Provide* means:

   a. avoid   b. waste   c. supply

6. There are various ways to **organize** and run a worker-owned business. *Organize* means:

   a. plan or set up   b. destroy   c. avoid

7. There are many worker-owned businesses in the world. The reading describes three **such** companies. *Such* means:

   a. of the kind just described **b.** on a regular basis **c.** in addition

8. The copy shop workers worried that their boss could **get rid of** them easily. *Get rid of* someone means:

   a. make someone leave **b.** increase someone's pay **c.** look after someone

9. According to a study in Italy, there is less **crime** in towns with many worker-owned businesses. *Crime* means:

   a. fun social activities **b.** actions that are against the law **c.** relationships among people

B These sentences use the target words and phrases **in new contexts.** Complete them with the words and phrases in the box.

besides	crime	customers	get rid of	none
organized	provide	such	take over	

1. The store went out of business because it didn't have enough

   _____.

2. There were three pay phones on the wall, but _____ of them worked.

3. _____ taking four courses, she is working 20 hours a week.

4. While the teacher is out sick, someone else will _____ the class.

5. I'm sure he can _____ an explanation for what he did.

6. People in the city are upset about the high _____ rate.

7. Al has to write a 20-page paper. He has never written _____ a long paper.

8. Beatriz _____ the class party. She knows who is bringing what food, who is in charge of the music, and all the other details.

9. The neighbors' dog keeps coming into our yard. We don't want him around, but we don't know how to _____ him.

C Read each definition and look at the paragraph number in parentheses ( ).
Look back at the reading to **find the target word** for each definition. Write
it in the chart.

Definition	Target Word
1. a powder made from wheat[1] or another grain, used for making bread, cakes, etc. (1)	
2. how good something is, its character (1)	
3. cook food inside an oven[2] (1)	
4. the people who work for a person or business (3)	
5. something that a person is allowed to do by law (5)	
6. all the things that affect the place someone lives or works (6)	
7. safety from having to change or from losing something (6)	

[1]*wheat*

[2]bread in an *oven*

Building on the Vocabulary

Studying Word Grammar

Remember: A **suffix** is a letter or letters added to the end of a word to make a
new word. Look at the words and suffixes in the word family for *employ* ("give a
job to"):

    *employ**er*** = a person who gives a job to someone

    *employ**ee*** = a person who works for another person, for a company, etc.

    *employ**ment*** = work; the fact or condition of having a job

    un**employ**ment = the opposite of *employment* (The prefix *un-* means "not" or
                      "the opposite of.")

A Complete the paragraph with the five words from the word family for *employ*.

The hospital is the biggest _____ in the community. It
(1)

has over 800 _____ s. It _____ s doctors,
(2)   (3)

nurses, office workers, cooks, and so on. Of course, the hospital is not the only

place to find _____ in town. There are many jobs available in
(4)

the area right now, so the _____ rate is low.
(5)

B The **boldfaced** words have the suffixes *-er* and *-ee*. Can you guess their meanings? Write the words next to their definitions.

a. He's a racehorse **trainer**.

b. On the first day at my new job, I met the other **trainees**.

1. _____ = a person who teaches skills, especially for a job or sport

2. _____ = people who are receiving training.

DEVELOPING YOUR SKILLS

Understanding Main Ideas and Supporting Details

Supply a detail from the reading to support each of the general statements below. Use your own words and write complete sentences.

1. Sometimes the employees of a company take it over. <u>For example, this</u>
   <u>happened at King Arthur Flour when Frank and Brinna Sands retired.</u>

2. Sometimes a group of employees work to create a business together. _____
   _____
   _____

3. Some worker-owned companies produce goods to sell. _____
   _____
   _____

4. Worker-owned businesses can have a good effect on their communities.
   _____
   _____

Summarizing

Do the following tasks on a piece of paper. Use information from the reading, but try not to copy sentences from the reading.

1. Summarize the history of King Arthur Flour, from 1790 to the present.
2. Describe the way Collective Copies began.
3. Describe Las Flores Metalarte.

Sharing Opinions

Talk about these questions in a small group.

1. The employees at a worker-owned business own a share of their company. How do you think this affects how they feel about their jobs? How do you think it affects the way they do their jobs?
2. The reading says, "According to a study in Italy, worker-owned businesses are good for their communities." How do you think such businesses help their communities?

Using New Words

Work with a partner. Choose five target words or phrases from the list on page 131. On a piece of paper, use each word or phrase in a sentence.

Writing

Choose a topic. Write a paragraph.

1. The phrase *working conditions* refers to all the things about your job that affect how you feel about it. They can include everything from the air quality in your workplace to your sense of job security. Imagine a job with great working conditions and describe it.
2. Are you good or bad at organizing things? Write about organizing something in your life—for example, your closet, your time on weekends, a party, or a trip.

CHAPTER 15

She Finally Did It

Elizabeth (Betty) Nice Weber presenting a check

GETTING READY TO READ

Talk with a partner or in a small group.

1. Would you like to be a millionaire?[1] Check (✓) your answer:
   ❑ Yes   ❑ No   ❑ Maybe

2. How do you think most millionaires get rich?

3. If you become very rich, what will you do with your money?

[1] a *millionaire* = a person with $1,000,000 or more

READING

Look at the words and definitions next to the reading. Then read without stopping.

She Finally Did It

1   While Betty Nice was growing up, her family did not have much money. They **could not afford** to buy a house, and the apartment they **rented** was in a bad part of town. Betty knew she wanted something better. She dreamed of living another kind of life, but how would she make it happen? She did not know. In fact, she had no idea what she wanted to do when she grew up. "All I knew," she says, "was I wanted to be a millionaire."

2   After high school, Betty went to college to study business. She took courses at four colleges, and although she came close, she never managed to get her **degree**. She says now, "I wasn't cut out for[1] the classroom."

[1] *not be cut out for = not have the right qualities for (a certain job or activity)*

3   Betty then went to work as a **secretary**. She spent years working for a law firm, doing all the usual office work. The job was nothing special, and she did not **earn** a lot. She and her husband could not save any money. With no savings in the bank, she had no sense of security. Betty wanted more.

4   During this period, she also had a series of part-time jobs in **sales**, sometimes going door-to-door, and sometimes organizing parties in the evening to sell things to friends and neighbors. In 11 years, she worked for nine different companies and sold lots and lots of different things. Brushes, **jewelry**, and skin care products were just a few. "I tried everything!" she says with a laugh. Betty made some money, but not much. She says, "It **wasn't worth** the hours I was putting in."[2] She did not know what to do. "I worked so hard, and I failed at everything. My husband paid the bills and supported me through it all." But all the time that Betty was "failing," she was learning. She was gaining business skills and becoming a better salesperson.

[2] *putting in = giving or spending (time)*

5   Betty was almost ready to give up when she heard about another company. It sounded different, so she **looked into** it and found out more about it. Then, after **thinking over**

continued

what she had learned, she decided to take a chance. She gave up her job at the law firm after 18 years as a secretary and became a full-time salesperson. She went on to sell everything from motor oil for cars to burglar alarms[3] for houses to **pills** for people trying to lose weight. She also recruited[4] other salespeople, and she became an **officer** in the company. After four years, Betty was a millionaire. Soon she was making over a million dollars a year!

6   At age 44, Betty was living a dream come true. She could afford **whatever** she wanted. She and her husband bought a **huge** house (it has 11 bathrooms), and they took their children on exciting trips all over the world. At that point Betty had everything she had ever hoped for. So, what does a person do when she has everything? Betty decided, "Now it's my **turn** to give."

7   Betty set up the Weber Foundation of Helping Hands. "There are a lot of families out there in need," she says, thinking especially of parents with very sick children. She wanted to help not only her own family but also people she did not know. Today, the Weber Foundation does that. In its first 18 months, it **gave away** more than $100,000. For Betty, it is another dream come true.

Betty Nice Weber's words come from Eileen McNamara, "Now a Boss but Still Nice," *Boston Globe,* October 15, 2000, B: 1, and from Phil Santoro, "Sharing Her Success," *Boston Globe,* March 3, 2002, North Weekly section: 9.

[3] *burglar alarms* = machines that warn people (by making a loud noise, for example) when someone enters a building

[4] *recruit* = find new people to work in a company, join an organization, etc.

Quick Comprehension Check

Read these sentences. Circle T (true) or F (false).

1.	Betty Nice grew up poor.	T	F
2.	She graduated from college with a business degree.	T	F
3.	She worked for many years as a secretary.	T	F
4.	Working at a law firm made her rich.	T	F
5.	Betty doesn't care about money.	T	F
6.	She gives away money to families who need it.	T	F

EXPLORING VOCABULARY

Thinking about the Vocabulary

Which target words and phrases are new to you? Circle them here and in the reading. Then read "She Finally Did It" again. Look at the context of each new word and phrase. Can you guess the meaning?

Target Words and Phrases			
could not afford (1)	earn (3)	looked into (5)	whatever (6)
rented (1)	sales (4)	thinking over (5)	huge (6)
degree (2)	jewelry (4)	pills (5)	turn (6)
secretary (3)	wasn't worth (4)	officer (5)	gave away (7)

Using the Vocabulary

A Complete these sentences. Write *jewelry, a pill,* and *a secretary.*

1. He's taking _____.   2. She's wearing _____.

3. She's _____.

B These sentences are **about the reading**. Complete them with the words and phrases in the box.

couldn't afford	degree	earn	gives away	huge
looked into	officer	rented	sales	thought it over
turn	wasn't worth	whatever		

1. Betty's family _____ a house. They didn't have enough money to buy one.

2. They didn't own their apartment. They _____ it from the owner.

3. Betty didn't finish her college studies, so she didn't get a _____.

4. She wasn't paid a lot at the law firm. She didn't _____ much money.

5. Betty also worked part-time in _____. She sold various products.

6. The money she got from selling things was not enough for all the hours she spent selling them. The money _____ the time.

7. She heard something about a company and she wanted more information, so she read about it and asked questions. She _____ it.

8. She took time to think carefully about joining the company. She

   _____.

9. Betty showed a lot of ability, so the company made her an _____, one of the people in charge.

10. Now she has money for anything she wants. She can afford _____ she wants.

11. Betty's house has many, many rooms. It is _____.

12. After Betty became rich, she decided it was her _____ to give. It was the right time for her to do something for others.

13. The Weber Foundation of Helping Hands _____ money to people in need. People who receive the money don't have to do anything for it, and they don't have to give it back.

C These sentences use the target words and phrases **in new contexts**. Complete them with the words and phrases in the box.

can afford	degree	earned	gave it away	huge
is worth	looked into it	officers	rented	sales
think it over	turn	whatever		

1. You have the right to say _____ you want.

2. He received his _____ from the University of Toronto.

3. They make a lot of money, so they _____ to eat in restaurants whenever they want.

4. In a company, the army, or the police, the _____ are the people who make decisions and give orders.

5. That's not cheap jewelry! It _____ thousands of dollars.

6. A career in _____ would be hard for a shy person.

7. They didn't take the train to Madrid. They _____ a car and drove.

8. The bus driver worked extra hours, so she _____ more money than usual.

9. You washed the dishes last night, so tonight is my _____.

10. I didn't try to sell my old bicycle. I _____.

11. They have invited him to join the firm, but he needs time to _____.

12. Yesterday I heard about an apartment for rent, so I _____ right away.

13. Going into business with my mother was a _____ mistake. We can't agree on anything!

Building on the Vocabulary

Studying Collocations

The adjective *worth* can follow *be* or another linking verb (such as *seem, sound,* or *look*). A thing can be worth:

- an amount of money: *The house is worth a million dollars.*
- time or effort: *Maybe we can fix it—it seems worth a try.*
- doing something: *The service is slow, but the food is worth waiting for.*

Write three statements with the adjective *worth*.

1. _____

2. _____

3. _____

DEVELOPING YOUR SKILLS

Reading Between the Lines

You cannot find the answers to these questions given in the reading. These are inference or opinion questions. To answer them, you must use what you already know in addition to information from the reading.

1. Was money the only thing that mattered to Betty? Explain your answer.

   _____

   _____

   _____

   _____

2. How would you describe Betty's character? Why do you see her this way?

   _____

   _____

   _____

   _____

3. Why do you think Betty didn't stop working after she became a millionaire?

   _____

   _____

   _____

   _____

Summarizing

On a piece of paper, write a summary of "She Finally Did It." Use no more than ten sentences. Include information about:

- Betty's life and dreams as a child
- her early career
- her part-time jobs
- her success as a salesperson
- the Weber Foundation of Helping Hands

Sharing Opinions

Talk about these questions in a small group.

1. Compare your answers to the three questions under **Reading Between the Lines**. In what ways do you agree or disagree?

2. What do you think of these two common sayings: "Money can't buy happiness" and "The best things in life are free"? Do you agree or disagree with these sayings? Why?

3. Why might someone not want to be a millionaire? Describe some reasons.

Using New Words

Work with a partner. Take turns completing these statements. Then tell the class something about your partner.

1. I can't **afford** . . .
2. I have never **rented** . . .
3. I would like to have a **degree** in . . .
4. The movie ". . ." **isn't worth** seeing.
5. A career in **sales** would be . . . for me.

Writing

Choose a topic. Write a paragraph.

1. For some people, success means making a lot of money. Is that true for you? Describe your idea of success.

2. Write a letter to a friend you haven't seen in a long time. Explain to your friend that you are now a millionaire and describe how you became so rich. Invite your friend to visit you.

CHAPTER 16

A Language on the Move

Doing business in English

GETTING READY TO READ

Answer the three parts of question 1 by circling a number from 1 to 5. Then talk about your answers to questions 1 and 2 in a small group or with your class.

Very ⟵⟶ Not at all

1. In your country:

   a. Are English classes common in the schools? 1 2 3 4 5

   b. Is English important for many jobs? 1 2 3 4 5

   c. Is English important in the business world? 1 2 3 4 5

2. When, where, and why do businesspeople from your country use English?

READING

Look at the words and definitions next to the reading. Then read without stopping.

A Language on the Move

1   Filiz Yilmaz works for a company in Istanbul and usually speaks Turkish at work. When she travels to England on business, she uses English. But when she goes to Germany or Brazil, she does not use German or Portuguese. She **deals with** people there in English, too. "And I use English in Japan and Thailand," she says. "English is the language of international business."

2   How did English get to be so **popular**? It is not the oldest living language, nor is it the most beautiful to the ear. It includes sounds that are hard to pronounce and many words that are hard to spell. So why has this language **spread** so far?

3   Some people would answer this question by pointing to the influence of music and movies. American films do seem to be everywhere now, but they often **appear** in other languages, and people can enjoy songs in English without understanding the words. So this cannot be the whole explanation.

4   Part of the answer can be found in the character of the language. English has certain **qualities** that make it especially useful. For one thing, its grammar is **quite** simple. It is relatively[1] easy to learn the **rules** of English—what is and is not allowed, or how the language works. For example, learners of English do not have to worry about the gender of a noun (that is, whether it is masculine, feminine, or neuter),[2] **while** learners of many other languages do. In German, for example, *der Mond* (the word for the moon) is masculine but *die Sonne* (the sun) is feminine. You would expect the words *girl* and *woman* (*das Mädchen* and *das Weib*) to be feminine, but they are neuter!

5   English also has a huge vocabulary. Early English developed from Germanic languages, which gave it the most common words we use today, such as *the, is, of, go, you, man,* and *woman.* However, from the beginning, English **borrowed** words from other European languages, including

[1] *relatively* = compared to others

[2] *masculine, feminine,* or *neuter* = male, female, or neither

continued

Latin (*secretary, attract, compete,* and *invent*) and Greek (*alphabet, mathematics,* and *technology*). After invaders[3] from France took over England in the year 1066, English gained a great many French words, such as *officer, foreign, crime,* and *service.* **Since** that time, English has welcomed useful new words from many other languages—from Spanish, Arabic, Turkish, Urdu, Chinese, and Japanese, to name just a few.

[3] *invaders* = people who enter and take over a country by force, as with an army

6   To understand the spread of English, we also have to look at **political** and economic[4] history. During the 1600s and 1700s, people from England **sailed** all over the world, taking their language to North America, Africa, India, and Australia. New **nations** were born, and their governments used English. In the 1800s, England led the Industrial Revolution: New machines were invented, factories were built, and the city of London became the world's great financial[5] center. That made English the language of money. In the 1900s, it became the language of science and air travel, too. All through the 1900s, the United States grew in power and influence, and the English language grew right along with it.

[4] *economic* = referring to money, goods, and services: how they are produced and used

[5] *financial* = relating to money or the management of money

7   Then came the Internet. As Filiz Yilmaz remembers it, "People at my company realized that the Internet could be quite useful to us. But at first, everything online was in English. It gave us another reason to know this language." Soon people in many countries were going online, both for business and for personal reasons. Some of them used to see English only in the classroom, but now they needed English on a regular basis, whenever they wanted to "surf the Net."[6]

[6] *surf the Net* = look quickly through sites on the Internet for things that interest you

8   Today, there are business schools teaching all their courses in English even in non-English-speaking countries. These schools want their students to have the language skills **necessary** for doing business in international **markets**. Companies around the world are **investing** in English classes for their employees. They believe in English as the language of the future.

9   There are over 300 million native speakers of English (that is, people who speak it as their first language). Many more speak Mandarin Chinese—almost 900 million. But few of them are outside of China, while there are people who know English all over the world. There may be a billion people who speak some variety of English as a second, third, or fourth language. Filiz says, "With so many people using English, I can't imagine any other language taking its place. I think English for business is here to stay."

Quick Comprehension Check

Read these sentences. Circle T (true) or F (false).

1. People around the world use English to talk business.   T   F

2. American movies are the biggest reason why English is so   T   F
   popular.

3. Many English words come from other languages.   T   F

4. England was a world power before the United States.   T   F

5. Companies around the world think English is the language   T   F
   of the future.

6. The same numbers of people speak Chinese and English.   T   F

EXPLORING VOCABULARY

Thinking about the Vocabulary

**Which target words and phrases are new to you? Circle them here and in
the reading. Then read "A Language on the Move" again. Look at the
context of each new word and phrase. Can you guess the meaning?**

Target Words and Phrases			
deals with (1)	qualities (4)	borrowed (5)	nations (6)
popular (2)	quite (4)	since (5)	necessary (8)
spread (2)	rules (4)	political (6)	markets (8)
appear (3)	while (4)	sailed (6)	investing (8)

Using the Vocabulary

Ⓐ **These sentences are about the reading. Complete them with the words
and phrases in the box.**

appear	borrowed	deals with	invests	markets
necessary	political	rules	since	spread

1. Filiz Yilmaz does business with people in several countries. She

   _____ people in Germany, Brazil, Japan, Thailand, and the

   United States.

2. The number of English speakers has grown. The language has

   _____ around the world.

3. American films are usually shown in English, but they _____ in other languages, too.

4. Languages have _____ (for grammar and spelling, for example). These tell us how to use words so that other people can understand us.

5. English has a big vocabulary because it has always _____ words from other languages. It has grown by copying useful foreign words.

6. Beginning in the year 1066, many French words entered the English language. _____ that time—in other words, starting then and continuing to the present—English has continued to add words from other languages.

7. To understand why English has spread over so much of the world, we have to study _____ history. This concerns power, governments, and relationships between countries.

8. Certain language skills are _____ for business. Businesspeople need them.

9. After finishing business school, some people go on to work in international _____, **i.e.,** in areas concerned with buying and selling.

10. When a company _____ in English-language training for its employees, it spends money. It does this because it expects the training to result in more money later.

> **Common Abbreviations**
> The abbreviation *i.e.* is short for the Latin words *id est*, meaning "that is." This abbreviation, like the phrase "in other words," is often used to introduce an explanation.

B These sentences use the target words and phrases **in new contexts.**
Complete them with the words and phrases in the box.

appeared	borrow	deal with	invested	market
necessary	political	rules	since	spreads

1. The verb _____ means "copy and use" when it refers to words or ideas. It can also mean "take something, use it, and then give it back," like a library book or money from a bank.

2. They _____ their money well and ended up rich.

3. You can't do that—it's against the _____ of the game.

4. News always _____ quickly among the employees.

5. Suddenly, a face _____ at my window. I was so surprised that it made me jump.

6. It is not _____ to wear a jacket and tie, but he can if he wants to.

7. The phrase _____ *science* refers to the study of government.

8. The company has customers in Europe and Asia, but the main _____ for their software is the United States.

9. Elizabeth has looked after her niece and nephew _____ her sister died last year.

10. I won't _____ that company again. They make high-quality goods, but their customer service is terrible.

C Read these sentences. Write the **boldfaced** target words next to their definitions.

a. It is hard to get to know her. She seems **quite** shy.

b. That song was very **popular** last year.

c. Almost 200 countries belong to the United **Nations**.

d. I'd like to **sail** around the Mediterranean Sea.

e. She likes foreign films, **while** her husband prefers Hollywood movies.

f. She has all the **qualities** the boss likes in an employee: She's smart, hard working, and creative.

Target Words	Definitions
1. _____	= countries
2. _____	= more than a little but not extremely
3. _____	= liked, accepted, or used by a lot of people
4. _____	= parts of the character of a person or thing that make that one different from others
5. _____	= but (used to present differences between two facts or ideas)
6. _____	= travel across the water on a boat or ship

Building on the Vocabulary

> ### Studying Word Grammar
>
> The word *since* is used to show when an action began. Use *since* + a point in time (for example, a time, a date, or an event). *Since* is usually used in sentences with verbs in the present perfect or present perfect progressive tense: *He has lived here since 1991. I have been waiting since 2:30. She's been avoiding him since the party.*

Complete the statements. Use *since* + a point in time.

Example: I have known my friend <u>Omar since our first day of school.</u>

1. I have studied English _____.

2. I've been using this book _____.

3. I have known my friend _____ _____.
                                   (name)

4. My family has lived in _____ _____.
                                  (place)

DEVELOPING YOUR SKILLS

Reading for Details

Read these sentences. Then reread "A Language on the Move" for the answers. If the reading doesn't give the information, check (✓) *It doesn't say.*

	True	False	It doesn't say.
1. Filiz Yilmaz uses English in Japan and Brazil.			
2. English has harder rules than most other languages.			
3. English has the largest vocabulary of any language.			
4. The Industrial Revolution started in England.			
5. English became the language of science in the 1800s.			
6. The Internet started in California.			
7. Some companies pay for their employees to learn English.			
8. More people speak English as their second, third, or fourth language than as their first.			

Understanding Topics of Paragraphs

(A) Where is the information about these topics in "A Language on the Move"? Scan the reading and write the paragraph number.

  _6_ **a.** political and economic influences

  _____ **b.** numbers of English speakers

  _____ **c.** the effect of the Internet

  _____ **d.** Filiz Yilmaz's use of English

  _____ **e.** the influence of American movies and music

  _____ **f.** how English developed its huge vocabulary

  _____ **g.** English for international markets

(B) On a piece of paper, write a sentence or two about each topic in Part A, beginning with the topic of the first paragraph and continuing in order. Do not copy sentences from the reading. Use your own words.

Example: <u>Filiz Yilmaz uses English when she travels to other countries</u>

<u>on business.</u>

Discussion

Work with a partner and take turns asking the questions below.

1. What English words can you list that sound like words in your first language? Where do you think the words came from?
2. How will knowing English affect your future? How much English do you need to know?

Using New Words

Work with a partner. Choose five target words or phrases from the list on page 147. On a piece of paper, use each word or phrase in a sentence.

Writing

Choose a topic. Write a paragraph.

1. People invest a lot of time and money in learning English, and nobody wants to waste either one. What advice would you give a new learner on how to invest his or her time and money well?
2. When, where, and why did you start to learn English? How did you feel about the experience?

Wrap-up

REVIEWING VOCABULARY

A Think about the meanings of the words in each group below. Cross out the one word that does not belong in each group.

1. nephew   uncle   ~~officer~~   niece
2. secretary   employee   director   quality
3. rules   customers   sales   markets
4. organize   sail   plan   set up
5. invest   earn   bake   borrow

B Match the words and phrases below with their definitions. There are two extra words or phrases.

deal with	foreign	goods	huge	industry	look into
nation	political	rent	think over	uncertain	whatever

1. _____ = very, very big
2. _____ = anything
3. _____ = not known or not sure
4. _____ = concerned with government or power
5. _____ = have a business connection with
6. _____ = things that are produced to be sold
7. _____ = from a country that is not your own
8. _____ = try to find out the facts about something
9. _____ = consider (something) carefully before making a decision
10. _____ = an area of business, usually dealing in the production of something

EXPANDING VOCABULARY

Some verbs are **transitive**. After a transitive verb, there is a direct object, usually a noun or pronoun. For example, the verb *take* is transitive and needs a direct object: *He took **a pill**. / He took **it**.* We cannot say *He took.*

Other verbs are **intransitive**, such as *sleep.* There can be no direct object after the verb *sleep: He slept.*

Some verbs can be used either way—with or without a direct object: *I drove **my car** to the beach* or *I drove to the beach.*

A **Underline** the verbs in the sentences below. Circle any direct objects after the verbs. Which verbs are transitive, which are intransitive, and which can be either? Check (✓) your answers in the chart.

	Transitive	Intransitive
1. a. I spread some (butter) on my bread. b. English spread around the world.	✓	✓
2. a. She often bakes on weekends. b. She baked a birthday cake.		
3. a. I'll trade my candy bar for yours. b. We trade with foreign countries.		
4. a. Can you sail a boat? b. The ship sails at 10:00.		
5. a. I can't afford the rent. b. Can they afford a new car?		
6. a. He finally appeared at 9:30. b. Stars appeared in the sky.		

B On a piece of paper, write at least six sentences with at least six different verbs. Use verbs that were target words in Unit 4. Mark each verb *T* for transitive or *I* for intransitive.

Example: <u>Let's organize a class party.</u> ᵀ

PLAYING WITH WORDS

There are 12 target words from Unit 4 in this puzzle. The words go
across (→)and down (↓). Find the words and circle them. Then use them
to complete the sentences below.

```
M  C  B  P  R  O  V  I  D  E
B  O  E  R  I  G  H  T  E  S
O  N  S  X  Z  C  V  X  G  E
R  D  I  K  H  R  Z  G  R  C
R  I  D  W  H  I  L  E  E  U
O  T  E  W  X  M  K  Z  E  R
W  I  S  V  Z  E  V  Q  X  I
P  O  P  U  L  A  R  X  K  T
M  N  E  C  E  S  S  A  R  Y
V  S  X  Q  U  A  L  I  T  Y
```

1. Working ____conditions____ were very bad, so many employees quit.

2. My friends are bringing the food and I'll _____ the drinks.

3. It took him four years to earn his college _____.

4. All patients must sign certain medical forms. They will give you the
   _____ forms at the hospital.

5. The _____ rate usually goes up during periods of high
   unemployment.

6. She buys cheap clothes. She can't afford anything of high
   _____.

7. Job _____ is worth a lot to him. He hates worrying about
   the future.

8. That color is very _____ this season. Everybody is wearing it.

9. Jack enjoys dealing with the customers, _____ his brother
   hates it.

10. I often _____ books from the public library.

11. At what age do people get the _____ to vote in your country?

12. She works 15 hours a week _____ going to school full-time.

BUILDING DICTIONARY SKILLS

Regular and Irregular Verb Forms

When a verb is **regular,** your dictionary may show only its **base form** (or **simple form**). Here are two examples:

> **ap·pear** /ə'pɪr/ *v* [I] **1** to begin to be seen: *Suddenly, clouds began to appear in the sky.* | *A face appeared at the window.* **2** to seem: *The man **appeared to be** dead.* | *The noise **appeared to** come from the closet.* **3** to take part in a movie...

> **earn** /ɚn/ *v* [T] **1** to get money by working: *Alan earns $30,000 a year.* **2** to make a profit from business, or from putting money in a bank, lending it etc.: *I **earned** $5000 **from** my investments last year.* **3** to get something that...

To form the simple past tense of a regular verb, add *-ed;* to form participles, add *-ed* (for the past) or *-ing* (for the present).

When a verb is **irregular,** dictionaries usually show the simple past tense form and the participles. Look at this example:

```
        Simple    Past      Present
        Past      Participle Participle
```

> **take**[1] /teɪk/ *v* **took, taken, taking** [T]
> **1** ▸ MOVE ◂ to move someone or something from one place to another: *I was going to take...*

Complete the sentences below. Write the simple past tense form of *deal, set,* or *spread*.

> **deal**[2] *v* **dealt, dealt** /dɛlt/, **dealing 1** [I,T] also **deal out** to give out playing cards to players in a game: *Whose...*

> **set**[1] /sɛt/*v* **set, set, setting**
> **1** ▸ RECORD/STANDARD ETC. ◂ [T] to do or decide something that other things...

> **spread**[1] /sprɛd/*v* **spread, spread, spreading**
> **1** ▸ OPEN/ARRANGE ◂ [T] also **spread out** to open...

1. He _____ the news to all his friends by e-mail.

2. I _____ with a new officer at the bank yesterday.

3. He _____ up a meeting, and everyone agreed to come.

UNIT 5

HEALTH MATTERS

CHAPTER 17

Living to 100 and Beyond

Ponce de Léon on his search for the Fountain of Youth

GETTING READY TO READ

Life expectancy means the number of years a person will probably live. The average life expectancy for a country is how long people in that country usually live. For example, for people in the United States, the average life expectancy is about 77 years. For Canadians, it is almost 80.

Talk with a partner or with your class.

1. What do you think the average life expectancy is for people in your country?

2. In what countries do you think people have the longest life expectancy? And the shortest? Why?

3. Do you think life expectancy is the same for both men and women? Tell why or why not.

157

READING

Look at the words and pictures next to the reading. Then read without stopping. Don't worry about new words. Don't stop to use a dictionary. Just keep reading!

Living to 100 and Beyond

1   Would you like to live to 100? Many people would. Some have dreamed of living even longer—perhaps **forever**. We know this has long been a popular idea because many cultures have legends[1] about ways to avoid growing old.

2   In Europe in the 1400s, people heard stories about a wonderful spring[2] somewhere in Eastern Asia. Drinking the water from this spring was supposed to make a person young again. It is **likely** that the Spanish explorer[3] Juan Ponce de Léon heard these stories. Maybe they were on his mind when he sailed to the Americas with Columbus. After arriving in Puerto Rico, Ponce de Léon heard about an island with a **similar** spring. So, he decided to look for it, and he invested in three ships. In 1513, he went searching for the island, but he ended up in Florida, never finding the island or the spring that people now call the "Fountain[4] of Youth." When Ponce de Léon died eight years later, he was 61 years old. That may seem young, but it was actually a very long life for a man of his times and his way of life.

3   Not long ago, scientists **generally** agreed that the human body could not **possibly** last more than 120 years. Nobody believes 120 to be the **limit** anymore. People have already lived **beyond** that age. A Japanese man, Shigechiyo Izumi, lived to almost 121, and a woman in France, Jeanne Louise Calment, **made it** to 122. People in many parts of the world are living longer lives now than people did in the past. This is partly because of better public health and safer water supplies. Greater understanding of how to **treat** heart problems has made a big difference **as well**. Scientists are learning more all the time about how we can live longer, healthier lives. Maybe someday they will even invent a pill to stop the aging **process** completely.

continued

[1] a *legend* = a well-known story from an earlier time in history

[2] a *spring* = a place where water comes up naturally from the ground

[3] an *explorer* = someone who travels to learn about unknown places

[4] a *fountain*

4   While you are waiting for that wonderful pill, there are things you can do to increase your life expectancy. You just have to follow these three simple rules:

Rule #1: Treat your body well.

Your everyday **lifestyle** influences how long you will live. For example, smoking can take years off your life. (Even if it doesn't make you sick, smoking will affect your skin and make you look older.) So don't smoke, get enough sleep, and lead an active life. Be sure to eat right, too. In other words, eat the kinds of food that are good for you, and don't eat too much.

Rule #2: Don't take **risks.**

Forget about motorcycles[5] and take the bus. Wear your seat belt when you travel by car. Also, choose a nice, safe job. Don't go to sea and work on a fishing boat—that's a dangerous way to **make a living**. If Ponce de Léon had followed Rule #2, he might have lived many more years. Instead, he ended up fighting Native Americans in Florida and died of his **injuries**.

Rule #3: Choose your parents carefully.

You say this one is not so simple? That's true. However, about 70% of your life expectancy depends on your genes,[6] and you get your genes from your parents. Genes control your hair and eye color and much, much more. If people in your family usually live long lives, then the chances are good that you will, too.

5   Scientists have already found genes that influence the aging process in fruit flies and in one kind of worm.[7] By changing these genes, they have managed to **double** the time that these flies and worms can live. Of course they are looking for ways to do that for humans as well.

6   Some final advice for anyone who wants to live to 100: It helps to be born in Australia or Japan, and it helps to be born female. Only one in 10,000 people in the United States lives to be 100, but people in Australia and Japan generally do better. The average Australian or Japanese man can expect to see age 77, while his sister can expect to reach 83.

[5] a *motorcycle*

[6] *your genes* = the parts of cells in your body that control qualities you get from your parents

[7] a *worm*

Quick Comprehension Check

Read these sentences. Circle T (true) or F (false).

1. Many cultures have stories from the past about ways to stay young.	T	F
2. Scientists all agree: Nobody can live past 120.	T	F
3. The reading gives "three simple rules" for living longer.	T	F
4. The way you live can add years to your life (or take years away).	T	F
5. People in certain countries often live longer than the average.	T	F
6. How long your family members live has no relationship to how long you will.	T	F

EXPLORING VOCABULARY

Thinking about the Vocabulary

Which target words and phrases are new to you? Circle them here and in the reading. Then read "Living to 100 and Beyond" again. Look at the context of each new word and phrase. Can you guess the meaning?

Target Words and Phrases			
forever (1)	possibly (3)	treat (3)	risks (4)
likely (2)	limit (3)	as well (3)	make a living (4)
similar (2)	beyond (3)	process (3)	injuries (4)
generally (3)	made it (3)	lifestyle (4)	double (5)

Using the Vocabulary

(A) These sentences are **about the reading**. Complete them with the target words and phrases in the box.

double	forever	lifestyle	likely	limit	made it
make a living	possibly	process	similar	treat	

1. Some people dream of a life without end. They want to live

   _____.

2. Juan Ponce de Léon probably heard the stories from Asia about a spring with special powers. It is _____ that he heard about it.

3. He also learned about an island with a _____ spring. The two springs were alike.

4. Scientists used to think no one could _____ live more than 120 years. They thought it could not happen in any way.

5. Now, no one thinks of 120 years as the longest anyone can live. No one sees 120 as the _____ anymore.

6. A French woman managed to reach the age of 122. She _____ to 122.

7. Today, doctors can deal with heart problems better. They can give heart patients new kinds of medical help. They can _____ these problems better now.

8. Our bodies change as we grow older. We go through the aging _____, a series of changes, actions, or events.

9. Your _____, or the way you live every day, affects how long you will live.

10. How will you earn enough money to live on? You may live longer if you choose a safe way to _____.

11. Researchers have managed to _____ the lifetimes of certain flies and worms. In other words, they got them to live twice as long as usual.

B These sentences use the target words and phrases **in new contexts.** Complete them with the words and phrases in the box.

double	forever	lifestyle	likely	limit	made her living
make it	possibly	process	similar	treat	

1. The speed _____ on this street is 35 miles per hour.

2. She _____ as a secretary.

3. The train won't leave for an hour. Don't worry, we'll _____ in time.

4. The two companies offer _____ services, so it's hard to choose.

5. I didn't need a doctor. I was able to _____ the cut myself.

6. They promised to _____ his pay, so he agreed to stay.

7. Getting a college degree is a long _____.

8. It's _____ to rain later, so take an umbrella.

9. Having a baby usually causes changes in a couple's _____.

10. The movie had a happy ending. The two main characters promised to love each other _____.

11. If the rent doubles, then I can't _____ afford it!

C Read each definition and look at the paragraph number in parentheses ( ). Look back at the reading to **find the target word or phrase** for each definition. Write it in the chart.

Definition	Target Word or Phrase
1. usually, in most cases (3)	
2. past or later than (a certain time or date) (3)	
3. too, also (3)	
4. chances that something bad may happen (4)	
5. hurt done to the body, as in an accident or an attack (4)	

Building on the Vocabulary

Studying Word Grammar

The adverb *possibly* usually means "perhaps, maybe": *He's going to buy a car soon, possibly this week.*

When *possibly* follows *can't* or *couldn't*, it means "in any way": *I can't possibly get there on time.*

What is the meaning of *possibly* in these sentences? Check (✓) your answers in the chart.

1. I'm sorry, but I couldn't possibly go out tonight.
2. This is possibly your best work ever.
3. You can't possibly mean what you're saying!
4. Is it going to rain? Possibly.

In any way	Perhaps

DEVELOPING YOUR SKILLS

Understanding and Using Supporting Details

Ⓐ **Supply a detail from the reading to support each of the general statements below. Use your own words and write complete sentences.**

1. People have told many stories about ways to avoid growing old. For example, _____

   _____

2. Some people have already lived to be more than 120 years old. _____

   _____

   _____

3. There are several reasons why people in many countries live longer lives now. _____

   _____

4. Some things beyond our control affect our life expectancy. _____

   _____

   _____

Ⓑ **Write a general statement that relates to each supporting example.**

1. <u>Take care of yourself. / Live a healthy lifestyle.</u>

   For example, eat well, get enough sleep and exercise, and don't smoke.

2. _____

   For example, take the bus instead of riding a motorcycle.

3. _____

   Don't choose a dangerous kind of career, like working on a fishing boat at sea.

4. _____

   For example, your hair and eye color depend on them, and about 70% of your life expectancy.

5. _____

   For example, people in Australia and Japan are more likely to make it to 100.

Thinking about the Main Idea

Complete this sentence to give the main idea of "Living to 100 and Beyond."

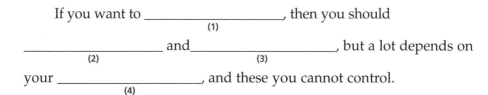

If you want to _____, then you should
(1)

_____ and_____, but a lot depends on
(2)   (3)

your _____, and these you cannot control.
(4)

Sharing Opinions

Talk about these questions in a small group.

1. Look again at Rules 1, 2, and 3 in the reading. Think about the things these rules say to do. What do you think is simple to do? What is hard?

2. The three rules in the reading say nothing about a person's relationships. Do relationships matter in living a long life? Explain your opinion.

3. The three rules say nothing about a person's state of mind—how he or she thinks and feels. Does this matter in living a long life? Explain your opinion.

4. What do you think the secret is to living a long life?

Using New Words

Work with a partner. Choose five target words or phrases from the list on page 160. On a piece of paper, use each word or phrase in a sentence.

Writing

Choose a topic. Write a paragraph.

1. Would you like to make it to 100 or beyond? Explain why or why not.

2. Imagine that today you celebrated your 100th birthday. Now you are writing in your journal about how you spent your day.

CHAPTER 18

The Placebo Effect

What are they thinking?

GETTING READY TO READ

Talk with a partner or in a small group.

1. When you are sick, what do you usually do? Do you take medicine? Do you see a doctor?

2. When you go to the doctor because you feel sick, do you expect to get a prescription?[1] Explain why or why not.

3. Does a sick person's state of mind (his or her thoughts and emotions) affect how quickly he or she gets well? Explain your answer.

[1] a *prescription* = a doctor's written order for a specific medicine for a sick person

READING

Look at the words and picture next to the reading. Then read without stopping.

The Placebo Effect

1   Harry S. wanted to quit smoking. So, when he saw an **ad** for a study on ways to **break the habit**, he called and offered to be part of it. The study was at a local university, where Harry and the other **volunteers**—all of them people who wanted to stop smoking—were divided into three groups. The volunteers in Group A received nicotine gum.[1] (Nicotine is in tobacco.[2] It is what gives smokers the good feeling they get from smoking.) When these smokers felt the need for a cigarette, they could **chew** a piece of this gum instead. It would give them the nicotine they were used to. The volunteers in Group B, including Harry, got some gum, too. It was just **plain** chewing gum, but the volunteers did not know that. The people in Group C got nothing. A group like this in a study is called the control group.

2   After a four-hour period without cigarettes, Harry and the other volunteers had to write answers to a set of questions. Their answers showed how much they wanted a cigarette at that point. Not surprisingly, the smokers in Group C—the group that got no gum—showed the strongest cravings.[3] The smokers in the other two groups did not feel such a strong need to smoke.

3   What surprised the researchers was that the results for Groups A and B were exactly the same. That meant that the plain chewing gum worked as well as the gum with nicotine. Why? The researchers say, "Maybe it was the placebo effect." In other words, the smokers in Group B *BELIEVED* that the gum would help them feel better, so they did feel better.

4   A placebo is something that seems like a medical **treatment** but does not contain any real medicine. The word *placebo* means "I will please" in Latin. The purpose of a placebo is to please a patient who doesn't really need medicine but wants some. Doctors have given placebos to patients in **situations** like these for hundreds of years. If the patient then feels better, the doctor may say it is because of the placebo effect.

continued

[1] a pack of *gum*

[2] *tobacco* = the plant whose leaves are used to make cigarettes and cigars

[3] a *craving* = a very strong wish for something (such as a certain food)

5   Not everyone believes that the placebo effect **exists**, but researchers in Houston, Texas, have found some interesting evidence[4] for it. They did a study on a certain type of knee **operation**. A lot of people have this operation—about 350,000 a year—and it is expensive, costing about $5,000. The study showed that a **fake** operation worked just as well as the real thing! There were 180 volunteers in the study, and they understood that they might get a real operation or they might not. The ones who had fake surgery[5] got only three small cuts around their knee. After two weeks, most patients believed that their surgery was real. Later, 35–40% of all patients reported that their knees felt better. The numbers were the same for those who had a real operation and those who had the "placebo surgery."

[4] *evidence* = facts that show something is true

6   Some researchers think that the placebo effect works only in a very few situations, possibly only in the case of pain. They have an idea how the placebo effect works in cases like these. According to some **recent** studies, when patients believe they are receiving treatment, their brains produce **natural** painkillers. The brain produces these when a person expects pain to go away. The brain's own painkillers then help **block** the pain.

[5] *surgery* = when a doctor cuts open the body to fix or take out something; an operation

7   Both the smokers in Harry's group and the fake surgery patients felt less pain than expected. Something happened that helped them feel better. Maybe the idea that they were getting treatment (a supply of nicotine or an operation) produced painkillers in their brains. Or perhaps something else was happening. For example, maybe the sugar in the chewing gum helped Harry and the others in his group feel better. Scientists agree that **further** research is needed. **So far**, no one has really **proven** that the placebo effect exists.

Quick Comprehension Check

Read these sentences. Circle T (true) or F (false).

1. Harry's doctor made him be part of a study on quitting smoking.   T   F

2. Chewing gum helped the smokers go without smoking.   T   F

3. A placebo has strong drugs in it.   T   F

4. The placebo effect depends on what a person believes.   T   F

5. Doctors have done only one study on the placebo effect.   T   F

6. Some studies show the brain can produce its own painkillers.   T   F

EXPLORING VOCABULARY

Thinking about the Vocabulary

Which target words and phrases are new to you? Circle them here and in the reading. Then read "The Placebo Effect" again. Look at the context of each new word and phrase. Can you guess the meaning?

Target Words and Phrases			
ad (1)	plain (1)	operation (5)	block (6)
break the habit (1)	treatment (4)	fake (5)	further (7)
volunteers (1)	situations (4)	recent (6)	so far (7)
chew (1)	exists (5)	natural (6)	proven (7)

Using the Vocabulary

A Complete these sentences. Write *an ad, blocking, chewing,* and *an operation.*

1. She's _____.

2. He's _____
   the way in.

3. This is _____
   (short for *advertisement*).

4. They're performing
   _____.

B These sentences are **about the reading**. Complete them with the words and phrases in the box.

break the habit	exist	fake	further	natural	plain
proven	recent	situations	so far	treatment	volunteers

1. For Harry, smoking was a thing he did repeatedly. He wanted to stop this
   behavior. He wanted to _____ of smoking.

2. The study on smoking used _____, people who offer to do something without expecting pay or anything else.

3. Some volunteers got a special gum with nicotine in it. The other gum was just _____ chewing gum, gum without anything added.

4. Doctors give placebos to patients in certain _____, meaning when certain conditions are present or certain things are happening.

5. Some people believe that the placebo effect doesn't _____. They say there isn't really any effect like this.

6. Some patients got a _____ knee operation. It wasn't a real operation.

7. _____ studies on the brain are studies that happened not long ago.

8. Patients go to doctors to get care or _____ for sickness or injuries.

9. Some painkillers are made by drug companies. The brain produces _____ painkillers.

10. We need more information about the placebo effect, so researchers need to do _____ studies.

11. _____, or until now, no one has really understood the placebo effect.

12. No one has shown clearly that the placebo effect exists. No one has _____ it.

C These sentences use the target words and phrases **in new contexts.**
Complete them with the words and phrases in the box.

break the habit	exist	fake	further	natural	plain
proved	recent	situation	so far	treatments	volunteers

1. Red isn't her _____ hair color. She was born with brown hair.

2. These firefighters are _____. They don't get paid.

3. I wish she would _____ of calling me every time she has a problem.

4. She is still in pain from a _____ operation.

5. We haven't had any trouble. Everything has gone smoothly _____.

6. He prefers _____ pizza: just cheese and tomato sauce, nothing else.

7. I _____ to my parents that I could deal with both school and work.

8. We'll make a decision after _____ discussion tomorrow.

9. Doctors are working on new _____ for patients with burns.

10. What is the political _____ in the country at the moment?

11. Dinosaurs[1] no longer _____.

12. When the police caught him, he had several _____ IDs.[2]

[1]*Dinosaurs* lived millions of years ago.   [2]An *ID* is an identification card.

Building on the Vocabulary

Studying Word Grammar

Farther and *further* are both comparative forms of *far*.

- Use *farther* when you mean a longer distance: *They ran/traveled/sailed farther than we did.*

- Use *further* when you refer to time, amounts, or processes: *We need to discuss/look into/study this further.*

These words can be adjectives (*a farther star, further research*) or adverbs (*it spread farther, we'll develop it further*).

A **Complete the sentences with *farther* or *further*.**

1. My classroom is _____ down the hall.

2. I need _____ practice.

3. They never developed the plan any _____.

4. Clear Lake is nicer than Heart Lake, but it's _____ away.

5. You can swim _____ than I can.

6. He will study math _____ when he goes to college.

B **Write your own sentences using *farther* and *further*.**

1. _____

2. _____

DEVELOPING YOUR SKILLS

Paraphrasing and Quoting

The following sentences paraphrase sentences in the reading. (They use different words to say the same thing.) Find the sentence in the reading with the same meaning and copy it here. Use quotation marks (" ") because you are quoting someone else's exact words.

1. The researchers were surprised that Groups A and B showed the same results. "What surprised the researchers was that the results for Groups A and B were exactly the same."

2. Harry S. didn't want to smoke anymore. _____

   _____

3. The volunteers in all three groups spent four hours without smoking and then had to answer some questions. _____

   _____

4. Scientists think that they need to look into the placebo effect some more.

   _____

5. Up to now, no one has shown that there really is such a thing as the placebo effect. _____

   _____

Pronoun Reference

Remember: A pronoun takes the place of a noun or a noun phrase. (A noun phrase is a group of words for a person, place, thing, or idea.) A pronoun generally refers back to a noun or noun phrase that came before it.

What do the boldfaced pronouns mean in these sentences? Look back at the reading.

1. Paragraph 1: . . . he called and offered to be part of **it**. _____

2. Paragraph 1: **It** is what gives smokers the good feeling they get . . .

   _____

3. Paragraph 3: . . . , so **they** did feel better. _____

4. Paragraph 5: . . . researchers in Houston, Texas, have found some interesting evidence for **it**. _____

5. Paragraph 5: The numbers were the same for **those** who had a real operation . . . _____

6. Paragraph 6: The brain produces **these** when a person expects pain to go away. _____

Discussion

Talk about these questions in a small group.

1. What was the purpose of the first study described in the reading? How were the three groups different? What surprised the researchers and why?

2. What was the purpose of the second study? How were the two groups different? What were the results?

3. Imagine that you are invited to be part of a study on a new drug. The drug is supposed to strengthen a person's memory and make him or her smarter. Some of the volunteers will get the drug, and some will get a placebo. Would you volunteer? Explain your answer.

Using New Words

Ask and answer these questions with a partner. Use one of the words or phrases in parentheses. Then talk about your answers with the class.

1. When have you (tried to/managed to) **break a bad habit**?

2. What **ad** on TV do you really (like/hate)?

3. (When/Where) are **volunteers** usually needed?

4. What are two things besides foods that (people/animals) sometimes **chew**?

5. What famous (person/thing) doesn't really **exist**?

Writing

Choose a topic. Write a paragraph.

1. Answer question 3 from **Discussion** above.

2. When do you go see a doctor? How do you feel about going to doctors?

CHAPTER 19

Tears

Why the tears?

GETTING READY TO READ

Talk with a partner or in a small group.

1. When was the last time you cried? Why did you cry?
2. When is it OK to cry? Are there times when a person *should* cry?
3. Do you agree with a, b, or c? Choose one and explain your choice.
   a. Crying is a healthy thing to do.
   b. Crying is bad for you.
   c. Crying doesn't help you or hurt you either.

READING

Look at the words and pictures next to the reading. Then read without stopping.

Tears

1   Tears are good for your eyes. In fact, without them, your eyes wouldn't even be able to move. Some people say tears help us in other ways, too. Maybe you know someone who likes to watch sad movies in order to "have a good cry." It hasn't been proven, but tears may be good not only for your eyes but for your emotional health as well.

2   We generally only notice tears when we cry, but we have them in our eyes all the time. Tears affect how we see the world while at the same time protecting our eyes from it. Without this **liquid** covering them, our eyes would be at risk of infection.[1] In addition, we need tears in order to see. The cornea[2] of the eye does not have a perfectly smooth **surface**. Tears **fill in** the **holes** in the cornea and make it smooth so that we can see clearly. Without tears, the world would look very strange to us.

3   There are three types of tears, and they are called basal, reflex, and emotional (or psychic) tears. These three types are different not only in purpose but also in composition.[3]

- Basal tears are the ones that we produce all the time. On average, our eyes produce these tears at a rate of five to ten ounces[4] a day. When we blink our eyes (quickly close and open them), we spread basal tears across the surface of our eyes. If we don't blink enough, like some people who spend long hours in front of a computer, then our eyes get dry.

- Have you ever cut up an onion[5] and felt tears come to your eyes? Tears of that type are called reflex tears. They are the ones that fill our eyes when a cold wind **blows**. These tears also protect our eyes, washing away **dust** and other **materials** that get into them.

- Emotional, or psychic, tears **flow** when we feel certain emotions. When we cry tears of sadness, disappointment, or happiness, we are crying emotional tears. Emotional tears are the tears we think of when we use the word *cry*.

continued

[1] *infection* = sickness in a part of the body

[2] the *cornea* = a covering for the eye; see the picture on the following page

[3] *composition* = the way something is made up of different things, parts, etc.

[4] an *ounce* = a small amount of liquid (eight ounces = one measuring cup)

[5] an *onion*

4   Tom Lutz, the author of *Crying: The Natural and Cultural History of Tears,* writes, "**Throughout** history, and in every culture, . . . everyone, everywhere cries at some time." Even men and women who say they never cry can usually remember crying as children. Most of us probably think it is **normal** for men or women to cry at certain times, and at such times, we may even **encourage** them to cry. For example, it is no surprise when someone cries during a sad movie, and we often expect people to cry when a family member dies. However, we don't always take this **view** of tears. Sometimes adults who cry—or even children who do—lose the respect of others. For example, what would you think of an adult who cried over losing a card game? Most people are **aware** of the social rules about when, where, and why it is OK to cry. These rules generally **differ** for children and adults, and often for men and women. They depend on things such as family, culture, and religion, and they change over time.

5   Some people think it is not just OK to cry but actually healthy to let the tears flow. Doctors in Greece over 2,500 years ago thought that tears came from the brain and that everyone needed to let them out. Today, many people still believe in[6] getting tears out. They say that through crying, we get rid of emotions we have stored up, which is good for our **mental** health. Some people report that they feel better after crying. This could be because of the **chemicals** in emotional tears. One chemical is a type of endorphin, a painkiller that the body naturally produces. Emotional tears increase the amount of endorphin that gets to the brain because tears flow from the eye into the nose and pass to the brain that way. This painkiller may make a person less aware of sad or angry feelings, and that could explain why someone feels better after "a good cry."

[6] *believe in* = trust in, feel sure that (a person or thing) is good

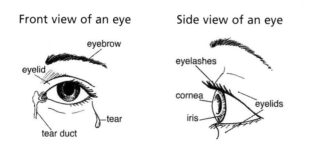

Front view of an eye   Side view of an eye

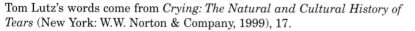

Tom Lutz's words come from *Crying: The Natural and Cultural History of Tears* (New York: W.W. Norton & Company, 1999), 17.

Quick Comprehension Check

Read these sentences. Circle T (true) or F (false).

1. Tears are important for keeping our eyes healthy.   T   F

2. Tears are important for our ability to see.   T   F

3. There are two different kinds of tears.   T   F

4. We have emotional tears in our eyes all the time.   T   F

5. People generally have the same ideas about when it is   T   F
   OK to cry.

6. Some people think it can be good for you to cry.   T   F

EXPLORING VOCABULARY

Thinking about the Vocabulary

Which target words and phrases are new to you? Circle them here and in the reading. Then read "Tears" again. Look at the context of each new word and phrase. Can you guess the meaning?

Target Words and Phrases			
liquid (2)	blows (3)	throughout (4)	aware (4)
surface (2)	dust (3)	normal (4)	differ (4)
fill in (2)	materials (3)	encourage (4)	mental (5)
holes (2)	flow (3)	view (4)	chemicals (5)

Using the Vocabulary

A These sentences are **about the reading**. Complete them with the words and phrases in the box.

are encouraging	aware of	blows	chemicals	dust
flow		materials	mental	normal	surface

1. The eye looks perfectly smooth, but it is not. Its _____ is irregular, with tiny holes and wrinkles (like your skin when you look at it closely).

2. When a wind _____ cold air into your eyes, they fill with reflex tears.

3. Sometimes you might get _____ in your eyes. It could happen when you are driving on a dry dirt road or cleaning under your bed.

4. Tears help wash away dust, dirt, sand, or any other _____ that might get into your eyes.

5. When you feel certain emotions, tears may start to _____, like water moving in a river.

6. At certain times it is not strange for someone to cry. It is _____. Everyone expects it.

7. People may tell someone, "Go ahead and cry." They _____ the person to cry.

8. Most people are _____ the social rules for crying. They know about them.

9. Tears are good for your eyes and may be good for your _____ health, too, meaning your emotions and state of mind.

10. There are different substances in the three types of tears. The _____ in emotional tears include a painkiller.

B These sentences use the target words **in new contexts. Complete them with the words in the box.**

aware	blew	chemicals	dust	encouraged
flows	materials	mental	normal	surface

1. The river _____ to the sea.

2. Only a few people have walked on the _____ of the moon.

3. The teacher's fingers were white with _____ from writing on the blackboard with a piece of chalk.

4. A strong wind _____ his hat off.

5. Ann says, "I have a _____ block against math. I don't understand it or enjoy it, and I never will."

6. It's _____ to feel nervous during a job interview.

7. To build a good house, you have to start with good-quality building _____.

8. There's a lot he doesn't notice. I bet he isn't _____ of her feelings for him.

9. My parents _____ me to think it over before deciding.

10. There are strong _____ in some of the cleaning products in the kitchen.

C Read these sentences. Write the **boldfaced** target words or phrases next to their definitions.

a. We need to dig a deep **hole** to plant the tree.

b. Water can take the form of a **liquid**, a gas, or a solid (ice).

c. I cried **throughout** the movie, from beginning to end.

d. The two companies **differ** in how they treat their employees.

e. Who did he vote for? Do you know his political **views**?

f. There is a bad hole in the street. Somebody should **fill it in**.

Target Words/Phrases	Definitions
1. _____	= be different or not alike
2. _____	= a substance that can flow and be poured
3. _____	= during all of a period of time
4. _____	= an open or empty space in something solid
5. _____	= opinions or beliefs
6. _____	= put something in a hole in order to make a smooth surface

Building on the Vocabulary

Studying Collocations

The noun *view* has different meanings:

- *View* often means "opinion, belief." Use *take* or *hold* with *view* to mean "have an opinion": *He takes the view that children should be seen and not heard.*

- *View* can also mean "the area someone can see." Use *have* with *view* when it has this meaning: *He has a view of the park from his house.*

A Complete the following sentences. Make true statements.

1. _____ and I hold similar views on _____.
   (name)

2. From my _____ window, I have a view of _____.
   (room)

B Write two more sentences with *view.*

1. _____

2. _____

DEVELOPING YOUR SKILLS

Paraphrasing and Quoting

 Answer each question by copying a sentence from "Tears." Use quotation marks (" ") before and after the sentence.

1. What would happen if we did not have tears in our eyes?

   "Without this liquid covering them, our eyes would be at risk of infection."

2. How do tears help us see clearly?

   _____

   _____

   _____

3. What are the different types of tears?

   _____

   _____

   _____

4. Social rules about crying differ for children vs. adults and often for men vs. women. What else affects the rules?

   _____

   _____

   _____

5. What effect does the painkiller endorphin possibly have on a person?

   _____

   _____

   _____

B On a piece of paper, write answers to these questions. Do not copy sentences from the reading. You will need to paraphrase (use your own words).

1. How do tears help our eyes?

2. When do our eyes produce basal, reflex, and emotional tears?

3. How does a person learn the social rules about crying?

4. Why do some people believe it is good to cry?

Summarizing

On a piece of paper, write a one-paragraph summary of "Tears." Include the answers to these questions:

- What are tears good for?
- Which kinds of tears protect our eyes?
- Which kind of tears do you produce when we cry?
- What do social rules about crying tell us?
- What do some people believe about crying?

Sharing Opinions

1. Check (✓) your answers to the questions below. Add a situation of your own to the list. Then share answers with a partner. Ask your partner about the situation you added.

Is it OK for a person to cry:

	An adult		A child	
	Yes	No	Yes	No
a. at the movies?				
b. when his/her team loses a game?				
c. when something bad happens at work/at school?				
d. when saying good-bye at the airport?				
e. at a religious service for someone who has died?				
f. _____?				

2. Do you think there are differences between the social rules about crying for men and those for women? Fill in the chart with situations. Compare charts with your partner.

When is it OK to cry?

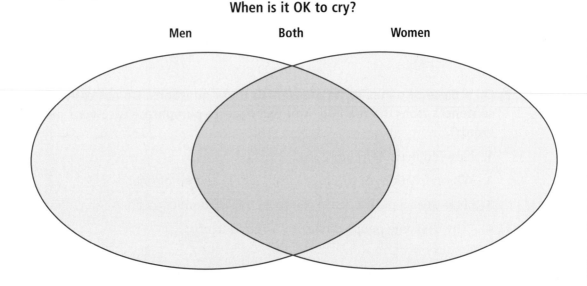

Men   Both   Women

Using New Words

Work with a partner. Choose five target words or phrases from the list on page 176. On a piece of paper, use each word or phrase in a sentence.

Writing

Choose a topic. Write a paragraph.

1. Do you remember crying as a child? Describe an experience that made you cry.

2. Is there someone in your life who encourages you to do things? For example:

   My friends encourage me to believe in myself.

   My father always encouraged me to get a good education.

   Describe the encouragement you have received from someone and its influence on you.

CHAPTER 20

Bionic Men and Women

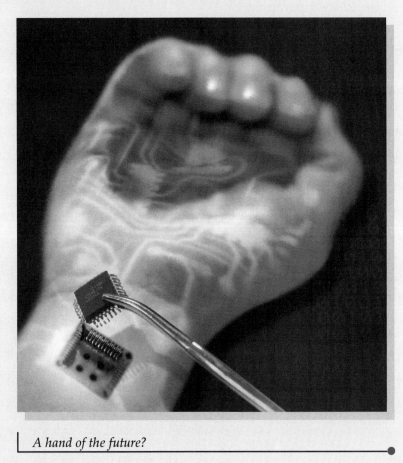

A hand of the future?

GETTING READY TO READ

Talk in a small group or with your class.

1. What movies or TV shows have you seen about a person who was part machine? What was the story about?

2. When a part of someone's body stops working, the person's life may depend on a machine, whether in the hospital or in everyday life. Give an example of a situation like this.

READING

Look at the words and pictures next to the reading. Then read without stopping.

Bionic Men and Women

1 In the movie *Star Wars: The Empire Strikes Back,* Luke Skywalker loses a hand, but he gets a new one, an **artificial** hand that looks and works just like a real one. This is not unusual in movies that take place far into the future. It is easy to believe that 100 years from now, doctors will be able to **replace** body parts with machines. But you don't have to go to the movies to see this happen.

2 Machines are already doing the jobs of various human body parts. There are people who can see, hear, walk, or pick up their children because of artificial eyes, ears, legs, and arms. These are all possible because of **developments** in the field of science called bionics. *Bionics* means the study of how living things are made and how they work. **Engineers** study bionics in order to **design** machines that are similar to living things. For example, in order to design airplanes, they have studied birds. The field of bionics also includes building machines to replace parts of the body or to support processes **within** the body.

3 One example of a bionic device[1] is the pacemaker. Doctors can put a pacemaker into the **chest** of someone whose heart **beats** too slowly or not regularly enough. They **attach** the pacemaker to the heart with wires, and the device gets its power from a **battery**. The wires carry small amounts of electricity to the heart and keep it beating as it should. Many thousands of people depend on pacemakers.

[1] a *device* = a small machine or tool that does a special job

4 Other bionic devices, like Luke Skywalker's new hand, take the place of a body part. A **major** problem in developing bionic parts has been setting up communication between the body and the machine. Normally, the brain tells parts of the body what to do by sending messages along nerves.[2] For example, your brain might send a message to your hand telling it to pick up a pen and write something. But how would it tell an artificial hand to do that? Dr. William

[2] *nerves* = thin parts like lines throughout the body that carry information to/from the brain

continued

Craelius, who has invented an artificial hand, says, "Communication is **key**, and it is getting easier."

5   Machines are not the only things that can replace a body part. There are also transplants. A transplant is an operation to move a body part, such as a heart or a kidney,[3] from one person to another. One major problem with transplants is that there aren't enough hearts, kidneys, and so on, available, so hospitals cannot **keep up with** the **demand** for transplants. Patients have to wait, and some have no time left. **Therefore**, many scientists see bionics as the best hope for the future. Using bionics, a patient could get a new heart or kidney right away instead of waiting for a transplant. Other scientists disagree. They say that bionics is already a thing of the past, and they have a better idea: They are working on ways to use animal parts for transplants.

6   Maybe in the future our choices won't be limited to bionic body parts and transplant operations. Maybe science will take us in another direction. Consider these facts: When a salamander[4] loses a leg, it can grow a new one, and if an earthworm[5] is cut in two pieces, the piece with the head can grow a new tail. Wouldn't it be great if a person who lost a hand or a kidney could grow a new one? This may sound like something from another sci-fi[6] movie, but it could happen. Researchers are now studying the genes[7] that let salamanders grow new legs, and they hope to learn how humans might do the same thing.

7   Growing a new body part could be the best way to go. On the other hand, some people might prefer bionic body parts if they had the choice. In the sci-fi movie *RoboCop*, a police officer has an operation that **turns him into** a cyborg—half man, half machine. His new body parts give him special powers, including superhuman strength. Think about it. If bionics could turn you into a superman, what would you do?

Dr. Craelius's words come from the article "Inventor of Artificial Hand Sees 'Bionic' Replacement Parts Becoming More Human," *Medical Devices & Surgical Technology Week* (March 10, 2002), 3.

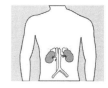

[3] the *kidneys*

[4] a *salamander*

[5] an *earthworm*

[6] *sci-fi* = (informal) *science fiction*, stories about imaginary worlds or imaginary developments in science

[7] *genes* = the parts of cells in your body that control qualities you get from your parents

Quick Comprehension Check

Read these sentences. Circle T (true) or F (false).

1. People can get new body parts only in the movies.   T   F

2. Bionics means studying living things: how they are made   T   F
   and how they work.

3. Giving a man a pacemaker for his heart is an example of   T   F
   using bionics.

4. Machines are our only hope for new body parts in the future. T   F

5. Some animals can grow new body parts if they need to.   T   F

6. In the movies, bionic body parts sometimes give people   T   F
   special abilities.

EXPLORING VOCABULARY

Thinking about the Vocabulary

Which target words and phrases are new to you? Circle them here and in the reading. Then read "Bionic Men and Women" again. Look at the context of each new word and phrase. Can you guess the meaning?

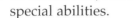
Target Words and Phrases

artificial (1)	design (2)	attach (3)	keep up with (5)
replace (1)	within (2)	battery (3)	demand (5)
developments (2)	chest (3)	major (4)	therefore (5)
engineers (2)	beats (3)	key (4)	turns him into (7)

Using the Vocabulary

Ⓐ **These sentences are about the reading. What is the meaning of each boldfaced word or phrase? Circle a, b, or c.**

1. Some people have to get **artificial** eyes, ears, hands, and legs. *Artificial* means:

   a. not available   **b.** not natural   **c.** not connected

2. People sometimes **design** machines to work like living things. *Design* means:

   a. draw plans for   **b.** deal in   **c.** take over

3. A machine may be needed to support a process **within** the body. *Within* means:

   a. beyond   **b.** according to   **c.** inside

4. A healthy heart **beats** slowly when a person is resting. *Beats* means:

   a. makes a regular movement   **b.** makes a living   **c.** makes an investment

5. Doctors **attach** a pacemaker to a heart with wires. *Attach* means:

   a. block   **b.** connect   **c.** avoid

6. A pacemaker gets its power from a **battery**. A *battery* is:

   a. a kind of software   **b.** a thing that provides electricity   **c.** a volunteer

7. The body and the bionic body part must communicate. Communication is **key**. *Key* means:

   a. necessary for success   **b.** not likely to exist   **c.** worth nothing

8. There is a great **demand** for transplants. *Demand* means:

   a. the lifestyle people want   **b.** the materials people use   **c.** the need people have

9. Transplants aren't always possible when patients need them. **Therefore**, some people think bionics offers more hope for the future. *Therefore* means:

   a. right away   **b.** because   **c.** for that reason

10. In the movie *RoboCop*, an operation **turned** a man **into** a cyborg. *Turn* (a person or thing) *into* (someone or something else) means:

    a. change into   **b.** chew up   **c.** fill in

B These sentences use the target words and phrases **in new contexts**.
Complete them with the words and phrases in the box.

artificial	attach	battery	beat	demand
designed	key	therefore	turns them into	within

1. She _____ and made her own clothes.

2. Please _____ a recent photo to your application.

3. The restaurant had _____ flowers on the tables.

4. Our hotel was _____ walking distance of the city center.

5. My little radio isn't working. It needs a new _____.

6. His heart _____ faster when he saw her.

7. The _____ thing is for the patient to believe in the treatment.

8. The army claims that it takes boys and _____ men.

9. The plan presented too many risks. _____, he decided against it.

10. The company went out of business because there wasn't enough
   _____ for their products.

C Read these sentences. Write the **boldfaced** target words or phrases next to
their definitions.

a. They want to **replace** their old car.

b. Recent **developments** in medical research encourage us to hope.

c. The computer, automobile, and airline industries all employ **engineers**.

d. The young father held his baby against his **chest**.

e. We couldn't **keep up with** the other runners, so we gave up.

f. The country has just two **major** political parties.

Target Words/Phrases   Definitions

1. _____ = change (one person or thing for another)

2. _____ = large or important

3. _____ = changes that make something more advanced

4. _____ = people who design machines, roads, bridges, etc.

5. _____ = move as fast or do as much (as someone else)

6. _____ = the front part of a person's body between the neck
   and the stomach

Building on the Vocabulary

Studying Collocations

Remember: Certain prepositions often follow certain adjectives. Use:

aware + of
key + to
normal + for
similar + to

A Complete each sentence with a preposition.

1. Certain players have been key _____ the success of the team.

2. He is aware _____ the risks of smoking.

3. The child's eating habits are normal _____ his age.

4. Her situation is similar _____ yours.

B Write a sentence using each adjective + preposition in Part A.

1. _____

2. _____

3. _____

4. _____

DEVELOPING YOUR SKILLS

Paraphrasing and Quoting

A Answer the questions by copying sentences from "Bionic Men and Women."
Use quotation marks (" ") before and after the sentences.

1. What has happened thanks to developments in the field of bionics?

   "There are people who _____

   _____ ."

2. Why has it been so hard to develop things like artificial hands?

   _____

   _____

3. What is a transplant?

   _____

   _____

4. Why are researchers studying salamanders?

_____

_____

B **Answer these questions without copying sentences from the reading. You will need to paraphrase.**

1. What is a pacemaker? What does it do? _____

_____

_____

_____

2. What is one problem with transplants? _____

_____

_____

_____

3. Why might some people like the idea of getting bionic body parts? _____

_____

_____

_____

Summarizing

On a piece of paper, write a one-paragraph summary of "Bionic Men and Women." Include the answers to the following questions:

- What does _bionics_ mean? (Copy the definition from the reading and use quotation marks around it.)
- How do bionic devices help people?
- What is another way to replace a body part that isn't working?
- What other way to replace body parts may be possible in the future?

Role-playing

Form a small group. Two of you are scientists. You work in the field of bionics. The rest of you are reporters, and you are here to interview the scientists about the most recent developments in their work. The reporters ask questions. The scientists answer the questions and ask their own questions. For example:

REPORTER: What are you working on right now?

SCIENTIST: We are developing a new . . .

Using New Words

Work with a partner. Take turns asking for and giving information.

1. Name two things that can run on **batteries**.
2. Name two things that **designers** work on.
3. Name two things that **engineers** work on.
4. Name two things that are **key** to doing well in school.
5. Describe something old that you'd like to **replace**.

Writing

Choose a topic. Write a paragraph.

1. Imagine that you could replace some part or parts of your body with artificial part(s) that would give you super powers, special powers that humans don't normally have. What would you replace and why?
2. Would you like a career as a designer or an engineer of some kind? Explain.

Wrap-up

REVIEWING VOCABULARY

A **Where would you find . . .**

_d_ **1.** a battery?   **a.** under a bed

____ **2.** an ad?   **b.** in a science lab

____ **3.** dust?   **c.** in the newspaper

____ **4.** chemicals?   **d.** in a clock

B **Complete the phrase.**

1. Write the noun *living, operation, risk,* or *treatment.*

  a. perform an ____operation____

  b. make a _____

  c. take a _____

  d. provide _____

2. Write the verb *blow, chew, replace,* or *treat.*

  a. _____ an injury

  b. _____ your food

  c. _____ your nose

  d. _____ a broken TV

3. Write the noun *chest, habit,* or *hole.*

  a. a deep _____

  b. a bad _____

  c. a hairy _____

4. Write the adjective *artificial, further, mental,* or *smooth.*

  a. _____ health

  b. _____ flowers

  c. _____ developments

  d. _____ surfaces

EXPANDING VOCABULARY

A We can add the prefix *un-* to *aware, likely,* and *natural* to form adjectives with the opposite meaning. Other prefixes can also mean "not."

Combine the prefixes meaning "not" with the adjectives in the box. Complete the sentences with the new words.

un- + aware   un- + likely   un- + natural   ab- + normal   dis- + similar

1. Her hair was an ____unnatural____ red.

2. The sky is perfectly clear, so I think it is _____ to rain.

3. The two scientists used the same process but had _____ results.

4. He is _____ of the problem. Someone has to tell him.

5. My cat's _____ behavior made me think she was sick.

B Sometimes a noun and a verb in the same word family look alike: *They design buildings. They showed us a design for a new house.* Sometimes they don't look alike: *He injured his leg. It was a serious injury.*

Read the following sentences and find the noun and verb from the same family. Complete the chart.

1. **a.** Attach one wire to each end of the battery.
   b. There is a strong attachment between the two sisters.
2. **a.** The players differ in their natural abilities.
   b. There are many differences between the two schools.
3. **a.** I encouraged him to see a doctor.
   b. Her friends gave her lots of encouragement.

Nouns	Verbs
attachment	attach

	Nouns	Verbs

4. **a.** What is the speed limit on this road?

   b. The school limits classes to no more than 15 students.

5. **a.** They hope to slow down the aging process.

   b. The factory processes fresh fruit. They put it in cans.

6. **a.** He will have to prove that he can do the work.

   b. A photo ID or passport shows proof of who you are.

7. **a.** Who will replace the director if she leaves?

   b. Our regular secretary is on vacation, but her replacement is doing a fine job.

C Write seven sentences with the noun or verb from each family in Part B.

1. _____

2. _____

3. _____

4. _____

5. _____

6. _____

7. _____

PLAYING WITH WORDS

Complete the sentences with words you studied in Chapters 17–20. Write the words in the puzzle.

Across

1. I'll love you <u>forever</u>_____.

3. The baby slept t_____ the trip.

6. What m_____ is the jacket made of?

8. Water is a l_____.

9. He couldn't prove it. T_____, no one believed him.

12. We can't let the party go on b_____ midnight.

13. We all agree the problem e_____.

Down

2. She's a v_____ at the hospital.

4. What would you do if you were in my s_____?

5. We watched the river f_____.

6. The m_____ problem is not enough money.

7. He lives w_____ a mile of his job.

10. I can't tell if it's real or f_____.

11. He's a k_____ member of the team.

BUILDING DICTIONARY SKILLS

Finding the Correct Meaning

Many words have more than one meaning. Look at the dictionary entries below. Read each sentence and write the number of the meaning.

1. a. __3__ The waves beat against the rocks.

    b. _____ Beat the eggs before you add the flour.

    c. _____ We beat them by a score of 3 to 1.

    d. _____ My heart was beating very quickly.

    e. _____ It's a crime to attack or beat someone.

> **beat**[1] /bit/ *v* **beat, beat, beaten**
> **1 ▸ DEFEAT ◂** [T] to defeat someone in a game, competition etc., or to do better than someone or something: *Stein beat me at chess in 44 moves.* | *Hank Aaron finally beat the record for home runs set by Babe Ruth.*
> **2 ▸ HIT SB ◂** [T] to hit someone many times with your hand, a stick etc.: *He used to come home drunk and beat us.*
> **3 ▸ HIT STH ◂** [I,T] to hit something regularly or continuously: *waves beating on/against the shore*
> **4 ▸ FOOD ◂** [I,T] to mix foods together quickly using a fork or a special kitchen tool: *Beat the eggs and add them to the sugar mixture.*
> **5 ▸ SOUND ◂** [I,T] to make a regular sound or movement, or to make something do this: *My heart seemed to be beating much too fast. . . .*

2. a. _____ You have no right to make demands like that.

    b. _____ The baker couldn't keep up with the demand for his bread.

    c. _____ He's in great demand as a speaker.

> **de·mand**[1] /dɪˈmænd/ *n* **1** [singular, U] the need or desire that people have for particular goods or services: *There isn't any demand for leaded gas anymore.* **2** a strong request that shows you believe you have the right to get what you ask for: *Union members will strike until the company agrees to their demands.* **3 be in demand** to be wanted by a lot of people: *She's been in great demand ever since her book was published.* —see also DEMANDS

3. a. _____ What's the best way to treat a burn?

    b. _____ Don't treat me like a child.

    c. _____ We must treat this situation carefully.

    d. _____ They have to treat the water before people can drink it.

    e. _____ They treated the children to ice cream.

> **treat**[1] /trit/ *v* [T] **1** to behave toward someone in a particular way: *Why do you treat me like an idiot?* | *She treats the children the same as adults.* | *Mr. Parker treats everyone equally/fairly.* **2** to consider something in a particular way: *You can treat these costs as business expenses.* **3** to give someone medical attention for a sickness or injury: *Eleven people were treated for minor injuries.* **4** to buy or arrange something special for someone: *We're treating Mom to dinner for her birthday.* **5** to put a special substance on something or use a chemical process in order to protect or clean it: *The wood has been treated to make it waterproof.*

UNIT 6

EXPLORING TECHNOLOGY

CHAPTER 21

A History of Telling Time

An atomic clock

GETTING READY TO READ

Talk with the whole class.

1. How many people in the class wear watches? What other ways are there to find out the time?

2. How many times a day do you look to see what time it is? What is the average for the class?

   a. 0–5   **b.** 5–10   **c.** more than 10

3. Do you agree with either of these ideas? Explain.

   a. Life without clocks would be beautiful.

   b. Life without clocks would be terrible.

READING

Look at the words and pictures next to the reading. Then read without stopping. Don't worry about new words. Don't stop to use a dictionary. Just keep reading!

A History of Telling Time

1   No one knows when people first thought about **measuring** time. We do know that they measured it by the sun, moon, and stars, and that they first divided time into months, seasons, and years. Later, they began dividing the day into parts, like hours and minutes, and they developed simple **technology** to help them do this. Today, we have much more advanced ways to tell time, such as the atomic clock pictured on page 197, and we can measure even tiny parts of a second. A great many things have changed in how people tell time—but not everything.

2   The Sumerians, who lived in the area of present-day Iraq, were the first to divide the day into parts. Then five or six thousand years ago, people in North Africa and the Middle East developed ways to tell the time of day. They needed clocks because organized religious and social activities had become part of their cultures. They needed to plan their days and **set** times to meet.

3   Among the first clocks were Egyptian obelisks.[1] The Egyptians used the movement of an obelisk's **shadow** to divide the day into morning and afternoon. Later, they placed stones on the ground around an obelisk to mark **equal** periods of time during the day, the way that numbers do on the face of a clock. That worked **fairly** well, but people could not carry obelisks with them. So the Egyptians invented something **portable**, a kind of sundial[2] that is now called a shadow clock. This came into use about 3,500 years ago, around 1500 B.C.E.[3]

4   There were many types of sundials in Egypt and in other areas around the Mediterranean Sea. All of them, of course, depended on the sun, which was no help in telling time at night. Among the first clocks that did not depend on the sun were water clocks. There were various types of these, too. Some were designed so that water would **drip** at a **constant**

[1] an *obelisk*

[2] one kind of *sundial*

[3] *B.C.E.* = Before the Common Era (also written *B.C.*, "before Christ")

continued

rate from a tiny hole in the bottom of a **container**. Others were designed to have a container slowly fill with water, again at a constant rate. It took a certain amount of time for the container to empty or fill up. However, the flow of water was hard to control, so these clocks were not very **accurate**, and people still did not have a clock they could put in their **pocket**. Hourglasses[4] filled with sand had similar problems.

[4] an *hourglass*

5   In the early 1300s, the first mechanical clocks—machines that measured and told the time—appeared in public buildings in Italy. Nearly 200 years later, around 1500, a German inventor, Peter Henlein, invented a mechanical clock that was powered by a spring.[5] Now clocks were getting smaller and easier to carry, but they still were not very accurate. Then in 1656, the Dutch scientist Christiaan Huygens invented a clock that was a big **step** forward. This was the first pendulum clock.[6] A pendulum moves from side to side, again and again, at a constant rate. Counting the movements of a pendulum was a better way to keep time. Huygens's first pendulum clock kept the time accurately to within one minute a day.

[5] two *springs*

6   Developments in clock technology continued as the demand for clocks increased. People began to need clocks for factories, **transportation**, banking, communications, and so on. Today, much of **modern** life happens at high speed and depends on having the exact time. We also have to have international agreement on what the exact time is.

[6] A grandfather clock is an example of a *pendulum* clock

7   Now we have atomic clocks, and the best of these are accurate to about one-tenth of a nanosecond[7] a day. But even with these **high-tech** clocks, we still measure a year by the time it takes the earth to go around the sun, as people did long, long ago. We say that it takes 365 days, but that is not exactly true. A year is actually a little longer—365.242 days, or 365 days and almost six hours long. So we generally add a day, February 29, every fourth year, and we call those years *leap years*. However, this creates another problem. The extra hours in four years add up to less than 24, so adding one day every fourth year would give us too many days. Therefore, when a year ends in -00 (for example, 1800, 1900, or 2000), we do not always make it a leap year. We do it only when we can divide the year by 4, as in 1600 and 2000. Remember that when you set your watch for the year 2100!

[7] a *nanosecond* = 1/1,000,000,000 (one-billionth) of a second

Quick Comprehension Check

Read these sentences. Circle T (true) or F (false).

1. People first measured time by the sun, moon, and stars.   T   F

2. People invented ways to tell time so they would know when to meet.   T   F

3. Water clocks depended on the sun.   T   F

4. Knowing the exact time is more important today than it was long ago.   T   F

5. Clocks have not changed in the last 200 years.   T   F

6. The earth takes exactly 365 days to circle the sun.   T   F

EXPLORING VOCABULARY

Thinking about the Vocabulary

Which target words are new to you? Circle them here and in the reading. Then read "A History of Telling Time" again. Look at the context of each new word. Can you guess the meaning?

Target Words			
measuring (1)	equal (3)	constant (4)	step (5)
technology (1)	fairly (3)	container (4)	transportation (6)
set (2)	portable (3)	accurate (4)	modern (6)
shadow (3)	drip (4)	pocket (4)	high-tech (7)

Using the Vocabulary

Ⓐ Complete the sentences. Write *containers*, *pockets*, *shadows*, and *transportation*.

1. You see _____ on a sunny day.

2. These are _____.

3. He has _____.

4. These are forms of _____.

B These sentences are **about the reading**. Complete them with the target words in the box.

accurate	constant	dripped	equal	fairly	high-tech
measure	modern	portable	set	step	technology

1. We use clocks to _____ time—to tell how much time has passed or how much time we have.

2. Thousands of years ago, people began developing the _____ for making clocks. (This word refers to the information, tools, and materials used to do something.)

3. As cultures became more advanced, people planned religious or social activities. They needed to _____, or decide on, specific times to meet.

4. The shadow of an obelisk took the same amount of time to move from each stone to the next. The stones marked _____ periods of time.

5. This way of telling time worked _____ well (less than "extremely well" or even "very well").

6. No one could carry an obelisk; obelisks were not _____. People wanted something they could carry.

7. Some water clocks were designed so that water _____, or fell little by little, from a tiny hole.

8. The water in a water clock would drip at a _____ rate. It never speeded up or slowed down.

9. Water clocks and hourglasses did not measure time exactly. They were not very _____.

10. In 1656, there was an important development. The invention of the pendulum clock was a big _____ forward.

11. The phrase _____ *life* refers to the way people live now or have lived in recent times.

12. Some clocks use very advanced technology, so we call them _____ clocks.

C These sentences use the target words **in new contexts**. Complete them with the words in the box.

accurate	constant	dripping	equal	fairly	high-tech
measure	modern	portable	set	step	technology

1. I have an old _____ radio that I take to the beach.

2. Getting married is a major _____ in anyone's life.

3. The course is on _____ Chinese history, just the last 100 years.

4. You won't believe all the things his new phone can do. It is very

   _____.

5. When you make a cake, you have to _____ the flour carefully.

6. He is studying computer _____. He wants to be an engineer.

7. They are going to get married some time next spring, but they have not

   _____ the date yet.

8. She does the same work he does, so they should get _____ pay.

9. Her Spanish isn't perfect, but she speaks it _____ well.

10. The shower in the upstairs bathroom won't stop _____. Can

    you fix it?

11. He gave the police an _____ report of the accident.

12. I drove the whole way there at a _____ speed of 55

    miles per hour.

Building on the Vocabulary

Studying Word Grammar

The *root* of the words *portable* and *transportation* is *port.* It comes from a Latin word meaning "carry." Something that is portable is something you can carry. *Transportation* refers to the process or business of carrying people and goods to other places. The verb form is *transport: We transported the computers by truck.*

Choose your own ways to complete the following sentences.

1. The first _____ were not portable, but now people can buy

   portable ones.

2. Modern transportation includes _____, _____, and

   _____.

3. In my country, businesses often transport goods by _____.

DEVELOPING YOUR SKILLS

Scanning

A Read these statements about "A History of Telling Time." Scan the reading for the information you need to complete them.

1. People in _____ and _____ were the first to develop ways to tell the time of day.

2. People started needing clocks and setting times to meet after they developed _____ and _____.

3. Obelisks and _____ depended on the sun.

4. A _____ measured time by emptying or filling up with water at a constant rate.

5. The first accurate clock was a _____ clock, invented in _____.

6. The best atomic clocks are accurate to _____.

7. It takes _____ days and _____ hours for the earth to travel around the sun.

8. A year with 366 days is called a _____.

B Scan the reading for these developments. Number them in chronological order from 1 (the earliest) to 8 (the most recent).

_____ Countries around the world had to agree on the exact time.

_____ People measured time by the sun, moon, and stars.

_____ Peter Henlein invented a spring-powered clock.

_____ The Egyptian shadow clock, the first portable clock, was invented.

_____ People used hourglasses.

_____ Christiaan Huygens invented a pendulum clock.

_____ The first mechanical clocks appeared in public buildings in Italy.

_____ The Egyptians built obelisks to help them tell time.

Reading for Details

Answer the following questions about the reading. Use your own words and write complete sentences.

1. What were two problems with using an obelisk or a sundial to tell time?

   _____

   _____

   _____

2. What were two problems with water clocks?

   _____

   _____

   _____

3. Why do we have leap years?

   _____

   _____

   _____

Discussion

Talk about these questions in a small group.

1. When is it important to be on time? How important is it?
2. If a friend is supposed to meet you, but he or she is late, how long are you likely to wait?
3. Although we need international agreement on what time it is, not everyone marks time by the same calendar. What examples can you list of calendars used by various cultures? What do you know about each one?

Using New Words

Work with a partner. Take turns asking for and giving information. Then tell the class something about your partner.

1. Name something you usually have in your **pockets**.
2. Name something **high-tech** that you would like to own.
3. Name something you own that isn't easily **portable**.
4. Name all the kinds of **transportation** you have ever used.
5. Name a time in your life when you took a big **step**.

Writing

Choose a topic. Write a paragraph.

1. There are many popular sayings about time in English— for example, "Time is money" and "Time flies when you're having fun." Give your opinion of one of these sayings, or explain a saying from your first language that refers to time.

2. Choose a topic from **Discussion** above.

CHAPTER 22

Out with the Old, In with the New?

Writing in Chinese

GETTING READY TO READ

Read the questions. Check (✔) your answers. Then find out how your classmates answered the questions, and write the numbers in the chart.

Questions	Class Survey Results
1. Did you use a calculator[1] in school when you were young? ❑ Yes ❑ No	_____ out of _____ people used calculators.
2. Did you spend much time in school practicing your handwriting when you were a child? ❑ Yes ❑ No	_____ out of _____ people worked hard on their handwriting.
3. Which statement is most true for you? ❑ I prefer to write by hand. ❑ I prefer to write on a computer.	_____ by hand _____ on a computer

[1] a calculator

READING

Look at the words and picture next to the reading. Then read.

Out with the Old, In with the New?

1   Modern technology is causing changes in our lives that have some people worried. Everyone agrees that new inventions have made life easier, but perhaps we need to ask, "Are we losing something along the way?"

2   Jack Riley is a fifth-grade student in Vancouver, Canada, and he is **annoyed**. His teacher has just said, "No more calculators in math class." Jack likes using a calculator to add, **subtract**, **multiply**, or divide, but his teacher is worried about her students' basic math skills. She wants them doing more math in their heads and on paper. She recently read about a study on the math skills of Canadian college students. Some of the students had lived and studied all their lives in Canada, while others had come to Canada from schools in China. The researchers found that the Chinese students were quicker at doing simple math problems and far better at doing **complex** ones. They also learned that the Chinese students had used calculators much less often during their early school years than the Canadians had. Jack's teacher has also read the report from the Third International Mathematics and Science Study (1999). According to this study, Canadian students are not keeping up with students from Japan, Korea, Singapore, or England. Jack's teacher **blames** technology.

3   Kate Gladstone of Albany, New York, has some similar feelings about technology. Gladstone is "the Handwriting Repairwoman." She helps people **improve** their handwriting so that others can read it better, and sometimes so that they can read it themselves. Businesses have asked her to work with their employees, and many doctors have taken her courses. People in the United States often **make fun of** doctors' bad handwriting, but Gladstone says it is nothing to laugh about. "We've got to be aware that handwriting is important," she says. Doctors have to write clear prescriptions[1] because their patients' lives may depend on them. Most of us have to be able to write notes to co-workers,[2] **fill out** forms, and write addresses that the post office can read. Gladstone

[1] a *prescription* = a doctor's written order for a specific medicine for a sick person

[2] *co-workers* = people who work together

continued

says that too many people never learned to write clearly in school, and too many people think it does not matter anymore. She feels that in the age of computers, handwriting is not getting the attention it **deserves**.

4   Li You lives in the city of Yangshuo in Guangxi, China. About eight years ago, he started using a computer to do word processing[3] in Chinese. Soon afterward, his memory for writing Chinese characters[4] by hand began to fail. He would pick up a pen and be unable to write something that he had learned as a child. Many of his friends have had the same problem. They used to be able to write thousands of characters. Now they often joke about how they try to write a character but cannot remember how to form it. At the computer, Li can easily **type** what he wants to say, so he is not worried. He does 95% of his writing at the computer now, and he says, "I can go for a month without picking up a pen." However, some people have a different view of the situation. "A long time ago, we all wrote much better," says Ye Zi, who works with Li. He says, "It's a cultural **loss**."

5   Are computers and calculators **robbing** people of **valuable** skills? Some people think so. Others say such questions just show that some of us cannot deal with change.

6   Jack's teacher thinks that students lose something when they depend on calculators, but other math teachers disagree. Kate Gladstone talks about the importance of handwriting, but she uses e-mail, too. Among writers of Chinese, opinions **vary** on the old way versus[5] the new. Some remember that until the 1900s, the brush—not the pen—was the **traditional** tool for writing Chinese, and writing was something that few people knew how to do. The pen replaced the brush because it was easier to use and carry around. Many people did not like this new development, but as the pen became more popular, it helped more people learn to write. We cannot avoid change, says Ming Zhou, a Microsoft researcher in Beijing. "It's just the way it is." He says the modern way is always to do things faster. "When culture and speed come into **conflict**, speed wins."

Kate Gladstone was quoted in "Why Farhad Can't Write" by Farhad Manjoo, August 16, 2000, <http:www.wired.com>. Li You, Ye Zi, and Ming Zhou were quoted in "In China, Computer Use Erodes Traditional Handwriting, Stirring a Cultural Debate" by Jennifer Lee, February 1, 2001, <http:www.nytimes.com>.

[3] *word processing* = the use of a computer and certain software to write

[4] the Chinese *character* for "Life"

[5] *versus* = (also *vs.*) as compared with, as opposed to

Quick Comprehension Check

Read these sentences. Circle T (true) or F (false).

1. All the people described in the reading feel the same way about technology.   T   F

2. Some people think the use of calculators hurts children's math skills.   T   F

3. A study was done in Canada on the math skills of college students.   T   F

4. According to the reading, handwriting does not matter anymore.   T   F

5. Some writers in China are forgetting how to write Chinese characters with a pen.   T   F

6. Some people worry about losing the old ways, and some do not.   T   F

EXPLORING VOCABULARY

Thinking about the Vocabulary

Which target words and phrases are new to you? Circle them here and in the reading. Then read "Out with the Old, In with the New?" again. Look at the context of each new word and phrase. Can you guess the meaning?

Target Words and Phrases			
annoyed (2)	blames (2)	deserves (3)	valuable (5)
subtract (2)	improve (3)	type (4)	vary (6)
multiply (2)	make fun of (3)	loss (4)	traditional (6)
complex (2)	fill out (3)	robbing (5)	conflict (6)

Using the Vocabulary

(A) These sentences are **about the reading**. Complete them with the words and phrases in the box.

annoyed	blames	complex	conflict	deserves	loss
make fun of	robs	traditional	valuable	vary	

1. Jack Riley is a little angry with his teacher. He is _____ about her new rule.

2. The Chinese students in the study were better than the Canadians at doing _____ math problems. These were difficult problems with many parts or steps.

3. Jack's teacher thinks technology is responsible for the Canadian students' poor scores on math tests. She _____ technology.

4. People in the United States often joke that no one can read what doctors write. They _____ doctors' handwriting.

5. Kate Gladstone thinks that the teaching of handwriting should receive more attention in schools. It _____ more attention, she says.

6. Ye Zi believes that the Chinese culture loses something when people forget how to write characters. "It's a cultural _____."

7. Are computers and calculators taking something away from us? Some people think technology _____ people of skills they need.

8. Some skills are very useful. They are worth a lot. They are _____.

9. Not all writers of Chinese have the same opinion. Opinions _____ from one person to the next.

10. The brush was the tool used by Chinese writers for a very, very long time. It was the _____ tool. The computer is a modern tool.

11. Culture and speed have come into _____. This means that a situation has developed in which people have to choose between opposite sides.

B These sentences use the target words and phrases **in new contexts**. Complete them with the words and phrases in the box.

annoyed	blamed	complex	conflict	deserve	losses
make fun of	robbed	traditional	valuable	vary	

1. Because he is the slowest runner, the other boys laugh at him and _____ him.

2. Two people doing equal work _____ equal pay.

3. The team has a record of six wins, no _____, and one tie.

4. I was _____ with my brother for not giving me the message.

5. Can the police prove that he is the one who _____ the store?

6. Do you understand the political situation? It's fairly _____.

7. Her band plays both _____ songs that everyone knows and new ones that she writes herself.

8. We hope the _____ between the two nations does not develop into a war.

9. Schools across the state _____ in what and how they teach.

10. When the artist became famous, his paintings became more

    _____.

11. His parents _____ him for the broken window, but it was actually his sister who did it.

C Read these sentences. Write the **boldfaced** target words or phrases next to their definitions.

a. When you **subtract** 20 from 30, you get 10.

b. When you **multiply** 20 times 30, you get 600.

c. You can **improve** your skills with practice.

d. You have to **fill out** this form to apply for the job.

e. My secretary can **type** over 100 words per minute.

Target Words/Phrases   Definitions

1. _____ = make something better

2. _____ = write using a typewriter[1] or computer keyboard

3. _____ = add a number to itself a specific number of times

4. _____ = take a number or an amount from another number or amount

5. _____ = write all the necessary information in the spaces provided on a form

[1] a *typewriter*

Building on the Vocabulary

Studying Word Grammar

The verb *rob* and the verb *steal* have similar meanings, but they are used differently.

- Someone robs a person or a company: *He robbed a bank.*
- Someone steals a thing (from a person or company): *He stole money from the bank.*

Write two sentences. Use *rob* and *steal*.

1. _____

2. _____

DEVELOPING YOUR SKILLS

Comparing and Contrasting

Use information from the reading to complete each diagram below. What do the people have in common? How do they differ?

1. The Canadian study:

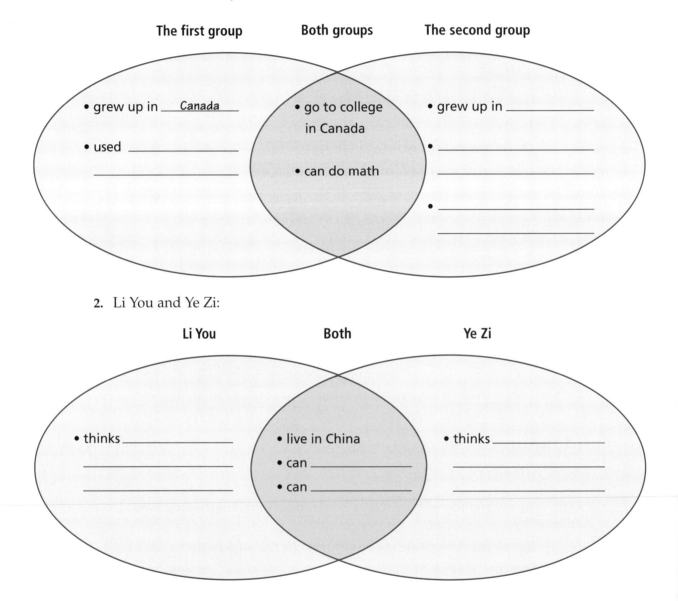

2. Li You and Ye Zi:

Reading Between the Lines

These are inference questions. The answers to these questions are not given in the reading, but you can answer them if you understand the reading.

1. What does Jack's teacher believe about calculators? _____

_____

_____

2. What does Kate Gladstone want schools to do? _____

_____

_____

3. What would Ye Zi probably want his children to learn in school? _____

_____

_____

Summarizing

On a piece of paper, write a summary of "Out with the Old, In with the New?" Begin with a statement of the main idea. Then give three examples from the reading.

Sharing Opinions

Talk about the following opinions in a small group. Tell why you agree or disagree.

Opinion 1	Children need to spend a lot of time in school developing good handwriting.
Opinion 2	Children in school should spend more time learning to write on a computer than learning to write by hand.
Opinion 3	Children should not waste schooltime practicing handwriting or typing. In the future, we will speak to computers and they will do any necessary writing for us.

Using New Words

Work with a partner. Choose five target words or phrases from the list on page 209. On a piece of paper, use each word or phrase in a sentence.

Writing

Choose a topic. Write a paragraph.

1. Think of a tradition that has changed in your country in recent years. Describe the change and give your opinion of it.
2. Some people love new technology, others aren't interested in it, and some are afraid of it. What about you? What is your relationship with modern technology? Give an example from your life.

CHAPTER 23

Appropriate Technologies

Keeping vegetables fresh in a cooler made from two clay pots with wet sand in between*

GETTING READY TO READ

Talk with a partner or in a small group.

1. What percentage of the people in the world do you think have no electricity?
   a. less than 10%   **b.** about 18%   **c.** about 33%

2. Do you know the phrases *developed countries* and *developing countries*? Read the definitions and list some examples of each.

   developed countries = rich countries with many industries, comfortable living for most people, and (usually) governments chosen by the people.

   Examples: _____

   developing countries = poor countries without much industry that are working to improve their people's lives.

   Examples: _____

* Developed by Mohammed Bah Abba of Nigeria for use in hot, dry places with no electricity

READING

Look at the words and pictures next to the reading. Then read.

Appropriate Technologies

1   You are probably reading this book in a developed country. So when you hear the word *technology,* you are likely to think of computers, high-tech phones, cars, and so on. Those of us who live in such countries can look forward to new **models** each year that may be even better. Modern technology has made life in developed countries much easier. Technology can make life easier in developing countries, too, but it has to be technology of another kind because the needs in such countries are very different. About two billion people—one-third of the people on Earth—do not even have electricity. What they need is technology that is **appropriate** for their situations, technology that will help them meet basic needs for food, water, clothes, housing, health services, and ways to make a living.

2   The **term** *appropriate technologies* means types of technology that:

- use materials available in the local area.
- can be understood, built, and **repaired** by the people who use them.
- bring communities together to **solve** local problems.

3   Some appropriate technologies are beautifully simple. For example, a project in Sri Lanka is using sunlight to make drinking water safe. Clear bottles are filled with water and placed in the sun for six hours. That is usually enough time for the sun to **heat** the water and kill germs.[1] If the weather is cool or cloudy, it takes two days. This **method** has already been proven to help people stay healthier.

4   Amy Smith is an inventor with a passion[2] for designing appropriate technologies. Smith studied engineering at MIT, the Massachusetts Institute of Technology (in the United States), and then spent four years in Botswana, in **southern** Africa. She taught math, science, and English there, and she trained farmers in beekeeping (looking after bees and getting honey[3] from them). In Botswana, she realized that she could help people more by using her skills as an engineer. Smith said, "The longer I was there, the more I realized there were **plenty** of inventions that could improve the quality of life."

continued

[1] *germs* = very small living things that can make a person sick

[2] a *passion* = a strong love

[3] Bees produce *honey.*

5   So Smith went back to MIT and started working on low-tech inventions. Her first great invention was a screenless hammermill. A hammermill is a machine that grinds grain[4] into flour. Usually a hammermill needs a screen[5] to separate the flour from the unwanted parts of the grain. But screens often break, and they are hard to replace, so regular hammermills are not of much use in **rural** Africa. Women there often end up grinding grain by hand and spending hours each day to do it. Smith's invention does not need a screen. It is cheap to build, simple to use, easy to repair, and it does not use electricity. With this machine, a woman can grind as much grain in a minute as she used to do in an hour.

[4] *grinds grain* = crushes the seeds of plants like corn or wheat between two hard, moving surfaces

[5] a *screen* = a wire net with holes that only very small things can pass through

6   Smith's invention has been a great success in Africa, but some other good ideas have not done so well. In **northern** Ghana, another project designed to help women failed partly for cultural reasons. The women in this area do most of the farming, and they spend a lot of time and energy walking to and from their farms. Most of the time, they are carrying heavy **loads** on their heads. They are very much in need of a better way to transport farm products, tools, water, and so on. Because bicycles are popular in the region, a bicycle trailer seemed to be a good **solution** to the problem. The trailer was like a shopping cart[6] but had two wheels and was attached to the back of a bike. However, the idea did not work. For one thing, it is the men in northern Ghana, not the women, who own and ride bicycles. In addition, the type of bicycle offered to the women was a bicycle with a crossbar.[7] A woman wearing a dress, as is traditional there, cannot ride such a bicycle.

[6] a *shopping cart*

[7] a bicycle with a *crossbar*

7   Amy Smith and others are trying to develop technologies that do not need a lot of energy, but most people agree that electricity would be valuable in developing countries. Electricity would improve education, allow greater communication, let doctors store medicines that must stay cold, and do much more. The **production** of electricity sometimes causes **pollution**, but creative engineers can find ways to produce it without destroying **the environment**, perhaps using the energy of the sun, wind, or water. Of course, the problems of developing nations cannot all be solved by thinkers like Amy Smith, but many can. As she says, "Technology isn't the only solution, but it can certainly be part of the solution."

Amy Smith was quoted in "MIT Grad Student Designs Low-Cost Solution for High-Tech African Problem" by Denise Brehm, November 29, 1999, <http://web.mit.edu/newsoffice> and in "Questions and Answers" March 2001, <http://alumweb.mit.edu/opendoor>.

Quick Comprehension Check

Read these sentences. Circle T (true) or F (false).

1. Today, only a few people in the world are without electricity.   T   F

2. The same technology will not work everywhere in the world.   T   F

3. *Appropriate technologies* means the most modern, high-tech machines.   T   F

4. Amy Smith is an engineer and an inventor.   T   F

5. Culture can influence how people use or feel about new technology.   T   F

6. Electricity would not help developing countries.   T   F

EXPLORING VOCABULARY

Thinking about the Vocabulary

Which target words and phrases are new to you? Circle them here and in the reading. Then read "Appropriate Technologies" again. Look at the context of each new word and phrase. Can you guess the meaning?

Target Words and Phrases			
models (1)	**solve** (2)	**plenty** (4)	**solution** (6)
appropriate (1)	**heat** (3)	**rural** (5)	**production** (7)
term (2)	**method** (3)	**northern** (6)	**pollution** (7)
repaired (2)	**southern** (4)	**loads** (6)	**the environment** (7)

Using the Vocabulary

A **These sentences are about the reading. What is the meaning of each boldfaced word or phrase? Circle a, b, or c.**

1. Each year, carmakers produce new **models** of cars. *Models* means:

   a. customers   **b.** habits   **c.** certain types
                                                                or designs

2. Technology for use in developing countries should be easy to **repair**.
   Repair means:

   a. blame   **b.** fix   **c.** drip

3. When the people in a community share a problem, they need to work together to **solve** it. *Solve* a problem means:

   a. find an answer to it   **b.** make fun of it   **c.** encourage it

4. People in Sri Lanka are using sunlight to **heat** their water and kill germs. *Heat* something means:

   a. measure it   **b.** keep up with it   **c.** make it warm or hot

5. They have a simple **method** for making their drinking water safe. *Method* means:

   a. a planned way of doing something   **b.** a conflict between two forces   **c.** a bad habit

6. Amy Smith realized there were **plenty of** inventions needed in Africa. *Plenty of* something means an amount that is:

   a. small or limited   **b.** enough or more than enough   **c.** decreasing

7. There is little modern technology in **rural** Africa. *Rural* means relating to:

   a. country areas, not the city   **b.** expensive goods   **c.** high-tech inventions

8. Water power is often used in the **production** of electricity. The *production* of something means:

   a. the investment in it   **b.** the explanation of it   **c.** the process for making it

9. Clean ways to make electricity do not hurt **the environment**. *The environment* means:

   a. all our land, water, and air   **b.** people's lifestyles   **c.** types of transportation

B These sentences use the target words **in new contexts**. Complete them with the words in the box.

environment	heat	method	models	plenty
production	repair	rural	solve	

1. He lives on a farm in a quiet, _____ area.

2. The accident was so bad that they can't possibly _____ the car.

3. You can get a TV at SuperBuy. There are lots of _____ to choose from.

4. I like her _____ of cooking rice. It has just a few, simple steps.

5. There's no need to rush—we have _____ of time.

6. He thinks money will _____ all his problems.

7. They burn wood to _____ their house.

8. The industry had to stop using chemicals that were bad for the

_____.

9. Demand for the game was high, so the company increased

_____.

 Read each definition and look at the paragraph number in parentheses ( ). Look back at the reading to **find the target word** for each definition. Write it in the chart.

Definition	Target Word
1. right for a certain purpose, situation, or time (1)	
2. a word with a specific meaning, especially in science or technology (2)	
3. in the south of an area, a state, a country, etc. (4)	
4. in the north of an area, a state, a country, etc. (6)	
5. amounts that are carried by a person, animal, truck, etc. (6)	
6. a way of solving a problem or dealing with a difficult situation (6)	
7. dangerous amounts of dirt or chemicals in the air, water, or soil (7)	

Building on the Vocabulary

Studying Word Grammar

The word *technology* can be:

- a noncount noun: *New technology is exciting.*
- a count noun, oft en plural: *Appropriate technologies are simple to use.* When it is plural, it means "types of technology."

Other nouns that are usually noncount, such as *fruit* and *cheese,* may also have a plural form meaning "types of."

Eat plenty of *fruits* and vegetables. = Eat plenty of types of fruits and vegetables.
My favorite *cheeses* come from France. = My favorite types of cheese come from France.

Circle the plural form when the noun means "types of." Circle the noncount form when it does not.

1. Some (food/foods) will affect the brain immediately; others won't.
2. Please give the cat her (food/foods).
3. They sell a variety of (coffee/coffees) from Latin America.
4. I'll have a cup of (coffee/coffees), please.
5. I use (shampoo/shampoos) to wash my hair.
6. The supermarket has lots of different (shampoo/shampoos).

DEVELOPING YOUR SKILLS

Understanding Cause and Effect

 A Complete each sentence about the reading.

1. The technology needs of developing countries are different from those of developed nations because _____

_____.

2. People in Sri Lanka put bottles of water in the sun because _____

_____.

3. Amy Smith's invention is a good example of an appropriate technology because _____

_____.

4. The women in Ghana did not use the bicycle trailers because _____

_____.

B These are inference questions. The answers to these questions are not given in the reading, but you can answer them if you understand the reading. Write complete sentences.

1. Why should appropriate technologies use materials available in the local area? <u>Materials available in the local area are easy to get and probably cost less than materials from far away.</u>

2. Why did the people in Sri Lanka have to use sunlight to heat their water?

_____

3. Why did Amy Smith leave Africa? _____

_____

4. Why have women in Africa welcomed the screenless hammermill? _____

_____

Understanding and Using Supporting Details

Write two statements with details that support each of the general statements below.

1. Technology means different things to people depending on where they live.

   <u>To people in developed countries, technology means high-tech inventions</u>
   <u>like computers and cars.</u>
   <u>To people in developing countries, technology means ways to meet</u>
   <u>basic needs.</u>

2. Appropriate technologies do not depend on high-tech machines or processes.

   _____

   _____

   _____

3. Bringing electricity to developing countries could have both good and bad effects.

   _____

   _____

   _____

4. Technology can make people's lives easier.

   _____

   _____

   _____

Discussion

Work with a partner or in a small group.

1. Fill in the chart with examples of modern technology that you use. Write what people had to do before the invention of each type of technology.

Modern technology:	In the past:
1. dishwashers	People used to wash dishes by hand.
2.	
3.	
4.	
5.	

2. Consider each of the types of technology in your chart. Which ones would you miss the most and the least if you didn't have them? Why?

3. Amy Smith spent four years living and working in a rural area of a developing country. Do you know anyone who has done something like that? Would you like to do it yourself? Why or why not?

Using New Words

Work with a partner. Take turns asking for and giving information.

1. Describe some kind of clothing that is not **appropriate** for school.
2. Name two things people can do to protect **the environment**.
3. Name something you can't **repair** if it gets broken.
4. Name two things you can find in **rural** areas.
5. Name something you have **plenty** of.

Writing

Write a paragraph that relates to question 2 or 3 from Discussion above.

CHAPTER 24

Technology in Science Fiction

A science fiction magazine cover from 1941

GETTING READY TO READ

Talk with a partner or in a small group.

1. *Science fiction* means stories about future developments in science and technology and their effects on people. Sometimes these stories include travel by spaceship.[1] There have been many popular science fiction movies, such as *Star Wars*. What others can you name?

2. **a.** Look at the magazine cover above. What is happening in the picture?

   b. An artist created this magazine cover in 1941. How well did the artist imagine the future? Explain.

[1] a *spaceship*

READING

Look at the words and pictures next to the reading. Then read.

Technology in Science Fiction

1   Facts are pieces of information we know to be true. When we read history, we want to know the facts—what really happened. Fiction is the opposite. Writers of fiction **make up** stories, telling of people and events that come from the writer's **imagination**. Science fiction writers imagine not only people and events but, perhaps most importantly, technology. They often write about the effects of that technology on a person, a group, or **society**. These writers usually set their stories in the future. Some of them have **predicted** technology that seemed impossible at the time but really does exist today.

2   An Englishwoman, Mary Shelley, was one of the first writers of science fiction. In 1818, she wrote the book *Frankenstein*. It tells the story of a young scientist, Dr. Frankenstein, who wants to create a human life. He puts together parts of dead people's bodies, including—by mistake—the brain of a **criminal**, and then uses electricity to bring the creature[1] to life. But he cannot control the creature, and it kills him. Since then, the idea of a "mad scientist" (someone who tries to use science and technology to gain power) has been very popular in science fiction, especially in the movies.

3   In 1863, the French writer Jules Verne wrote the first of his many great science fiction **adventure** stories, *Cinq Semaines en Ballon* (*Five Weeks in a Balloon*). It is the story of three men traveling across Africa by hot air balloon.[2] Readers loved it, but many were **confused**: Was it fact or fiction? The story sounded unlikely, but the **style** of the writing and the **scientific** details made it seem true.

4   Later, Jules Verne wrote *Paris au Vingtième Siècle* (*Paris in the Twentieth Century*), a story he set 100 years into the future, in the 1960s. This story has **descriptions** of high-speed trains, gas-powered cars, calculators, skyscrapers,[3] and modern methods of communication, including fax machines. Verne imagined all these things at a time when **neither** he

continued

[1] a *creature* = a living thing (but not a plant)

[2] a *hot air balloon*

[3] a *skyscraper* = an extremely tall building

nor anyone in Paris had even a radio! In another book, *De la Terre à la Lune* (*From the Earth to the Moon*), he predicted that people would travel in **outer space** and walk on the moon, a prediction that came true on July 20, 1969. Verne even got some of the details right. Both in his book and in real life, there were three astronauts[4] making the **flight** to the moon, they **took off** from Florida, and they came down in the Pacific Ocean on their return.

5   Space travel continued to be a popular subject for science fiction in the twentieth **century**. The best writers based the science and technology in their stories on a real understanding of the science and technology of their time. Computers, robots,[5] and genetic engineering[6] all appeared in the pages of science fiction long before they appeared in the news.

6   The following quotation comes from a story by the great science fiction writer Isaac Asimov. He wrote these words in 1954. When you read them, remember that at that time, people had no computers in their homes. In fact, the few computers that existed were as big as some people's homes. In "The Fun They Had," Asimov describes a child of the future using a personal computer to learn math:

7   Margie went into the schoolroom. It was right next to her bedroom, and the mechanical teacher was on and waiting for her. . . .

8   The screen was lit up, and it said: "Today's arithmetic lesson is on the addition of proper fractions. Please insert yesterday's homework in the proper slot."

9   Margie did so with a sigh. She was thinking about the old schools they had when her grandfather's grandfather was a little boy. All the kids from the whole neighborhood came, laughing and shouting in the schoolyard, sitting together in the schoolroom. . . .

10   And the teachers were people. . . .

11   In 1954, readers probably found Asimov's story hard to believe. Fifty years later, his ideas don't seem so strange, do they? Maybe we should pay more attention to what science fiction writers are saying today about the world of tomorrow. But we should also remember that their predictions have been wrong more often than right. Here we are in the twenty-first century without flying cars, vacations on the moon, or robots cooking our dinner. And **in spite of** computers, people still do go to school.

Isaac Asimov's story "The Fun They Had" appears in *The Best of Isaac Asimov* (New York: Doubleday & Company, 1974), 153–155.

[4] an *astronaut* = someone who travels and works in outer space

[5] a *robot*

[6] *genetic engineering* = the science of changing the genes of living things

Quick Comprehension Check

Read these sentences. Circle T (true) or F (false).

1. Science fiction is often about the technology of the future.   T   F

2. People began writing science fiction in the 1900s.   T   F

3. A lot of science fiction is about people traveling in outer space.   T   F

4. Science fiction writers have imagined technology before it was invented.   T   F

5. A writer 50 years ago imagined computers replacing schools and teachers.   T   F

6. The predictions of science fiction writers are generally correct.   T   F

EXPLORING VOCABULARY

Thinking about the Vocabulary

Which target words and phrases are new to you? Circle them here and in the reading. Then read "Technology in Science Fiction" again. Look at the context of each new word and phrase. Can you guess the meaning?

Target Words and Phrases			
make up (1)	criminal (2)	scientific (3)	flight (4)
imagination (1)	adventure (3)	descriptions (4)	took off (4)
society (1)	confused (3)	neither . . . nor (4)	century (5)
predicted (1)	style (3)	outer space (4)	in spite of (11)

Using the Vocabulary

Ⓐ These sentences are **about the reading**. Complete them with the words and phrases in the box.

adventure	century	confused	criminal	imagination
in spite of	make up	predicted	society	took off

1. Writers of history shouldn't invent anything, but writers of science fiction _____ almost everything.

2. The people and events in fiction come from the writer's _____ (his or her ability to think of new ideas or form mental pictures).

3. Science fiction often deals with the effects of future technology on _____, meaning people in general.

4. Writers have imagined technologies of the future and described them in their stories. They _____ that we would have these types of technology.

5. By mistake, Dr. Frankenstein gave his creature the brain of a _____, a person who broke the law and committed crimes.

6. Jules Verne's science fiction stories are full of _____. In other words, they are about exciting experiences in which dangerous or unusual things happen.

7. Readers of *Five Weeks in a Balloon* didn't know whether or not the story was true. They didn't know what to think. They were _____.

8. In both the book *From the Earth to the Moon* and in real life, the astronauts _____ from Florida. That is, their spaceships went up into the air from Florida.

9. Science fiction books and movies were popular during the twentieth _____ (the 100 years from 1900 to 2000).

10. Computers have not replaced teachers and classrooms. _____ computers (that is, even though computers exist), people still go to school.

B **These sentences use the target words and phrases in new contexts. Complete them with the words and phrases in the box.**

adventure	century	confused	criminals	imaginations
in spite of	made up	predicted	society	took off

1. Jules Verne died in 1905. He died a _____ ago.

2. The actor didn't like his real name, so he _____ another.

3. Some people enjoy taking risks. They want exciting experiences. They go looking for _____.

4. We _____ that they would solve the problem, and soon they did.

5. She told her students to use their _____ to find a solution.

6. It is the job of the police to catch _____.

7. _____ expects people to obey the law and respect the rights of others.

8. The twins look so much alike that I can't be sure who's who. I get

_____.

9. He volunteered to do the job _____ the danger.

10. The plane _____ from Madrid several hours ago. In a little while, it will land in Mexico City.

C **Read these sentences. Write the boldfaced target words or phrases next to their definitions.**

a. I like the **style** of that car but not the color.

b. What time is the next **flight** to Paris?

c. H_2O is a **scientific** term for water.

d. He gave the police a **description** of the robber.

e. Sales have **neither** increased **nor** decreased. They have stayed exactly the same.

f. He dreamed of traveling in **outer space**, of going to the moon and beyond.

Target Words/Phrases   **Definitions**

1. _____ = not (one person, thing, or action) and not (another) either

2. _____ = the way something is made or done

3. _____ = relating to science or using its methods

4. _____ = a trip in a plane or space vehicle, or a plane making a trip

5. _____ = the area outside Earth's air, also called simply *space*

6. _____ = a piece of writing or speech giving details of what someone or something is like

Building on the Vocabulary

Studying Word Grammar

After the phrase *in spite of,* you can use:

- a noun: *In spite of his injury, he stayed in the game and kept playing.*
- a pronoun: *The weather was bad, but we went out in spite of it.*
- a gerund (an *-ing* form of a verb used as a noun): *I went to class in spite of feeling sick.*

Write three statements using *in spite of.*

1. _____

2. _____

3. _____

DEVELOPING YOUR SKILLS

Using Context Clues

The paragraphs in the reading from Asimov's story "The Fun They Had" contain words you may not know. Answer these questions about the story using the context to guess word meanings.

1. On the computer screen, Margie can read these words:

   Today's arithmetic lesson is on the addition of proper fractions.

   Which words are related to math? Circle them.

2. The computer tells Margie to "insert yesterday's homework in the proper slot." A slot is a long, narrow hole in a surface. We sometimes put letters into a mail slot or money into a coin slot.

   a. What is the meaning of *insert*? _____

   b. Do you think Margie does her homework on paper or on something

      else? Why? _____

      _____

3. Margie put her homework into the computer "with a sigh." These words show how she was feeling. Consider what Margie is thinking about. What do you think *a sigh* means? Check (✓) your answer.

   ❏ a big smile   ❏ an angry shout   ❏ a sad or tired sound

4. How do you think Margie feels about the way education has changed since

   the school days of her grandfather's grandfather? _____

   _____

Summarizing

On a piece of paper, write a one-paragraph summary of "Technology in Science Fiction." Include answers to the following questions:

- What does *science fiction* mean?
- Who was one of the first writers of science fiction?
- Who was Jules Verne?
- What were some of the things that Jules Verne accurately predicted in his stories?
- What happened with science fiction during the twentieth century?

Sharing Opinions

Answer the following questions. Then form a small group and find out the answers of the others in your group. Share the information about your group with the class.

1. Do you like to read science fiction:
   In your first language? ❑ Yes   ❑ No
   In English? ❑ Yes   ❑ No

2. Do you enjoy science fiction movies?   ❑ Yes   ❑ No   ❑ Sometimes
   Examples of sci-fi movies you have seen: _____
   _____

3. What do you like or dislike about science fiction? _____
   _____
   _____
   _____
   _____

Using New Words

Work with a partner. Choose five target words or phrases from the list on page 226. On a piece of paper, use each word or phrase in a sentence.

Writing

Choose a topic. Write a paragraph.

1. Margie, the little girl in Asimov's story "The Fun They Had," knows a little about her grandfather's grandfather's life when he was a boy. What do you know, and what can you imagine, about the lives of any of your great-great-grandparents?

2. Become a science fiction writer! Imagine your life 30 years from now. Think especially about the technology you will use every day. Describe something from your daily life.

Wrap-up

REVIEWING VOCABULARY

Complete the phrase.

1. Write *methods of, a solution to,* or *steps in.*

    a. _____ a problem

    b. _____ a process

    c. _____ transportation

2. Write the verb *predict, repair,* or *type.*

    a. _____ a car

    b. _____ a letter

    c. _____ the future

3. Write the adjective *complex, rural,* or *valuable.*

    a. _____ jewelry

    b. a _____ situation

    c. a _____ area

4. Write the noun *applications, flour,* or *stories.*

    a. make up _____

    b. fill out _____

    c. measure _____

5. Write the adjective *accurate, equal,* or *modern.*

    a. an _____ report

    b. _____ amounts

    c. _____ society

6. Write the verb *rob, solve,* or *subtract.*

    a. _____ an amount

    b. _____ a problem

    c. _____ a bank

EXPANDING VOCABULARY

A In Unit 6, you learned *load, model,* and *step* as nouns and *blame, drip, heat,* and *repair* as verbs. In the following sentences, they are used differently because each of these words can be either a noun or a verb. Fill in the correct word. Is it a noun or a verb? Circle the answer.

1. My car is in need of _____repair_____. (*n.*/*v.*)
2. Our bags are all packed. Let's _____ them into the car. (*n./v.*)
3. I cleaned up a _____ of paint that fell on the floor. (*n./v.*)
4. They asked everyone standing in line to _____ to one side. (*n./v.*)
5. Whenever anything goes wrong, he gets the _____. (*n./v.*)
6. They go to the mountains to get away from the summer _____. (*n./v.*)
7. She put on the dress she bought to _____ it for her friend. (*n./v.*)

B On a piece of paper, write seven sentences with the words from Part A. Use the verbs as nouns and the nouns as verbs.

Example: My cousin can repair his own car.

C Sometimes an adjective forms its **antonym** (a word with the opposite meaning) by adding a prefix. For example:

accurate—inaccurate	appropriate—inappropriate	equal—unequal

Sometimes the antonym of an adjective is a different word. For example:

high-tech—low-tech	northern—southern	rural—urban	valuable—worthless

Use one word from each pair of adjectives to complete the sentences.

1. You can't wear that shirt to your job interview! It's _____.
2. The report was full of mistakes. It was highly _____.
3. The car was in such poor repair that it was almost _____.
4. North America, Europe, and most of Asia are in the _____ hemisphere.
5. There are many people, businesses, and big buildings in _____ areas.
6. My favorite method of writing is fairly _____—I use a pencil.
7. I broke the candy bar into two _____ parts and gave her the bigger one.

PLAYING WITH WORDS

There are 13 target words from Unit 6 in this puzzle. The words go across
(→) and down (↓). Find the words and circle them. Then use them to
complete the sentences below.

```
X   K   Q   P   O   R   T   A   B   L   E
A   C   O   N   F   U   S   E   D   O   Z
D   O   P   L   E   N   T   Y   E   S   X
V   N   P   W   X   Z   W   K   S   S   M
E   S   X   S   S   T   Y   L   E   X   P
N   T   M   Q   Z   K   V   Z   R   Z   O
T   A   Z   I   M   P   R   O   V   E   C
U   N   X   Z   M   X   K   X   E   Q   K
R   T   C   E   N   T   U   R   Y   Y   E
E   N   V   I   R   O   N   M   E   N   T
L   P   O   L   L   U   T   I   O   N   S
```

1. He's always traveling to exciting places. He loves _____adventure_____.

2. We are living in the 21st _____.

3. You can easily move a _____ TV.

4. Cars are bad for the _____.

5. No one can swim in that lake anymore. There's too much

   _____.

6. She got her hair cut in a new _____.

7. Your boss doesn't pay you enough. You _____ more.

8. Bring your friends to eat with us—we have _____ of food.

9. Living near the airport, they have the _____ sound of planes
   overhead.

10. I didn't understand what was happening. I felt _____.

11. I want to be a better player. How can I _____ my skills?

12. When my friend moved away, I felt a great sense of _____.

13. I put my hands in my _____ to keep them warm.

BUILDING DICTIONARY SKILLS

Look at the dictionary entries below. Then read each sentence and write the number of the meaning.

1. _____ **a.** I'm sorry, but I can't make it to the meeting tomorrow. I have a conflict.

   _____ **b.** The two partners ended up in constant conflict.

   _____ **c.** At first, the conflict was limited to just those two nations.

> **con·flict**[1] /ˈkɑnˌflɪkt/ *n* [C,U] **1** disagreement between people, groups, countries etc.: *The two groups have been* **in conflict with** *each other for years.* | *a* **conflict between** *father and son* | **conflicts over** *who owns the land* **2** a situation in which you have to choose between opposing things: *In a* **conflict between** *work and family, I would always choose my family.* **3** a war or fight in which weapons are used

2. _____ **a.** Do they treat their employees fairly?

   _____ **b.** It was a fairly traditional wedding.

> **fair·ly**[1] /ˈfɛrli/ *adv* **1** more than a little, but much less than very: *She speaks English fairly well.* **2** in a way that is honest or reasonable: *I felt that I hadn't been treated fairly.*

3. _____ **a.** The plane took off on time.

   _____ **b.** I took off my coat.

   _____ **c.** He was here a moment ago, but then he took off.

   _____ **d.** She took a month off after having her baby.

> **take off** *phr v* **1** [T **take** sth ↔ **off**] to remove something: *Your name has been* **taken off** *the list.* | *Take your shoes* **off** *in the house.* **2** [I] if an aircraft or space vehicle takes off, it rises into the air **3** [I] INFORMAL to leave a place: *We packed everything in the car and* **took off**. **4** [T **take** sth **off**] also **take off work** to not go to work for a period of time: *I'm* **taking** *some time* **off** *work to go to the wedding.* . . .

4. _____ **a.** The teacher varied the class, so we didn't get bored.

   _____ **b.** The weather varies a lot in the spring.

   _____ **c.** The movies he makes don't vary much, do they?

> **var·y** /ˈvɛri, ˈværi/ *v* **1** [I] if several things of the same type vary, they are all different from each other: *Teaching methods* **vary greatly/enormously** *from school to school.* | *wines that* **vary in price/quality** **2** [I] to change often: *His moods seem to vary a lot.* **3** [T] to regularly change what you do or the way that you do it: *You need to vary your diet and get more exercise.*

Vocabulary Self-Test 2

Circle the letter of the word or phrase that best completes each sentence.

Example:

The radio isn't working. It needs new _____.

a. pills   (c.) batteries

b. nephews   d. degrees

1. I like exciting movies that are full of action and _____.

   a. adventure   c. flour

   b. service   d. investment

2. He needs a car, but he says he can't _____ one.

   a. beat   c. sail

   b. subtract   d. afford

3. The airplane was invented more than a _____ ago.

   a. flight   c. model

   b. century   d. space

4. The boss _____ me whenever anything goes wrong.

   a. robs   c. predicts

   b. blames   d. bakes

5. She left school at a young age. She didn't go _____ eighth grade.

   a. beyond   c. throughout

   b. within   d. besides

6. Those flowers do not need water. They are not real. They are
   _____.

   a. foreign   c. portable

   b. appropriate   d. artificial

7. Your heart is inside your _____.

   a. chest   c. market

   b. dust   d. lifestyle

8. They _____ money from the bank to buy their house.

   a. provided   **c.** borrowed

   b. attached   **d.** designed

9. We divided the bill so that we all paid _____ amounts.

   a. southern   **c.** equal

   b. mental   **d.** rural

10. Let's _____ a date for our next meeting.

    a. set   **c.** heat

    b. rent   **d.** blow

11. The two brothers think alike. They hold the same _____ on most things.

    a. sales   **c.** pockets

    b. firms   **d.** views

12. The company produces cars of high _____, so of course they are expensive.

    a. risk   **c.** production

    b. crime   **d.** quality

13. _____ the long trip and the late hour, the children didn't seem tired.

    a. Whatever   **c.** In spite of

    b. Since   **d.** Therefore

14. You have worked hard. You _____ some time off.

    a. appear   **c.** flow

    b. deserve   **d.** treat

15. If he practices, he will _____.

    a. prove   **c.** improve

    b. solve   **d.** invest

16. The reporters took notes on the _____ parts of the president's speech.

    a. key   **c.** such

    b. worth   **d.** aware

17. Drive slowly—the road is in bad _____.

    a. condition   **c.** pollution

    b. description   **d.** operation

18. Their research led to new _____ in medical care for patients with burns.

    a. loads   **c.** limits

    b. developments   **d.** surfaces

19. Who _____ your cat when you are away?

    a. thinks over   **c.** looks after

    b. fills out   **d.** deals in

20. He goes to all the games, so it isn't _____ that he would miss this one.

    a. scientific   **c.** huge

    b. valuable   **d.** likely

21. She is afraid of losing her job. She has little job _____.

    a. industry   **c.** injury

    b. society   **d.** security

22. Farmers are in a bad _____ after ten weeks of no rain.

    a. trade   **c.** situation

    b. material   **d.** method

23. I go to my grandfather for advice. He has always had a _____ influence on my life.

    a. recent   **c.** political

    b. confused   **d.** major

24. Everything around us is part of our _____.

    a. shadow   **c.** environment

    b. flight   **d.** term

25. His new haircut didn't look good, so his brothers _____ it.

    a. kept up with   **c.** took over

    b. looked into   d. made fun of

26. We don't know what will happen. The future is _____.

    a. plain   **c.** normal

    b. uncertain   **d.** political

27. A person who shops in a store is a _____.

    a. customer   **c.** criminal

    b. director   **d.** officer

28. You can both come in our car. We have _____ of room.

    a. none   **c.** fairly

    b. plenty   **d.** possibly

29. I cleaned out my notebook and _____ old papers I did not need.

    a. got to know   **c.** set up

    b. made up   **d.** got rid of

30. Computers did not _____ 100 years ago.

    a. spread   **c.** exist

    b. demand   **d.** encourage

31. The students _____ a lot of money at their summer jobs.

    a. repaired   **c.** measured

    b. doubled   **d.** earned

32. You don't have to do that. It isn't _____.

    a. similar   **c.** further

    b. necessary   **d.** annoyed

33. Water, oil, and juice are all _____.

    a. liquids   **c.** containers

    b. rules   **d.** processes

34. What is the first _____ in finding a job?

    a. loss   **c.** ad

    b. step   **d.** nation

35. I need to _____ my closet so that I can find things easily.

    a. multiply   **c.** organize

    b. block   **d.** drip

36. She has a small business with fewer than 20 full-time _____.

    a. nieces   **c.** volunteers

    b. employees   **d.** criminals

See the Answer Key on page 239.

VOCABULARY SELF-TESTS ANSWER KEY

Below are the answers to the vocabulary self-tests. Check your answers, and then review any words you did not remember. You can look up words in the index on the next three pages. Then go back to the readings and exercises to find the words. Use your dictionary as needed.

Vocabulary Self-Test 1 (Units 1–3; pages 115–118)

1. d	10. d	19. a	28. a
2. b	11. c	20. a	29. c
3. d	12. d	21. b	30. b
4. c	13. b	22. b	31. d
5. d	14. a	23. a	32. d
6. d	15. b	24. d	33. a
7. a	16. a	25. c	34. b
8. b	17. b	26. c	35. c
9. c	18. a	27. c	36. c

Vocabulary Self-Test 2 (Units 4–6; pages 235–238)

1. a	10. a	19. c	28. b
2. d	11. d	20. d	29. d
3. b	12. d	21. d	30. c
4. b	13. c	22. c	31. d
5. a	14. b	23. d	32. b
6. d	15. c	24. c	33. a
7. a	16. a	25. d	34. b
8. c	17. a	26. b	35. c
9. c	18. b	27. a	36. b

INDEX TO TARGET WORDS AND PHRASES

THE ILLUSTRATED
STAR WARS
UNIVERSE

ART BY RALPH McQUARRIE
TEXT BY KEVIN J. ANDERSON
ADDITIONAL ART: MICHAEL BUTKUS · HARRISON ELLENSHAW · CHRIS EVANS
NILO RODIS-JAMERO · JOE JOHNSTON · MICHAEL PANGRAZIO · NORMAN REYNOLDS

BANTAM BOOKS
NEW YORK · TORONTO · LONDON · SYDNEY · AUCKLAND

THE ILLUSTRATED

STAR WARS

UNIVERSE

THE ILLUSTRATED STAR WARS
A Bantam Spectra Book

PUBLISHING HISTORY
Bantam Spectra hardcover edition published in December 1995
Bantam Spectra trade paperback edition / October 1997

DEDICATION
To my grandfather, JENS T. ANDERSON, who was never much of a
reader, but always kept my books proudly displayed along with all his
other mementos from his grandchildren. He taught me many things,
including the small measure of common sense I might once have had.

I think he would have liked this book.
Kevin J. Anderson

ACKNOWLEDGMENTS
Thanks to George Lucas, Lucy Wilson, Sue Rostoni, Allan Kausch,
Halina Krukowski, and Janet Silk at Lucasfilm;
STAR WARS authors Dave Wolverton, Timothy Zahn, and Tom Veitch;
Bill Smith and West End Games; Scott Usher, Peter Landa and Megan
Rickards Youngquist at the Greenwich Workshop for their design skills;
Betsy Mitchell; and last but not least—Tom Dupree for imagination
and editorial assistance.

ISBN: 0-553-37484-2

Published simultaneously in the United States and Canada

Bantam Books are published by Bantam Books, a division of Bantam Doubleday
Dell Publishing Group, Inc. Its trademark, consisting of the words ''Bantam Books''
and the portrayal of a rooster, is Registered in U.S. Patent and Trademark Office and
in other countries. Marca Registrada. Bantam Books, 1540 Broadway, New York,
New York 10036.

PRINTED IN THE UNITED STATES OF AMERICA
KPP   10 9 8 7 6 5 4 3 2

CONTENTS

TATOOINE

ABOUT THE AUTHOR:

(*Indeterminate*) *Hoole*—Senior Anthropologist Hoole has taken great advantage of his species' astonishing shape-changing and mind-fogging abilities, vastly enriching our knowledge of the galaxy's varied worlds through his unique powers of investigation. His skill at imitating and infiltrating alien cultures—not to mention interpreting them for our readers—has earned him many honors. Unfortunately, there are few like him; his race, the Shi'ido, is rare.

In this report, written before Tatooine was thrown into prominence as the homeworld of Luke Skywalker, (Indeterminate) Hoole describes his fascinating and sometimes harrowing experiences on the remote and little-known desert planet.

TATOOINE

Two suns burn down on the planet Tatooine, rising and setting over the harsh desert landscape. The system contains the binary stars Tatoo I and Tatoo II, similar yellow G1 and G2 stars that would have made for a pleasant climate…if the planet had not orbited on the hot inner edge of the life zone.

One can find this information in any star gazetteer. But I wanted to know more, not just a list of statistics and astronomical quantities. I wanted to know the real Tatooine, this place of mystery. And because of my unique biology, I could discover knowledge hidden from even the best anthropologists and survey teams. I could observe like the proverbial mace fly on the wall.

Other members of my shape-changing race have given my entire species a disreputable air. My people are most commonly thought of as spies and assassins, able to disguise themselves and blend in with any group of sentients. We can fog the minds of those around us, erasing suspicions and distracting people from asking embarrassing questions. Naturally, we are greatly sought after by powerful crime lords as well as the Empire itself for espionage and covert operations.

I have chosen, however, to turn my skills to the advancement of knowledge. As an "invisible" anthropologist, I am able to blend in with any culture and observe it from the inside, discovering valuable details hidden from blundering, intrusive teams with their electronic imagers and keypads and blunt questions.

No, I work alone. I slip in and play my role. I watch, and learn.

I reached Tatooine by impersonating a crew member on a long-distance cargo hauler. With my abilities of distraction, I made sure no one particularly noticed me or realized that I seemed to have no defined duties. I wasn't there to deceive anyone. I just wanted passage to the planet, where I could begin my studies.

During the brief passage, I reviewed what other databases already contained about the arid desert planet. Much of the information was dry and uninspired, as if the original survey teams had not been much interested in the place, and no one had bothered to expand the write-ups.

Tatooine has the fortune—or *mis*fortune, some might say after learning of the planet's tortured history—of being located in the remote Outer Rim, yet near a prime nexus of hyperspace routes. This makes the planet easy to get to…but nobody particularly wants to go there. Given the world's low profile and strategic location, a significant amount of smuggler traffic has always passed through the Tatooine system—even before the recent Imperial crackdown on commercial spice freighting.

Tatooine has been settled by outside colonists for only a few hundred years; but in that time the desert world has been the site of countless battles between rival gangsters and smuggling lords.

According to anecdotal reports, the uncharted landscape is scattered with the debris from burning ships, crashed fighters, and the broken hulks of mercenary battle cruisers. Scavenger races in the desert arm themselves with all manner of weaponry, from archaic bombs and projectile weapons to contraband double-blasters dumped by gunrunners fleeing the Empire.

As we approached the silent, orange-tan sphere of Tatooine, I stood on the observation deck, completely unnoticed, while the other crew members bustled about in their preparatory work for landing. The planet looked stained and desolate, practically featureless, blazing in the reflected light from its double suns.

The geography of Tatooine has never been precisely mapped, probably because no one really cares. The planet is sparsely inhabited with well-defined settlements and holds few resources of galactic interest. Titanic sandstorms roar across the face of Tatooine every year, altering the landscape and erasing landmarks.

From my vantage at the observation windows, I watched one of Tatooine's few prominent features orbit beneath our ship—the wide expanse of the

Dune Sea, a harsh basin left from the drying of an ancient ocean. I had seen grainy images showing how the alkaline sands glitter under the binary sunlight, without so much as a rock outcropping to break the monotony for kilometers.

Bordering the Dune Sea lay the badlands of the Jundland Wastes, rocky canyons and mesas in which roam the Sand People, or Tusken Raiders, a violent and secretive race who inspire fear among the local settlers. The caves and crannies in the Jundland Wastes supposedly house an unknown number of fugitives, hermits, and marauders. I had also read overblown, boastful reports of local flyers who spent their free time practicing aerial combat and gunnery skills in the steep and winding gorges, such as Beggar's Canyon.

I couldn't wait to get to work down there. I was ready for anything.

We landed in the seedy spaceport of Mos Eisley—Tatooine's only "big city"—which seemed identical to a thousand other spaceports on a thousand other backwater worlds. I overheard one of the crew members muttering that the place was a "wretched hive of scum and villainy," but that didn't seem to bother him in the least.

After the long-distance cargo hauler had landed in one of the docking bays, I slipped off the ship. No one noticed me, and no one would ever remember me. With my slim electronic notepad in hand, I entered the city, eager to jot down my impressions.

Mos Eisley is a haphazard array of low, gray steelcrete structures and semidomes at the bottom of a wide, windy basin surrounded by bluffs.

Large, shabby spaceship hangars line the actual spaceport district near the Spaceport Traffic Control Tower, the beacon that guides shuttles and small cruisers down to land. Because of the small amount of "official" traffic, the traffic control tower rarely does anything beyond negotiating landing fees at the various docking bays. Unofficial traffic usually consists of smugglers hauling glitterstim or ryll

spice or other contraband through the black-market centers on Tatooine.

In the town center I found the large wreck of a crashed spacecraft, the *Dowager Queen*, a mess of tangled girders and falling-apart hull plates that had been picked over by generations of scavengers. From what I could tell, the wreck provided a home for all manner of strange creatures, vagrants, and scavengers lurking inside the cool shadows.

Near the center of the dusty town, I saw the corroded hulk of a large space freighter half-buried in the sands, much more intact than the *Dowager Queen*. From the visitors' information I had taken from the docking bay, I recognized this as the *Lucky Despot*, a ship no longer spaceworthy that had been converted into a hotel and casino, now run by the long-faced, tusked Whiphid female, the Lady Valarian, reputed to be one of the powerful crime lords on Tatooine.

Officially, Imperial law is enforced on Tatooine

Tatooine offers vistas as sweeping as any in the galaxy. From a distance it may seem that nothing could live in such a hot, dry place—but the spaceport at Mos Eisley thrives with activity (both legal and illegal).

through a small contingent of stormtroopers; however, it is obvious the Empire does not consider the place worth a major effort. The man in charge, Prefect Talmont, seems to spend most of his time trying to get himself reassigned, ignoring the blatant crime in the streets of Mos Eisley.

It took little time for me to pick up details of how this city works. Much of the business—legal or otherwise—is conducted in the seedy cantinas near the docking bays. Like all spaceports, Mos Eisley is a melting pot of sentient creatures, from honest traders to fugitives to bounty hunters. Many of the inhabitants have taken up spying as a profession, keeping careful tabs on every being who comes and goes, hoping to find someone else willing to pay for the information they've gathered.

An efficient network of brokers connecting buyers and sellers has fallen into place. If you need to hire a starship or a guide, you can find the right person by asking a few discreet questions. If you need to sell illegal imported weaponry or buy a personal supply of glitterstim, someone will take care of you.

Most of the businessmen in Mos Eisley have become accustomed to bribing Prefect Talmont or other city officials to avoid being harassed about permits or code compliance. Though many of the people there have no love for the Empire, the stormtrooper outpost is considered a necessary evil. With the influx of regular water tankers and supply ships to stock the garrison, the standard of living in Mos Eisley is now higher than it has ever been.

I spent only a day in this city, since Mos Eisley interested me little. I wanted to go out and see the real Tatooine.

As a stepping-stone to the great barren wilderness, I traveled to one of the smaller settlements, Anchorhead, which serves as a central trading point for moisture farmers and others eking out a living on the edge of the Dune Sea. It was once the site of a deep, reliable well frequented by pilgrims crossing the wasteland, but the well has long since dried up.

Many support services survive in Anchorhead, but the economy is tied directly to the vagaries of the desert air. When the wind blows hotter and dryer than usual, decreasing the water harvest, the crops wane, credit accounts get thinner, and everyone suffers.

With the automation of vaporators and reclamation systems, the younger generation often has little to do except dream about the lives they could have had elsewhere in the galaxy. I infiltrated a group of teenagers near the popular hangout of Tosche Station, a power and water distribution complex, and listened to their rebellious dreams of running away from home, making their way to Mos Eisley, and finding a ride that would take them to the Imperial Academy. Their impossible but heartfelt talk disturbed me, though, and I made my way out of Anchorhead toward one of the outlying moisture farmer settlements.

Unless the blaster fire is particularly loud or a brawl gets out of hand, in seedy establishments such as this cantina most customers barely notice a disturbance.

On a desert planet such as Tatooine, the most precious commodity is water. The people who have adapted to the arid conditions have developed drastic measures to acquire and conserve water. Living in underground dwellings, moisture farmers deploy

water collection devices of all kinds along the broad perimeters of their stake, harvesting the scant droplets and hoarding them in armored underground holding tanks.

Posing as a hired hand who had lived with them for the past season, I stayed with one such family for a week. I observed their daily routine and how the moisture farmer's very existence is tied to barely functional technology, the best equipment they can scrounge on such an out-of-the-way planet.

The most common water collection device is the vaporator: three meters tall and made of multiple refrigerated cylinders. The hot wind of Tatooine blows through the open tubes, and the vital moisture condenses out upon striking the chilled metal surface. All day long, drop by drop, the distilled water fills small catchbasins buried in the base unit beneath each vaporator.

Some sophisticated-model vaporators can adapt to wind speeds, external temperature, and moisture content in the air, regulating the refrigeration unit to require the minimum power necessary to extract the maximum moisture. The programming of most vaporators, however, is done in an archaic binary language that is no longer understood by many repair droids.

Part of a moisture farmer's daily work is to travel the perimeter of his property to harvest the vaporator network. Occasionally, desperate Sand People will break into deployed vaporators and steal the collected water, but the Tusken aversion to technology usually proves as effective a barrier as the farmers' perimeter shields.

Moisture farmers sell some of their hard-won water in small containers for personal use in the towns of Anchorhead and Bestine. Most of the moisture harvest, however, is piped to extended subterranean agricultural complexes. In small artificial caverns, botanical engineers grow extended crops in intensive cultivation, using carefully regulated drip systems to add just enough precious water and concentrated nutrients directly to the root masses.

The invigorating light from the two suns of Tatooine is piped underground through prisms and mirrors, keeping the plants well nourished. This type of agriculture does not allow for much profit, but it provides enough food for the population of Anchorhead and the outlying moisture farmers.

Some of Tatooine's water, I learned, is also obtained by roving, solitary prospectors who search the uncharted desert for their wet treasure. After I had lived with the moisture farmers for a week, one of these water prospectors came to the dwelling, asking for a meal and some supplies before he journeyed out into the Jundland Wastes again. Seeing an opportunity to explore the deep desert, I changed my appearance and fogged the memories of those around me.

The following day, disguised as the water prospector's longtime partner, I journeyed out into the baking desert, riding in the passenger compartment of a battered old XP-30 speeder.

Water prospectors roam the wastes in search of undiscovered catchtraps that have formed reservoirs near enough to the surface to be reached by laser drills. Though my companion was human, I learned that water prospectors are frequently aliens with a high tolerance for Tatooine's heat and baking dryness.

I inferred from my nameless companion's sketchy conversation that prospectors rarely find more than

Whether in the stillness of the afternoon's peak heat or in the chill of a deep desert night, the backstreets of Mos Eisley are the site of any number of underhanded dealings.

a mere trickle, which is pumped at great effort from beneath the ground. A persistent legend, though, tells of a great underground river that can be heard rushing under the rocks of certain winding, wind-carved canyons far to the north. To me it sounded typical of the "lost treasure" myths frequently told by desperate people.

Many hermits live by hidden springs deep in caves or fissures in the labyrinthine badlands, such as Beggar's Canyon, which is aptly named for the beseeching sound made by the wind as it whistles through the crevices.

He told me that the Sand People also know where water sources can be found, and these are jealously guarded; any hapless stranger who ventures too close to a secret Tusken oasis is sure to be killed.

Day after day we cruised over the landscape, studying delicate moisture sensors or just following his instincts. If we did happen to strike an underground spring, my partner carried three repulsorlift cargo platforms in the cargo bay of his vehicle. When deployed, these platforms could carry tough bladders filled with the valuable water.

However, during all the time I spent with him, we found nothing; and so I left him to set off on my own. I blurred the memory of the water prospector so that he remembered being alone all the time. Then, confident and fascinated, I strode into the sprawling desert.

At first glance, Tatooine may seem like a desolate and unforgiving place—but the persistence of life throughout the galaxy has left a rich and varied ecosystem even in the most hellish places.

Cliffborer worms, found among arid rocks.

I saw many astonishing adaptations during my time alone in the hot, rocky sands, but I managed to sketch only a few.

Tatooine's razor moss chews into shadowed rock and uses corrosive root tendrils to break down crystals and chemically extract water molecules hydrated into certain minerals. Tiny arthropods known as sand-jiggers feed on the razor moss, as do long, armored cliffborer worms.

Another interesting species, the funnel flower, sports a brilliant cone of flapping petals on each end of a long strawlike stem; the hollow stem dips through a shadowed crevice in a cliff wall, then bends back upward. Hot air sucked in through one end of the funnel flower plunges through the cool crevice, where the faint moisture condenses out in

The palace of Jabba the Hutt, originally constructed by the reclusive and mysterious B'omarr monks, is an unmistakable citadel at the edge of the Dune Sea. In its shadowy interior *(right)* many creatures have taken refuge... or vanished.

Inside Jabba's throne room, various entertainers—such as Max Rebo, Droopy McCool, and Sy Snootles, shown above—play to amuse their Hutt master...or else.

the temperature differential, collecting in the crook of the stem. Root systems spread out from the moisture-laden elbow, seeking nutrients in the rock. Deep in a crevice, this water is not directly accessible to desert people. Later I found out that Jawas have become masters at inserting long, thin hoses down the stem to siphon off the reservoir.

The hubba gourd, a tough-skinned melon studded with small reflective crystals to deflect the harsh sunlight, is a difficult-to-digest fruit, but it is a primary food of the Jawas and Tusken Raiders. In the Jawa language, hubba means "the staff of life."

I also came upon larger animals, such as a family

of scuttling womp rats, camouflaged as gray-brown boulders while they foraged along canyon bottoms. From my initial eavesdropping in Mos Eisley, I knew that though they are slow movers, the womp rats' relative invisibility has made them favorite practice targets for flyers and stormtroopers, and these creatures are becoming increasingly scarce.

Herbivorous reptilian dewbacks are used by moisture farmers as beasts of burden and by desert storm-troopers as patrol animals. Though sluggish in the cool of the night, dewbacks can be urged to bursts of great loping speed in the daytime heat. At full run, they have been able to pace landspeeders for a

(pages 26-27) In the undesirable levels of Jabba's palace—rooms that are clean and brightly lit— the wives and children of Gamorrean guards make the best of their airy but miserable quarters.

25

R. McQUARRIE/'77

short distance—and (I heard one stormtrooper say), unlike mechanical vehicles, dewbacks do not break down in sandstorms.

Herds of furry, shuttle-sized banthas run wild in the badlands of Tatooine.

While passing through Anchorhead nearly two weeks earlier, I had heard the tale of one trader who had attempted to sell captured Tusken banthas as beasts of burden; but the banthas became listless and could not be trained to perform even simple duties, though the animals are thought to be quite intelligent. Not until I saw how the Sand People domesticate wild banthas in a strange familial relationship did I understand why the trader had encountered so many difficulties.

After some time surviving alone in the desert, wishing again for the companionship of other sentient beings (as well as the amenities civilization

Tusken Raiders *(above)* are occasionally visitors to Jabba's palace, secretly trading with the B'omarr monks or others in the fortress. Their huge bantha mounts are skittish and rarely allow the curious to approach. Inside the palace, many strange creatures *(right)* can be found, some of which have not yet been classified by galactic xenobiologists.

offers), I came upon a towering citadel at the far edge of the Dune Sea. I had not come here consciously, but I counted myself very fortunate to come upon the imposing palace currently owned by the gangster and smuggling kingpin Jabba the Hutt.

Currently an odd assortment of creatures, clingers, "business associates," sycophants, and slaves live in Jabba's palace, along with their families. Gamorrean guards are totally loyal—if a bit unimaginative—defenders of the palace, while their wives spend their days lording over their households in other parts of the palace. Among Jabba's strange companions are never-before-seen species, bounty hunters, and assassins found only on wanted posters throughout the galaxy.

I was forced to use my abilities of disguise and deception to the utmost just to divert attention from myself. The inhabitants of Jabba's palace are accustomed to suspecting everyone and everything because they are embroiled in so many plots. Reading their thoughts and learning their intended plots made me literally dizzy as I went about

studying the palace itself and its history—which I found far more interesting than the petty underworld squabbles.

The enormous citadel has actually been on Tatooine for centuries, as was obvious from the generational structure of the outside, with modifications and additions constructed over the years. Centuries before a few hardy colonists arrived to scrape out a living in the desert, the mysterious religious order of the B'omarr monks moved their followers to Tatooine. Out in the harshest wastelands, the monks sought a place of suitable isolation among the crags; there, over the generations, the monks carved for themselves a labyrinthine palace of grim solitude.

A legend dimmed by time claims that the monks built their fortress in this area of Tatooine with some assistance from roving bands of Tusken Raiders, though I encountered no one who understood the connection between the Sand People and the B'omarr order. Occasionally, though, the grim and mysterious Tusken Raiders will

A Gamorrean guard in full work regalia.

Walkways and observation towers allow a full view of the desert surrounding Jabba's palace. For a few hours during the long, hot day, some people willingly go outside for some fresh air.

ride their banthas to the gate of the palace and just stare, making no attempt to communicate, and then they depart as silently as they have come.

It frightened me to discover that the B'omarr monks saw through my deception with ease and observed my real nature. I could keep no secrets from them—but they did not seem to care. They accepted my presence as part of the natural order of things.

The belief system of the B'omarr monks is centered on physical denial; by cutting themselves off from all sensation, they can focus and enhance the power of the mind, embarking on journeys made possible through inner space. Thus the rugged, unwelcoming climate of Tatooine seemed a perfect exile to them.

Once built, the citadel remained silent and mysterious, mostly hidden within the rock face, showing only battlements and great doors from the outside. Seeing the huge gates, travelers across the desert often wondered what might be hidden inside. The dark silhouetted forms occasionally seen on the ramparts never spoke, never gestured in greeting.

Over the years the B'omarr monks had no contact whatsoever with the local moisture farmers or representatives from other religious orders, such as the bantha-worshiping Dim-U monks in Mos Eisley.

The inner citadel of the monastery was so vast and empty, and the place so isolated, that renegades and smugglers soon broke in and became squatters in abandoned alcoves and corridors.

The first usurper to occupy the B'omarr monastery was the great bandit Alkhara, who once allied himself with the Sand People to wipe out a small police garrison near the former capital of Tatooine, and then butchered the Sand People who had helped him—thereby beginning the centuries-long blood feud the Tusken Raiders have toward humans.

Alkhara and his band fled into the desert from military retribution and stormed the citadel, intending to take it as a place against siege. He was surprised to find the gates unlocked, and the monks were unimpressed by his arrival. One of the monks apparently told Alkhara to make himself at home and stay as long as he liked. The monks themselves had other concerns.

B'omarr acolytes rarely speak to each other, pondering their own philosophies, except during times when they all sit in tea-rooms and sip their only nourishment, a potent tea made from herbs stored in caches somewhere in the citadel. During this time, the monks talk in snatches of conversation, entire lectures boiled down to an obscure word or phrase that they somehow seem to understand. I listened in on one of these abbreviated, esoteric conversations and walked away shaking my head, unable to fathom just how the palace's monks could be communicating.

The higher up the monks went in their studies, the fewer words they used and the less they moved…the less they needed their own bodies. Even with all the shocking things I have seen in my varied anthropological investigations, I was still shocked to discover the monastery's horrible secret.

When a B'omarr monk reaches the stage of final enlightenment, he has no further use for his body, his eyes, his ears, his senses. Nothing at all. The monk has achieved a stage of pure mental power, at one with the cosmos. When this occurs, the other, "lesser" monks help the enlightened one to shed his body, *surgically*. The enlightened brain is removed and placed in a nutrient-filled jar, forever freed from the distractions of the flesh and able to spend the years in perpetual thought. The monks showed me their wall cases filled with brain jars as they proudly explained their technique.

Even these enlightened brains still occasionally have business to attend to along the monastery corridors. Mechanical, spiderlike walking legs are available if ever an enlightened one feels the need to "go for a walk." Telepathically, the brain in a jar summons the walking legs, which approach the storage alcoves, pick up the appropriate brain jar, and attach it under the walking legs. When such a mechanical walker comes clicking along the corridors, the other B'omarr monks give it a wide, reverent berth, as did I.

Recently it has been said that Jabba the Hutt captured one of his rivals and, as punishment, demanded that the monks surgically "shed" his body and place his brain in a jar among their own. For his own amusement, Jabba wanted to see whether the hapless enemy would survive. Unfortunately for

the victim, he did. Now, blind, confused, and unable to communicate, this brain has commandeered a set of the spider legs and wanders the palace, lost and without purpose.

When the monks graciously offered to help me on the way to my own enlightenment, I declined—perhaps a bit too vehemently—and decided I would be safer in the upper levels of Jabba the Hutt's palace, among the cutthroats, bounty hunters, and assassins.

The bandit Alkhara used the citadel as his head-

The B'omarr monks ignore all their unwanted visitors, preferring instead to discuss esoteric subjects (top). The most enlightened monks— merely disembodied brains in jars—move about on robotic legs (right).

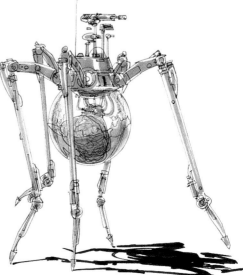

quarters for thirty-four years, improving many of the rugged corridors and great halls. His followers fixed many of the living quarters and added a deep network of dungeons and underground chambers, which the monks adored. So vast was the citadel and so few were the monks that they rarely noticed

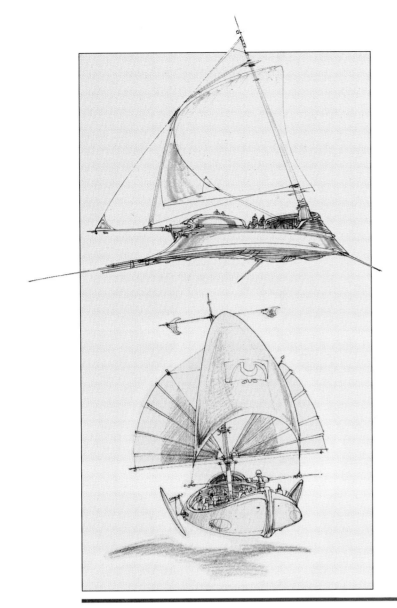

Many vehicles are used to cross the desert, such as these sand-sailing skiffs (above) or the immense and corroded sandcrawlers used by the scavenger Jawas (right).

their unwanted visitors were even there.

Over the years other bandits, revolutionaries, and crime lords took over the B'omarr monastery, occupying it under the same terms. In payment for this lodging and protection, the visitors each built another portion onto the sprawling complex: perhaps a cistern in the bluffs beneath the palace, an observation tower, or more extensive dungeons.

Jabba the Hutt has been the most recent and extravagant follower of this tradition, converting the rugged facades into a towering but elegant palace built out of sandrock reinforced by ditanium plating and reflective shielding.

Jabba constructed a vast hangar wing and garage to house his sail barge along with the sandskimmers and other vehicles. The Hutt and his retinue frequently go out across the sands on pleasure rides—usually to watch hapless victims die in various ways out in the desert.

One of his favorite styles of execution is to toss his prisoners into the gullet of a strange and fearsome creature, the Sarlacc, which makes its nesting place at the bottom of a slippery-sided basin called the Great Pit of Carkoon. The only portion of the sand dwelling creature visible aboveground is its pink, mucus-lined mouth opening, more than two meters in diameter.

Tentacular appendages can whip out and snare spectators from the rim of the pit, and inward-pointing spearlike teeth make escape impossible. Though the Sarlacc does not get frequent prey, its extremely long digestive cycle sustains it through

lean times. Legend has it that the Sarlacc may bear a rudimentary intelligence, and that it intentionally keeps its victims alive for a hideous sort of companionship even as it feeds on them.

Much as he enjoys feeding the Sarlacc, though, Jabba seems prouder still of his pet monster, the rancor, which he keeps in a slimy, dank pit beneath his throne room. The rancor is one of the most hideous beasts I have ever encountered, best described as a walking collection of fangs and claws, with no thought other than to kill and eat. Jabba frequently delights in plunging random cronies or unwanted guests through a trapdoor just to watch their death struggles.

After some time surrounded by the Hutt's weak-minded cronies with their poisoned thoughts, I found myself being looked at with more and more suspicion. Everyone, it seemed, had plans in motion

to kill Jabba, and the Hutt himself seemed able to resist some of my mind-muddling attempts.

When a passing group of chittering, hooded Jawas took their leave of Jabba's palace to continue their endless scavenging journey across the sands, I joined them in their sandcrawler. I was glad to get out of there, before Jabba fed me to his rancor just to see what color my blood really is.

After spending days in the fearsome cesspit of Jabba's palace, I found the company of the Jawas quite refreshing. The Jawas are a small-statured, rodentlike people, hardworking but eager to take advantage of any opportunity they spot. They have earned their place as Tatooine's master scavengers, salvagers, and tinkerers.

Our sandcrawler ground its way across the Dune Sea, leaving broad tracks across the sand. A team of hooded spotters stared out the narrow window high up on the pilot's observation bridge. With their

glowing yellow eyes, they searched for any usable garbage exposed by time and weather. After I had quickly assimilated their language, I heard some of the clan members speak of foolhardy Jawa family units that actually venture out during sandwhirl season, tracking the paths of the great storms to see what the winds and scouring dust uncover.

The Dune Sea is studded with the crashed hulks of spacecraft from centuries of warfare. Escape pods, shuttlecraft, attack cruisers, even luxury passenger liners have been buried under the desert. The Jawas find them.

One of their legends tells of a huge Old Republic water tanker that soft-landed out in the desert, its

crew killed by a poison gas leaking from a cracked hyperdrive chamber. Any Jawa expedition that finds this wrecked tanker with its cargo holds unbreached would be wealthier than even Jabba the Hutt.

Jawa resourcefulness can be seen in their abilty to survive by picking over wreckage and debris long since discarded by other races. These little people

The Jawas set up portable smelters to break down salvage they pick up on their travels. Such smelters can be dismantled in a hurry in the face of an impending sandwhirl storm.

can make workable devices from the most corroded components, the most battered engines.

Decades ago the Jawas took their sandcrawlers from a fleet of abandoned ore-hauler vehicles, left behind as junk from a failed mining expedition in the days before Tatooine was colonized. Each sandcrawler started out looking identical, but more than a century of repairs, embellishments, and quick fixes cobbled together from the engines and hull plates of other excavated wrecks has given them an individualistic appearance. The mechanical drives are steam-powered nuclear fusion engines, sufficient to propel the giant vehicles across the desert for centuries to come.

As an anthropologist, I found the Jawa social structure fascinating. About half of each clan spends time out in the sandcrawlers scavenging, while the remainder of the family unit lives in thick-walled fortresses erected for protection against attacks by Tusken Raiders or ferocious predators such as krayt dragons. The walls of these fortresses are made from large chunks of wrecked spacecraft, pitted and corroded by the desert winds.

Posing as a member of the Nkik clan, I made the journey from Jabba's palace in our sandcrawler. Over the course of the previous year, the vehicle had made a great circular sweep across the desert landscape, crisscrossing swaths across the empty wastelands, searching for any useful item. About half the volume of a sandcrawler is used for cargo space, storage areas to hold the junk the Jawas have managed to collect during their journey. The rest of the sandcrawler contains workshops where Jawas tinker with and repair their prizes.

Only a small amount of space is wasted on amenities for the crew and the pilot's compartment. The Jawas are expected to sleep six in a cabin the size of a closet. When not working, they strap themselves upright into coffinlike cubicles for peace and solitude—of which they need little because their family units are accustomed to being close.

Jawa sandcrawlers roam the edges of civilization on Tatooine. Emissaries from the family unit seek to barter with moisture farmers, trying to sell reconditioned droids, asking to buy malfunctioning equipment or scrap metal. They usually manage to acquire discarded items for very few credits, which they then fix and sell again,

Each year, all the Jawa clans gather for a chaotic swap meet in an isolated section of the desert *(above)*. Elsewhere, Jawa fortresses have been erected from large hunks of salvaged metal *(below)*.

although I understand that humans do not like to deal with Jawas because of their offensive smell. Master tinkerers, Jawas know how to make their wares work *just enough* that they can sell them, knowing they will be long gone before an item breaks down again.

The Nkik clan seemed relieved to be leaving Jabba's palace, though, because of a grim incident that befell another group of Jawas. The Rkok clan foolishly unloaded a cargo of questionable merchandise on Jabba the Hutt, who was neither pleased nor forgiving. The Nkik clan later found the smoking hulk of their brothers' sandcrawler utterly destroyed out in the Dune Sea, with no Jawas to be found, only a few torn brown Jawa cloaks blowing

around the lip of the Great Pit of Carkoon. The stench of Jawa terror clung to the golden sands, and the hideous Sarlacc appeared to have feasted....

We spent days out on the desert, driving and searching, driving and searching, until finally we entered more rugged territory and suddenly came upon the family fortress. The sandcrawler spent days unloading treasures behind the safety of the thick fortress walls, where the rest of the family members sorted and assessed the wealth. I even deigned to help a little bit as I continued my observations.

While many of the sandcrawler crew members were proficient at repairing equipment, I realized that most of the true experts remained inside the fortress, working at the items the crew members could not fix. For truly unsalvageable debris, the

Jawas have highly efficient solar smelters to melt down the junk and process the raw metal into ingots.

Jawa society is tightly knit, with large family units spreading out along tangled family trees. In their chittering language, the Jawas have forty-three different terms to describe relations and lineage, such as *father's-sister's-son's-son-by-second-wife,* and so on. Bloodlines are carefully recorded, though, and Jawa families are not interbred; each family unit mingles its marriage line with other Jawa groups.

As I lived invisibly among them, I learned of an impending celebration, the greatest event in the Jawa calendar: the great swap meet. Once each year, just before the storm season, Jawas from across the continent make a pilgrimage to the great basin of the Dune Sea for a huge, secret rendezvous, "the greatest swap meet in the galaxy." Here Jawas exchange salvaged items, haggling and trying to outsmart each other. Jawas can find missing components to otherwise repaired items, tell stories, and even exchange sons and daughters as "marriage merchandise" with much dickering over bloodlines and how the family unit will be strengthened by the union.

Though I eagerly looked forward to this exciting opportunity to see Jawa culture in its purest form, my time among them was destined to be cut short by an exciting turn of events.

The Jawas are a skittish people, downtrodden and preyed upon by their enemies for as long as they can remember. Even in their heavily defended fortresses they post regular guards to watch for impending attacks—but unfortunately, even with the diligence of the Jawas, it turned out that the Sand People were stealthier warriors.

Appearing out of nowhere, it seemed, a Tusken war party attacked in the long shadows of first dawn, leading a thunderous group of banthas that rammed the crumbling walls until the armored plates fell away. The Sand People charged into the breach, wielding their long, sharp pikes called gaffi sticks. The banthas trampled the carefully sorted Jawa salvage material, and the Sand People howled as the panicked Jawas squealed and fled, making no attempt whatsoever to fight back.

The Sand People showed no interest in grabbing booty for themselves; they seemed intent merely on causing damage and maintaining the impression of fear usually associated with any mention of their vicious race.

I believed I had already learned much from the Nkik clan, and I doubted if I would ever again get the chance to spend time with the elusive Sand People. And so I became one, and followed the Tusken Raiders off to their secret encampments.

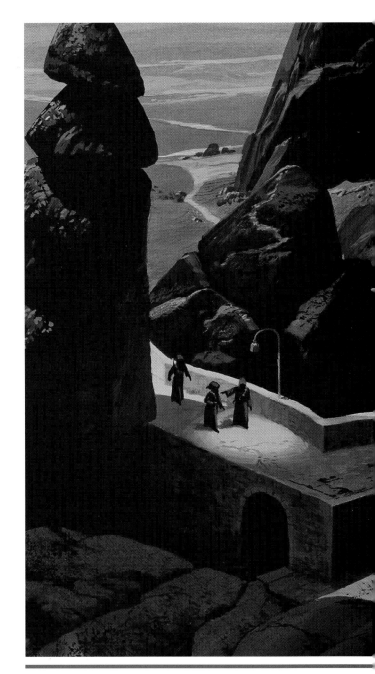

Because of the threat of attacks from Tusken Raiders *(right)*, Jawas maintain tight security at their mountian fortresses. Sentries keep regular patrols at all hours of the day and night.

From speaking with the inhabitants of Mos Eisley and Anchorhead and the moisture farmer family, my impression was that the Tusken Raiders were called Sand People in a derogatory fashion, yet always the speakers' voices carried a hidden fear. The Sand People are violent, nomadic, and extremely mysterious. Roving in skilled hunting bands, they eke out a harsh life on the fringes of civ-

ilized areas, taking from the desert in good times, taking from other people in bad times.

Even as I departed the Jawa fortress with the victory cries echoing in my ears, I got the distinct impression that the Raiders sensed something amiss, though they could not pinpoint the source of their uneasiness. It took all my skill to divert their thoughts, and I knew then that this could be my greatest challenge—but ah, to be the first anthropologist in the galaxy ever to describe the Tusken Raiders from firsthand knowledge! It was a risk I was willing to take.

Tusken clans roam the deserts of Tatooine. The Sand People keep only meager possessions, which are considered a liability when they are moving across the burning sands, especially during flight from an enemy. The Tusken Raiders have built no permanent shelters, although I followed them to a traditional encampment among the rocky badlands in the Jundland Wastes, in an area called the Needles. These caves and fissures in the hot rock are sheltering places for Tusken clans during the sandstorm season.

Sand People have no compunctions about killing anything in battle, hand to hand, with primitive weapons, because that is the bravest way to fight. Tusken Raiders prefer, however, merely to subdue a captive and take him as a prisoner back to the encampment. There they will use the captive as part of their vicious "sport" and to hone their skills at inflicting pain on an enemy.

Tusken Raiders ride in single file to hide their numbers, and even though the deserts of Tatooine are flat and featureless, somehow they manage to sneak up on their prey—no simple thing while riding a huge bantha or other large desert creature! They demonstrated this skill amply with their attack on the Jawa fortress.

Though they are nomadic and have no permanent settlement, the Sand People allow no change in their lives. This perhaps explains their resistance against adopting high technology and against adapting to the new weapons they have been able to take from the stormtroopers and the outlying moisture farmers. They

rely instead on their wits and their "traditional" weapons: their gaderffii, or gaffi sticks—double-edged spear-axes made from scavenged metal—and an occasional blaster rifle.

The more time I spent observing these strange people, the more I grew to admire them, in an analytical sort of way, of course. Their cultural heritage is rich and rigid, unchanged after many difficult centuries on Tatooine.

I learned how important "coming of age" is to the Sand People. Children are guarded by the adult Tuskens, but youngsters are not considered truly "people" until they have endured the ceremonies that make them valuable adults. Many babies die because of difficult desert conditions, and the Sand People take great pride in knowing that only the strongest reach adulthood—and fewer still survive the rigorous rites of passage.

To earn a place among the Tusken adults, a candidate must perform some great feat of skill or prowess, the magnitude of which determines his or her station among the clans. A common adventure involves ambushing stormtrooper squadrons and taking home their armor as trophies.

Tusken lore has it that four youths once banded together and single-handedly slew a krayt dragon without bantha assistance. Many other Tusken youths have attempted the same feat, with predictably gruesome results. Judging from the size of a single krayt dragon skeleton I saw atop a dune during my solitary journeys, these monsters must be formidable indeed.

The krayt dragons, usually found in mountainous areas, are the largest and most feared of all creatures on Tatooine. Krayt dragons continue to grow throughout their lifetimes, and they do not become weaker with age. At high summer each year, the mountains ring with the bellowed challenges of krayt dragons. Upon hearing a nearby dragon mating cry, all wise people flee—because a dragon in such a frenzy kills everything within reach.

Tusken Raiders ride any serviceable desert beasts, such as the rangy creatures shown at left, to reach remote and uncharted encampments (above).

To prove their bravery, young Tusken Raiders try to hunt the krayt dragon, the most ferocious beast on Tatooine—perhaps in the entire Outer Rim.

From early childhood, the Sand People wrap themselves in ritual rags and protective gear. They wear loose and flowing robes, letting no part of themselves show. They see through eye filters protruding from their bandaged faces; across their mouths they wear breath masks to filter sand particles.

Tuskens make no distinction between males and females, and only the clan elders keep records of the sexes, so that they can arrange marriages. (As one can imagine, some rather embarrassing mistakes have been made, unfortunately.)

Once each year, all newly recognized adults are assigned mates. In a bonding ceremony that involves mixing the blood of husband and wife, and of their respective bantha mounts, they become joined for life. Sheltered in the privacy of their tent, the new husband and wife are allowed to unwrap the bindings from their faces and view their true selves. Then, for the rest of their lives, only a Tusken's mate is allowed to know his or her true appearance. Matters of personal hygiene are attended to in the utmost privacy; one Tusken seeing another's face, even accidentally, is cause for a blood duel. I took great care to keep my distance.

Much to my amazement, I learned that the Sand People have developed a tight symbiosis with the huge, hairy banthas, an emotional bond stronger than any I have previously seen between master and beast.

Banthas may be intelligent, although in captivity they have never shown any signs of communication or behavior beyond that of a domesticated beast of burden. Wild banthas also show no initiative other than a kind of feral violence toward their captors. However, I was amazed to see that among the Sand People banthas act much differently.

Tusken children tend young banthas, but upon reaching adulthood, one Tusken and one bantha team up in a kind of deep emotional bonding, as strong as a marriage. It is as if bantha and rider become extensions of the same person. When a Tusken is killed, the suddenly "widowed" bantha will fly into a vicious suicidal frenzy; the same is true if a bantha mount is killed, leaving the rider alive.

If a bantha is left without its Tusken companion, the Sand People turn the bantha out into the desert to survive alone. Likewise, when a bantha is killed, the bereaved Tusken wanders off into the desert on a vision quest. There the Tusken must come to terms with the spirit of his bantha partner—if the bantha partner wishes to drag his companion into the afterlife, then the Tusken will die out on the sands. If, however, the bantha spirit guide is generous, he will lead the Tusken to another wild bantha, a riderless bantha, whom the Tusken will take back to the tribe as a new companion. When such a Tusken returns "reborn," he is much esteemed by the other Sand People.

Tusken Raiders have no written language, relying instead on long and complex chants to keep track of their lineage and of their legends. Handing their chants down from generation to generation, they remember the great and devastating space battles that laid waste much of Tatooine and strewed the desert with wrecked battleships.

The most revered person in the camp is the storyteller, whose duty is to retell the old tales, allowing no word to be changed. It is the storyteller who chronicles the coming-of-age stories of each mem-

The most revered member of any Tusken clan is the storyteller, who speaks the old legends by firelight, never daring to alter a single word.

ber of the clan; once he tells the tale the first time, not one word is allowed to deviate—not ever. This practice, which may sound harsh, makes an anthropologist want to jump for joy because the records are preserved intact from generation to generation, without the distortion that comes from sloppy mistakes.

The storyteller takes an apprentice and begins hammering in the vast amount of verbal knowledge. The apprentice is not allowed to recite any of this, or to practice out loud—since the words may *never* be spoken incorrectly, even during the learning process. When the apprentice feels he is ready to become the master, he is called upon to recite what he has learned. If the apprentice makes so much as

one mistake, he is killed outright—it is blasphemy to speak the wrong words. If, however, the apprentice has learned every word, every tale, every lineage, then he becomes the tribe's next storyteller—and the old storyteller, no longer needed, wanders off alone into the desert to die.

This rigid and violent people, however, proved more volatile than even I had anticipated. Perhaps I erred, or I asked too many questions, or my smell wasn't quite right, or the Tuskens just decided to kill someone that day—but I found myself fleeing across the desert with my disguise in tatters as Sand People charged after me on their banthas, waving their wicked gaffi sticks at me.

I had little hope of surviving, but I continued to run in dismay, greatly disappointed that all my newly uncovered knowledge would not now be published and available to my colleagues. Nevertheless, I fled to the best of my ability.

By sheer luck I stumbled upon a deep desert stormtrooper patrol and, as a desperate ploy, made them think I was a lost comrade. They fought against the Tuskens and rescued me, at the cost of three of their own party.

They brought me back to Mos Eisley, where I now sit in a cantina writing this account, waiting for passage out of the system and back to where I can begin the lecture circuit, describing my adventures on this harsh world.

There are plenty of ships at the docking bays, but I want to find one with a reasonably good chance of not falling apart as soon as it enters hyperspace. As time goes by, though, I am growing less selective, anxious to be away from here.

I have had enough of Tatooine!

IMPERIAL CENTER
CORUSCANT

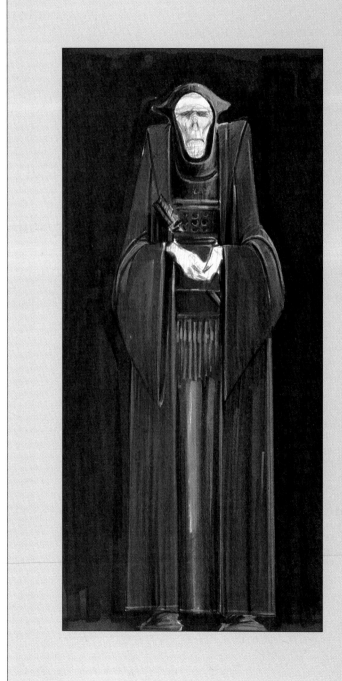

ABOUT THE AUTHOR:

Pollux Hax served for several years as chief of the Emperor's propaganda dissemination section. We are honored to present this report exactly as Emperor Palpatine wishes it published.

Being an enlightened man, the Emperor has read many articles on the cultures, life-forms, and land forms of other planets, the better to understand them so that his benevolent rule could be more attentive to the needs of his subjects. He commissioned Pollux Hax to write a similar article about the wonders of Imperial Center, which was called Coruscant in the days of the Old Republic.

We are pleased to present this report verbatim. Not one word has been changed from the original text.

CORUSCANT

The illustrious planet Coruscant, now renamed Imperial Center to reflect the progress of the times, has been the hub of the galaxy's government for millennia. Naturally, since Emperor Palpatine wishes to minimize displacement of his subjects, the planet continues to serve in this capacity, as it did during the days of the Old Republic and perhaps even before. The recorded history of Coruscant stretches back so far that it becomes indistinguishable from legend, and we in the Imperial administration are proud to be part of this continuing legacy.

Galactic governments have changed over the ages, but Coruscant has always been the center of power. Though poor in resources, the planet thrives on the changing tides of politics, providing a stable anchor through damaging rebellions, the long-overdue fall of the corrupt Old Republic, and the sweeping introduction of the Emperor's resplendent New Order.

After many thousands of years of constant construction and expansion, Coruscant's entire planetary surface has been covered with layer upon layer of buildings, like crystalline growths on a rock. Portions of the unending city have been rebuilt, demolished, and rebuilt again over the centuries. As part of the Emperor's new efficiency programs, not a square meter of space is wasted, and the people are happier than before.

The rooftop of virtually any building offers a truly breathtaking view unparalleled on any other world. Towering skyscrapers, built of transparisteel and smoked duracrete, stretch to the horizon like a great forest of structures built by hundreds of different architects, both human and alien. The city dazzles the imagination, and has rightfully been the subject of much poetry and music commissioned by the Emperor himself.

Many of the huge buildings are identical—nondescript and functional, population centers where people live, work, and sleep. Other gigantic constructions are wildly exotic, designed by alien minds accustomed to worlds with less gravity or other resources. At the tops of the skyscrapers lighted shuttle landing pads welcome visitors. Everything gleams, everything is clean. Never before in all of history has a city such as this existed.

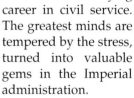

Our planet is a interminable metropolis that twinkles with power systems, city lights, traffic landing beacons. Seen from orbit, Imperial Center is a blaze of light and sparkling colors, reminding some spacers of gemlike corusca stones, after which this planet was named long ago.

Because of its importance in galactic politics, offworlders view an assignment to Imperial City as a marvelous opportunity to promote bureaucratic careers back on their home worlds. It is a challenging but rapid career path, with the rewards of a satisfying career in civil service. The greatest minds are tempered by the stress, turned into valuable gems in the Imperial administration.

Other workers, unfortunately, succumb to "government fever," which catches them up in the hypnotic bustle of galactic politics. Obsessed, they work practically round the clock, as if their own small involvement in running the Empire were some kind of drug. They become wrapped up in their jobs to the exclusion of all else, obsessed with politics. Those who suffer from government fever rarely leave Imperial Center, requesting extension after extension on their "temporary" assignments. Most of these staffers die young, squeezed dry by

the demands of their profession...much to the Emperor's dismay, of course.

The buildings of Imperial Center are densely packed, with major thoroughfares slicing like deep canyons through the metropolis. Hawk-bats ride thermals flowing up from the bowels of the city, swooping down to prey upon granite slugs and other creatures that have adapted to survive on the vertical surfaces of the tall buildings. It is a magnificent sight to see these efficient and successful predators attacking these destructive parasites on our city.

The complex terrain of towering metal and transparisteel pinnacles makes our weather difficult to predict, even with the best Imperial climate modeling routines. Occasionally, unexpected storms coalesce out of water evaporating from millions of rooftop exhaust vents, condensing and rising from the skyscraper forests, creating squalls that dump rain upon the hard surfaces of the buildings.

Each section of our vast, unending city has high-

Cruising over Imperial City for the first time is a breathtaking sight, sure to cause awe and wonder in even the most inferior species.

(left) Imperial City rooftops provide convenient walkways and open-air meeting places for small assemblages with appropriate permits. Even taller skyscrapers rise like landmarks in the distance.

lights and attractions for visiting dignitaries and off-planet sightseers. The marvels of Imperial City are sung from planet to planet. Automated tourist stations provide information on cultural activities that cater to different interests. The numerous entertainment centers are clusters of bright lights and exotic pleasures ranging from the hedonistic to the enlightening and educational. No one has ever been disappointed with the spectrum of enjoyment available on Imperial Center.

For example, the Skydome Botanical Gardens rest on the level roof of an isolated skyscraper. Constructed by an Old Republic philanthropist who had grown rich by establishing the Galactic News

The greatest city in the galaxy extends from horizon to horizon. The rooftops are glorious *(top)*, and the vertical levels seem to go to the core of the world itself *(right)*.

Service (one of the more prominent news services that help disseminate all the information appropriate for the Emperor's subjects), this giant terrarium is a carefully tended place with compartmentalized environments to display exotic and otherwise extinct flora from those worlds that have sworn fealty to the Empire.

Tour droids, fluent in most known forms of communication, are available for hire, although special guide/guards are required for entry into our

renowned Carnivorous Plants section. Because the Skydome Botanical Gardens are such a popular attraction, and because they are so near the Imperial Palace, the facility is often used for receptions thrown to honor important arriving diplomats.

Learned scholars from all corners of the galaxy come to study at the spacious Galactic Museum, which houses records dating back thousands of years, through the stages of the Old Republic, preserving artifacts from lost civilizations. Popular displays include relics from the Sith culture and tokens of the old order of Jedi Knights. Though the Emperor has been forced to eliminate funding for the museum, due to costs incurred in snuffing out the damaging

Seen from space, the planet Coruscant gleems like a brilliant corusca gem, from which it draws its name *(left)*. In the street levels *(below)* open-air mezzanines offer Imperial-approved cultural opportunities.

Skylanes and transit systems provide for rapid travel and efficient courier traffic on important Imperial business.

rebellion against his rule, he has given his verbal support for the museum to continue to preserve the heritage of his subjects.

Another of Coruscant's popular attractions—built during the days of the Old Republic so that now it appears rather dated and rough at the edges—is the Holographic Zoo for Extinct Animals. Inside a labyrinth of small chambers, dramatic three-dimensional dioramas are projected, showing spectacular (perhaps even fanciful) life-forms from other planets, such as the mammoth krabbex, the manticore, and the singing fig trees of Pil-Diller.

A recreational area frequented by the civil servants and other planet-bound inhabitants of Imperial Center is Monument Park—a protected mall built around what was once a tall peak in the Menarai Mountains visible from the Imperial Pal-

ace. Since practically every square meter of land on the planet has been built over, Monument Park gives the people a chance to touch the naked ground.

Layers and layers of construction have erased most topographical features from view, but the single jagged outcropping of this one mountain peak still protrudes from the surrounding buildings, to the amazement and delight of all. Emperor Palpatine himself often goes to this place for his own solitude and communion with nature.

A small group of meditative religious followers has made a shrine of the rock outcropping, however, protecting it from souvenir gatherers who might chip off a flake of stone as a memento to take

back to their crowded cities. The meditative followers stand vigil around the mountaintop, touching the living rock and communing with the sleeping core of Coruscant. From the bare stone they attempt to draw a reminder of the peace and serenity the world experienced before the sprawling cities. The Emperor, naturally, tolerates all such forms of religious expression.

Some libelous and illegal reports have claimed that the Emperor has a clear prejudice against nonhuman species, but this is demonstrably not true. Sentient beings from the Empire's arctic worlds make their homes in the planet's colder latitudes, while aliens from hotter tropical worlds live closer to the equator. Species accustomed to subterranean settings inhabit the lower, shadowy levels of the Imperial Center's huge buildings.

To understand the depth of the Emperor's tolerance, one needs only to observe the cultural areas he has allowed to exist in segregated parts of the city. In carefully bordered sectors designated for particular cultures and life-forms, these honored nonhuman visitors can live their lives as they would on

The architecture of Imperial City is as varied as the species serving the Empire, from open-air stadiums for every citizen to hear important speeches *(below left)* to information exchange and confidential intelligence centers *(below).*

(pages 58-59) **The night life in Imperial City is renowned throughout the galaxy. Regular security patrols ensure that everyone has a good time.**

their homeworlds. There they are protected from the hazards of genuine prejudice by guardian contingents of stormtroopers who patrol the borders of the alien sections.

Architecture varies to reflect the different cultures and their social preferences in colorful pockets of "ethnic neighborhoods" like charming islands in the midst of Imperial City.

Often these alien neighborhoods are dominated by tall statues erected to honor offworld heroes and planetary legends from other parts of the galaxy. Humans are frequently confused to see towering monuments of bizarre multilegged heroes riding equally bizarre mounts in these permanent reenactments of unforgotten glory.

Unfortunately, due to the extended diplomatic families and retainers from alien planets who do not

Monument Plaza—one of the gems of Imperial City, where visitors can actually touch bare rock, which was once on a mountaintop.

The approach to Monument Plaza is a cavalcade of quaint ethnic banners and memorials erected by stubborn races who still attempt to retain their individual identities.

understand Imperial customs and rules, many personal squabbles erupt. The Emperor has brought in crack squadrons of stormtroopers to quash any such short-lived disturbances.

As part of his New Order, the Emperor has abolished the outdated Old Republic concept of diplomatic immunity. All troublemakers are responsible for the problems they cause, and disobedience is dealt with sternly. We are proud to note that there are very few repeat offenders. Thanks to the protective stormtrooper presence, Imperial City is one of the safest places in the galaxy.

Because the surface of Coruscant has been completely built over, resources and food are a precious commodity, and our people work together to make the whole system function efficiently. Transportation and delivery systems have been perfected,

out of necessity. Giant thoroughfares carry shipments continuously and at high speed, distributing needed items throughout the planetwide city. These shipments are generally shuttled through the lower levels of the metropolis, where they will not disturb the more important government officials.

New raw materials are brought down from asteroids on the fringes of the Coruscant system, as needed. Heavy lifters drop the massive rocks down through the atmosphere—but this is an extremely expensive way to get new supplies of metals for underground processing stations.

Instead, the people of Imperial City have developed closed-loop ecosystems inside their giant buildings. Major recycling efforts have resulted in an efficient operation monitored by multiarmed droids, sorting through the garbage of Imperial Center to select out even tiny scraps of useful material.

A metropolis as large and as old as Imperial City is in a constant state of urban renewal. Central planners in the Imperial Palace monitor the decay of old buildings and sections of the city. One entire central computer is devoted to updating and maintaining a master plan of the world-city. With our constant vigilance and preplanning, we have made Imperial Center the envy of all urban areas in the Empire.

On Coruscant, enormous walking factories—construction droids—wade through older sections of the city designated for renewal. These construction droids are fully as tall as the skyscrapers themselves, moving at a ponderous pace. Both the front and the back ends of these machines are a blur of moving mechanical arms, conveyor belts, demolition equipment, and sensors.

A construction droid tears down a condemned

building in front, shoveling the debris into its vast furnaces and material sorters, where useful items are extracted, recycled, and smelted. The corresponding factory on the opposite half of the droid extrudes new girders and transparisteel sheets. The rear side of the droid assembles a brand-new building from a preprogrammed blueprint while the front side tears down the ruined hulk. As these independent construction droids march through old sections of the city, they leave in their wake a gleaming swath of polished new skyscrapers.

Only rarely has it happened that the directional sensors of these droids have malfunctioned, causing them to rip the wrong buildings apart, much to the dismay of the unfortunate inhabitants.

Dedicated Imperial functionaries are given the task of delivering the proper eviction notices to those still living within condemned structures; reports that these notices are often misdelivered, or not delivered at all, are grossly exaggerated. While it is true that occasionally people have had to flee as their building began to topple into wreckage around them, there are no casualties on record resulting from this inconvenience.

Surrounded by immense buildings, the deep lower levels of the city entrap air and create a sheltered microclimate. Moisture rises partway into the air up the sheer sides of the skyscrapers, condensing into small clouds, then drizzling a mist of lukewarm rain back down into the murk. Convective wind whistles through the narrow, building-lined canyons.

Deep in the lower, forgotten levels, in the oldest subbasements of ancient buildings, an entire shadowy culture has developed. Coruscant's underworld is dank and oppressive, never seeing the sun or the night sky because of the looming shadows of kilometer-high buildings. Low-flying shuttles traveling near ground level must fly with all their running lights on and weapons powered up. Otherwise, the underworld is never traveled alone.

The shadowy streets of Imperial City's underworld were once a dangerous haven for criminals and fugitives, but the Emperor has stepped up efforts to clean up the lower levels.

Some have said that down here the Emperor keeps private detention centers where black IT-0 interrogation droids extract every scrap of valuable information from a victim. It is time to put these rumors to rest once and for all. The Emperor has no need of such barbaric practices, and he has no need to keep secrets.

Because all space traffic to and from Imperial Center is tightly controlled, many criminals flee to the lower levels to escape the Emperor's justice:

bureaucrats who have made a fatal mistake in their paperwork, ambassadors from a planet reprimanded by the Emperor, even clumsy personal servants from the Imperial Palace...all vanish into the lower levels, where, amazingly, they think they must hide for the rest of their lives.

Judging from signs found by stormtrooper commando teams, these clever fugitives have established a tolerable lifestyle by revamping some of the abandoned underbasement rooms, tapping into elec-

trical conduits, and stealing energy from the Imperial Center power grid. They have formed their own pathetic civilization from scraps of the shining world that has been forever forbidden to them.

We believe there may even be descendants of exiles from the Old Republic who do not know that the political order has changed for the better, that the Emperor's New Order has replaced the corruption and unpleasantness. Emperor Palpatine would welcome these refugees with open arms if only they would return and ask his pardon.

These poor people know no other life, not even in their imagination. Living like troglodytes, sleeping in abandoned alcoves, these shaggy semihumans have never seen the sun. Clothed in tatters, they walk

Coruscant's water needs are met by huge pipelines carrying melted ice from the polar caps of the planet.

hunched from bone diseases and nutritional deficiencies; their skin is clammy and corpse-white. The Emperor's benevolence would extend even to such unproductive members of society, but the troglodyte specimens flee and somehow manage to elude all attempts to capture and reeducate them. Several troglodytes—unfortunately killed during capture— have been preserved and are now on display in the Galactic Museum.

The inhabitants of the underworld must live on scraps, or harvest the fungus that grows in the sodden shadows. Duracrete worms, shadow-barnacles, and granite slugs also inhabit the protected corners of the underworld.

Larger creatures, too, have made their homes in the forgotten tunnels, including gigantic mutated rodents that will attack and eat anything they can find—whether it fights back or not. The troglodytes must occasionally hunt these rat-things, then eat the flesh raw or sizzled on a burst-open power coupling. Before any of the automatic mainte-

nance/repair droids can come to fix the ruptured power coupling, though, the troglodytes vanish into their hiding places.

Our failure to bring these poor people back into the fold of society remains the Empire's great shame.

The Imperial planet is too far from its small white sun to have a climate truly comfortable to humans, which leaves even the temperate zones of Coruscant rather cold and bleak.

However, because of our technological advances,

The bustling shuttle ports in all parts of the city are busy day and night, transporting valuable diplomatic personnel.

the vast, self-contained metropolis is mostly immune to the climate outside. The attitude of most inhabitants is that Coruscant exists for the business of government, not for vacations and sunbathing and sightseeing...although many facilities have sprung up by necessity, simply because of the sheer numbers of people assigned to Imperial Center.

R. McQUARRIE

The most spectacular show in the night sky is the flaming veils of aurorae in shimmering gray-green and red curtains. The enormous amount of space traffic to and from Imperial Center continuously dumps residual field discharges and broken debris into orbit around the planet, energizing the aurorae even when Coruscant's sun is not in one of its active phases.

The densest population centers are clustered around the temperate zones, as are the main business areas, political centers, and commercial hubs. Unsightly manufacturing and industrial facilities have been relegated to the less habitable zones, or beneath the planet's surface.

The extreme northern and southern areas are great plains of crystal and metal buildings covered

with hoarfrost. Plumes of steam curl upward from heating and ventilation systems. Transportation conduits from the northern to the southern areas of the planetwide city are so efficient that people can live near the arctic circle and attend weekly meetings at the Imperial Palace.

The polar caps are the planet's only water reservoir. All inland seas and oceans have been drained

Rooftop landing pads in the tallest skyscrapers of Imperial City receive shipments of matériel and duly acquired items of tribute to the Emperor.

and consumed over the thousands of years of overpopulation, leaving no other water than what is locked inside the ice. Large stations have been established on the rim of the ice shelves, with huge

mechanical borers to mine the ice, self-contained furnaces to melt it, and an intricate network of pipelines to distribute the recovered water. Our amazing recirculating systems and purification facilities connected to the plumbing labyrinths allow for recycling of the vast majority of water used, so that the polar ice caps are only slowly becoming depleted. The Emperor has appointed a powerful commission and workgroup to study this problem.

On the other end of the spectrum, at the planet's equator most of the upper levels of the metropolis are glassed-over greenhouses devoted to agriculture. Fully automated, the agricultural roof-landscapes glint with brilliant reflections visible even from orbit. Our planet is by no means self-sufficient, but the Emperor does what he can to minimize the

amount of food and water required from offworld, so that his subjects can keep the fruits of their labor for their own enjoyment and the strengthening of their planetary economies.

The orbital activity around Imperial Center is a constant blur of shuttles arriving and departing, weather and communications satellites, starship construction yards, and military staging areas. The space navigation systems used by every ship in the galaxy are based on the coordinates of Coruscant, defined as zero-zero-zero on all recorded maps.

Pumped up on stimulants and mind-focusing drugs to improve their personal efficiency and to minimize human error, space-traffic controllers crowd around giant holoprojections. These teams monitor the location of each vessel or large piece of debris, tracking its path in a complex intercon-

nected dance that brilliantly keeps the traffic flowing smoothly while avoiding collisions.

Orbiting climate-control mirrors focus sunlight on the extreme northern and southern latitudes of the planet, warming the environment by a few degrees to make more of the land area hospitable. These mirrors are usually monitored and piloted by low-ranking Imperial Navy troopers sworn to do even this grueling duty. Among troopers, "riding the mirrors" is considered the loneliest, most tedious assignment on Coruscant, but all are happy to serve the Empire in whatever capacity they are needed.

Spidery docking and starship repair yards ride high above the planet, providing reconditioning facilities for the largest of spaceliners. Spherical self-contained colony vessels, Imperial Star Destroyers, and huge luxury yachts are built in the space-dock

Coruscant's space construction platforms are remarkable examples of Imperial industriousness. Here giant-size habitation spheres are designed and assembled strictly for peacetime purposes.

centers. The Emperor has commandeered other, more sophisticated space construction centers in other systems, notably the Kuat Drive Yards and the Rendili and Loronar space construction facilities, for assembling his largest battleships and special weapons platforms.

The most prominent building on the face of Coruscant, indeed the centerpiece of the entire gleaming city, is the Imperial Palace.

The Palace stands like a hybrid cathedral and pyramid, rising higher than any other structure on

the planet. Its tallest spires reach up into the rarefied atmosphere, occasionally sparking discharges from the hovering aurorae in the sky. Made of polished gray-green rock and mirrored crystals, the home of Emperor Palpatine sparkles in the hazy sunlight, a fitting example of the glory of our leader.

Even in the deepest hour of night, the Imperial Palace never grows dark. Blazing illumination from phosphorescent panels, glowspheres, and electroluminance strips keeps the Palace in a shower of shifting light up and down all the corridors.

After Senator Palpatine took on the cowl of Emperor in the crumbling days of the Old Republic, he decided to show clearly the enormous difference between his New Order and the stagnant, thousand-generations-old Republic. The Emperor programmed

Communications and surveillance stations keep an ever-vigilant eye on the populace below, making every citizen feel safe and cared for.

construction droids to tear down portions of the ancient Presidential Palace and ordered it reconstructed and "enhanced" as a new facility. His Imperial Palace was erected in record time.

The Palace is enormous, with some of its open areas large enough to house a *Victory*-class Star Destroyer. The Palace looms high over the old Senate Hall in an adjacent sector of the city—and the Senate Hall itself towers over everything else on Coruscant.

Within the cyclopean palace, the Grand Corridor is like an enclosed canyon, populated by thousands of bureaucratic functionaries, diplomatic runners,

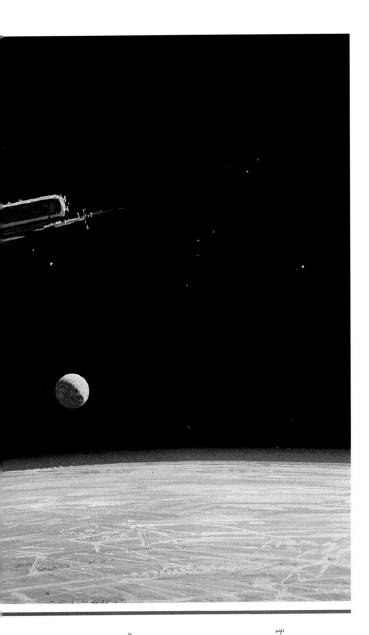

staffers, and ambassadors of all races and species, as well as specialized droids of many fantastic configurations. Insectile maintenance droids ride hoverlifts over the crowds, polishing and cleaning the intricate carvings or richly colored transparisteel insets.

The corridor is lined with exotic purple-and-green ch'hala trees, the transparent bark of which is sensitive to vibrations in the air, responding to each noise with a turmoil of color. The Emperor himself expressed a personal fondness for these trees, claiming that watching their changing hues reminded him of changing patterns in the universe. No one knows the name of the planet from which the ch'hala trees were originally transplanted, or if they were genetically manipulated in the Emperor's finest laboratories.

Above the Grand Corridor, much business is carried out on promenade balconies, where sentient beings sit in high cafés to stare down at the flowing bustle of traffic below. Lift platforms requiring special key access prevent unauthorized creatures from reaching secluded areas. Stormtroopers patrol the corridors, enforcing security and tranquility in the halls of government.

Important visiting dignitaries are housed on the President's Guest Floor, a vestige of the old capitol building that has been engulfed by the much larger Palace structure. These shielded inner rooms are well protected and nearly impregnable from outside attack, should violent criminals from the Rebel Alliance attempt terrorist acts or sabotage.

Deep inside the structure of the Palace, in the most protected rooms at the core of the building, are several "artificial penthouse" suites, with window walls made of projection screens, displaying realistic images from cameras mounted at the top of the

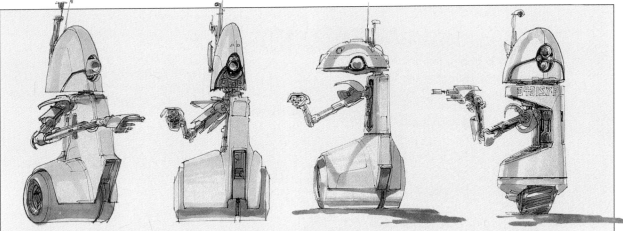

Many new model droids, from cleaning models to fast courier droids, assist in the efficient running of Imperial City.

The Imperial Palace *(top)* is the largest structure on Coruscant, perhaps on any planet. Its interior *(above)* is a breathtaking monument to the grandeur of human capabilities.

Imperial Palace. In this way the Emperor can hold meetings in total security and privacy, yet still enjoy a sweeping view of his planet.

Numerous architectural styles and design motifs can be found throughout the Palace. In some sections the structure is open and airy, with much illumination and transparisteel; other sections are dark and brooding, with carved friezes along the ceiling. Some rooms have old-fashioned hinge doors, made from exotic wood carved with intricate figures.

The Emperor's throne room is a sunken auditorium like a great crater dug into the bedrock. In the audience decks, flat stone benches are arranged in long arcs, where visitors can come to hear Imperial pronouncements directly from the Emperor himself. Acoustics are perfect, allowing the audience to hear the barest whisper from the Emperor; the reverse is also true, and the Emperor is able to hear any question spoken to him from the highest row of benches,

even whispered comments from one audience member to another.

At the pinnacle of the throne room is an angled, prismatic skylight, which pours rainbows of light onto the Emperor as he lounges back in his levitating chair, bathing him in glorious colors as he speaks. . . .

The Empire's business never slows down, and some say the Emperor himself never sleeps. Palpatine has many private rooms, studies, audience chambers, libraries, and retiring alcoves hidden throughout the labyrinth of the Palace.

One of his well-known personal haunts is a transparisteel-enclosed observation deck on the tallest spire, where he can recline in a comfortable chair and stare out at the glittering chaos of the world he holds in his benevolent grasp, merely one planet at the heart of a great web of planets that comprises his glorious Empire.

DAGOBAH

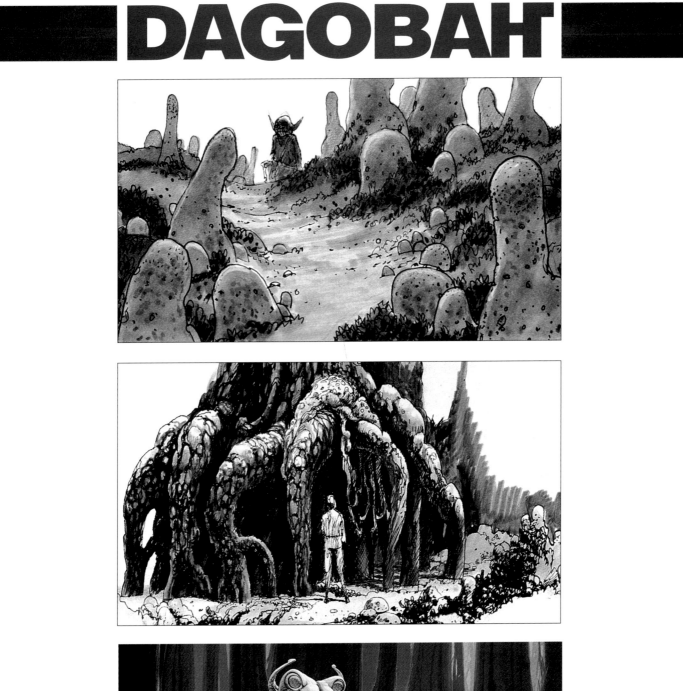

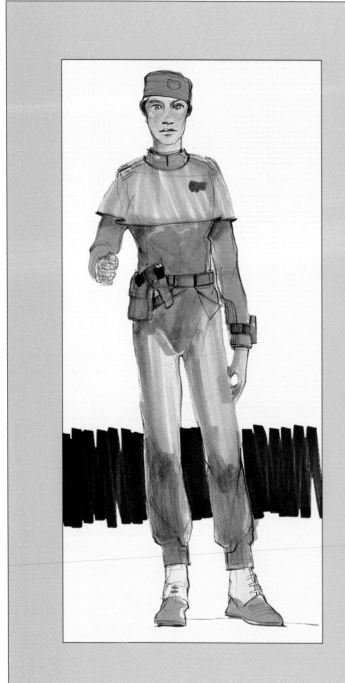

ABOUT THE AUTHOR :

Halka Four-Den kept these detailed journals of her experiences in command of a forgotten Republic research team stationed on the swampy world of Dagobah. Her previous record of service is exemplary, and she was placed in the role of supervisor of this team as her first command assignment. Unfortunately, the supposedly simple scientific survey of Dagobah was not to be a routine mission.

Halka Four-Den's account gives a vivid view of the exotic flora and fauna her team studied during their overlong assignment, as well as the hazards associated with performing straightforward scientific research during a time of great political upheaval.

DAGOBAH

*[**Ed. Note**—Even as its government structure began to crumble, the Old Republic continued to send ambitious exploratory expeditions to study and catalog little-known worlds, such as Dagobah. We can now see it as an effort made through momentum and established bureaucracy, with no real scientific drive; after all, the Republic had sent out missions like this for centuries, then dutifully cataloged and forgot all the survey reports. We are only now beginning to mine the treasures of information buried deep within the databases on the Imperial capital world of Coruscant.*

The commander of the Dagobah research team, Halka Four-Den, kept an account of the expedition, as she was required to do; but unfortunately all her records were misplaced during the upheaval of the Emperor's New Order. Now, though, after many years, Halka Four-Den's fragmented log entries have been located and are being published here for the first time.]

FIRST WEEK SUMMARY

The planet Dagobah—who named it, and why, is told in no existing record. Dagobah itself seems to avoid mention, as if some invisible power deflects all inquiries. As a result, the swampy planet is cloaked in mystery.

We—my team and I—were chosen to shed light on the enigma of Dagobah. It is an honor to add our discoveries to the greater knowledge of all sentient beings. The task ahead of us seems great, but we are enthusiastic and dedicated.

Dagobah is the only inhabitable world in a system of the same name in the Sluis sector. Shrouded in thick clouds over a dense gray-green blanket of foliage, Dagobah looks grim from space.

Two of my team members expressed uneasiness as we approached and entered orbit, somewhat concerned to be stranded here alone and self-sufficient for our allotted standard year in the field, but I tolerated none of that talk. Perhaps I was too harsh, but I could not allow a drop in morale before we even landed at our objective!

The cargo pods detached first from the main freighter, burning down through the atmosphere and carrying transportainers of supplies and armored self-erecting shelters and laboratory enclosures.

Then the eight of us suited up and took our meager personal possessions. We said our good-byes to the other passengers, who would continue to a distant star system, climbed aboard the robotic dropship, and strapped in. I gave the order to launch, and we fell toward Dagobah, which would be our home for the next standard year.

At ground level, the smell of rot permeates the air. The buzzing, chirping, crunching sounds of billions of living things make a constant, pounding hum of white noise.

The swamp looked the same and endless for kilometers. One site seemed as good as any other, so we used heavy laser burners and plasma fusers to clear a camp, where we established our permanent base. Working together, we set up our prefabricated shelters, sealed our supplies in airtight armored containers, and took inventory.

My seven companions comprise a small botanical and zoological research team, dedicated to compiling all possible information about the world. In its ancient days of expansion, the Republic had established a venerable tradition of mapping and cataloging all known planets—but in such a vast galaxy with hundreds of millions of star systems, this was no simple task, and many had slipped through the cracks. Dagobah was one such planet, and we would be the ones to rectify that mistake.

On this swampy, inaccessible world, we were supposed to summarize and comment on the characteristics of the primary indigenous species—plant, animal, insect, and…other. Our survey team was woefully understaffed for the job, eight researchers to catalog and understand a world, using only old and questionable equipment…but it was the best the Republic could spare for us. We were enthusiastic xenobotanists and naturalists, so we attempted the task, regardless.

As commander of the expedition, I gathered the team in the main shelter and slipped the data chip into the reader. I played the pre-recorded message given to me by the Republic Senate. A bureaucrat none of us had ever seen before wished us good luck, but it sounded as if he was reading from a prepared statement that had been used many times before. I did not point this out to my companions. The message ended, and we set to work.

Initial Impressions: Dagobah is absolutely covered with life, swarming with creatures and plants large and small. Within the tiers of the ecological system can be found every conceivable form of stalking technique, defense mechanism, and camouflage. We learned quickly that if you don't watch where you sit, you may well find the rock or log to be alive and scuttling away under you!

As near as we can tell, all creatures we have seen so far are nonsentient. The planet's ecosystem must have spent its energy on quantity and diversity, filling every possible natural niche, rather than developing intelligence.

Sometimes, though, as I stand alone in the noisy but weirdly silent swamp, I wonder if the world itself resents our presence, wanting to keep the mystery that shrouds it. Perhaps Dagobah is gathering its malevolent forces to resist our work at unraveling its secrets.

I shouldn't be thinking like this.

SECOND WEEK SUMMARY

Our two entomologists began to collect specimens. As part of the plan established in our expedition protocol, we all assisted them in rigging up bright lights around the clearing of our settlement, along with nets connected to very weak stunner fields. In the dim underworld of the Dagobah swamps, we assumed that the bright lights would attract various nocturnal insects, but we weren't prepared for the magnitude of the response.

The brilliant lamps stabbed through the thick mist, burning like a target. The entomologists sat waiting, electronic logpads in hand, ready to record what they saw; the rest of us joined them, prepared to offer our assistance.

After only a few moments, the spotlights brought swarms of creatures from every direction, whining and buzzing, smothering the lamps, dropping dead in their frenzy to batter themselves against the glow. The stunner nets clogged in moments. The entomologists could barely restrain their delight.

More insects came, and more, followed by leathery flying things that feasted on the swarms. The noises of the swamp grew deafening, an incredible crescendo. Then the disoriented creatures began to swoop down and attack us. My team members and I frantically tried to keep ourselves safe under the protective cover of the nets.

Out among the wall of shadowy trees, we heard larger predators stomping through the undergrowth, attracted by the light and sound, coming closer. In the shadows they roared and snarled hungrily.

Before everyone could panic and run inside our flimsy shelters, I ordered the lights switched off. We ran inside our dwellings, barricaded the doors, and pressed our faces against the armored ports, staring out into the tepid darkness, but by the time our eyes had adjusted to the sudden shadows, the swamp creatures had forgotten about the disturbance, and we saw nothing unusual for the rest of that long, sleepless night.

The following morning, I insisted that the spotlights be dismantled and stowed away. We never used them again. The murky fog, frequent torrential downpours, boggy ground, and dense undergrowth make lengthy expeditions from our modular base extremely difficult. Though four members of the team wanted to range far from our site, I advised them to cut back their expectations for the time being, until we had learned some of the basic information about Dagobah. Grudgingly, it seemed, they fell to the simple chore of cataloging and imaging as many of the various specimens as possible.

Specimen sketches: many creatures on Dagobah seem unclassifiable. These, for instance, seem to be animated, carnivorous fungi.

With only eight people to dissect the life-forms on an entire planet, I sent a tight-beam transmission back to Coruscant, beseeching the Republic for assistance, but my requests either were ignored or were given low priority. It is a shame, because with all the plants and fungi, insects and venomous creatures, a further investment in Dagobah would repay itself a hundredfold with unimaginable advances in med-

Gnarltree roots provide a habitat for many camouflaged predators.

ical science, pharmacology, and genetics. But receiving nothing but static in response to our pleas, we dutifully returned to work.

In only two weeks we have already filled our archives with massive amounts of data on thousands of strange organisms.

THIRD WEEK SUMMARY

A great botanical discovery this week, as we began to explore beyond the fringes of our camp. Our researchers went out in two groups of three, fully armed, with the remaining two people left behind and prepped as a rescue squad, should emergency measures be needed.

The most prominent living things in the swamp are the ancient petrified forests of "gnarltrees," huge roots rising out of the bog, buttressed in the muck, gathering into wide trunks. The knobby roots and outer layers of the trunk have been calcified through centuries and centuries of slowly growing and rising toward the forest canopy high above. Because of their obvious importance to the Dagobah ecosystem, these trees were our first focus of investigation.

Each gnarltree itself is a microcosm of life-forms, with lichens, moss, and shelf fungus filling the crannies in the calcified trunk. These parasitic growths draw nutrients by breaking down outer layers of the gnarltree and absorbing moisture from the mists in the air. Insectlike organisms build nests in the

knotholes and tangles of the webbed branches, while larger animals take shelter in the cave-sized hollows beneath the overhanging loops.

One common creature, the knobby white spider, is intimately connected with the ecology of the gnarltrees. Understanding the life cycle of the fearsome-looking albino spider proved quite a challenge to us, and upon learning its secret we realized how alien this world was, how evolution had taken a bizarre and unexpected path here.

All the specimens of knobby spiders we obtained were about the same size, as big as a landspeeder, each with a lumpy, large body and gnarled legs that seemed designed for camouflage among the towering roots. Though the white spiders are common, nearly to the point of being pests, our field teams found no nests or eggs or young that would give a clue as to the spiders' development.

Finally, by dissecting one of the knobby spiders, our arachnid specialist discovered that the creature's body core was made primarily of calcified wood, the same as the trees. The knobby spiders *are* part of the gnarltrees' life cycle!

I cannot describe to you our arguments and discussions, the skepticism we held, during our evening summary reports inside the main camp dwelling under the comforting glow of artificial light, surrounded by the wildness.

As we gathered more and more data, the evi-

Striking example of gnarltree root structure.

(pages 82-83) **The knobby white spider, the mobile predatory stage of the gnarltree life cycle.**

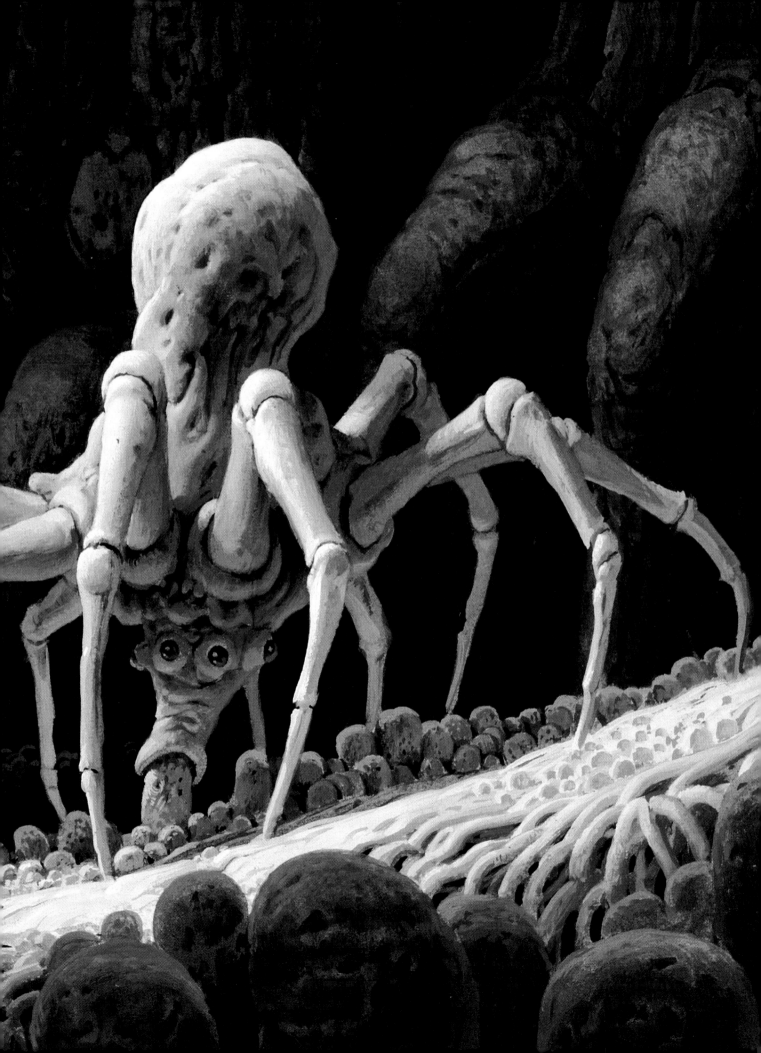

dence became incontrovertible; even the most vehement skeptics accepted the theory: In much the same way as some familiar plants send out runners to reproduce and spread, the gnarltrees grow a special kind of detachable, *mobile* root—the knobby spider—that breaks free of its parent gnarltree and begins the predator phase of its life.

The knobby spider roams the swamps, hunting and devouring other animals, storing energy in its

The titanic dual between two of the most fearsome creatures we discovered on Dagobah. The swamp slug and the dragonsnake are natural enemies. At right, preliminary sketches of swamp slug anatomy.

bloated, bulbous head. When it has gathered enough nutrients to support itself during its metamorphosis phase, the knobby spider searches for a clear spot in

the undergrowth, where it will remain for centuries.

In preparation for its anchored phase, the spider uproots all competing plant life within about ten meters—sometimes even including other implanted knobby spiders—and then plunges its eight sharp legs deep into the spongy ground. As the spider drains its stored energy, the gangly legs transform into roots, tapping deeper into the soil. The bloated head shrinks and hardens, and then begins extending upward into a rudimentary trunk, eventually reaching the canopy above.

We know this hypothesis will be challenged by other members of the scientific community, so we have redoubled our efforts to image this transformation in progress and to place a wealth of specimens in our stasis boxes for transport when our assignment here is finished.

Some members of our team have already begun counting down the days.

FOURTH WEEK SUMMARY

Plenty of new discoveries again. This planet's penchant for exotic life-forms seems inexhaustible!

One multilegged armored creature—which we named the butcherbug—spins a tough, microfine wire between the roots of the towering gnarltrees. The wireweb is invisible unless seen under exactly the right conditions. When a flying creature blunders into this trap, the microwire slices it into pieces, which the butcherbug then scuttles down to devour before meticulously cleaning the gore from its invisible web.

In the dimmest underworld of the swamp, some animals have developed bioluminescent patches to light their own way through the undergrowth or to attract prey.

One hairy herbivore, the spotlight sloth, patiently forages until it finds a large succulent plant on which it prefers to feed. When it has located a succulent studded with tough-skinned flower-fruits, the sloth illuminates bright glowing patches on its chest. Then it waits. After an hour or so, the tough skin of the flower-fruit unfolds to bask in the light, revealing a treasure of sticky purplish berries, on which the spotlight sloth feeds.

Larger predators are rare in the bogs, but deadly. This week we had the great good fortune to observe the titanic battle between a giant swamp slug and a mammoth dragonsnake. Both huge creatures inhabit the water channels through the swamp, swimming through the black, peaty water and rooting out their food.

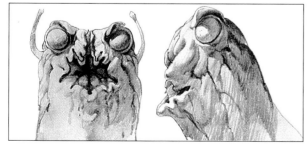

The giant swamp slug is an omnivore, eating anything it can pull into its lipless gash of a mouth. Small animals, decaying vegetation, even larger aquatic life-forms, are sucked through a long throat/mouth lined with thousands of tiny, grinding teeth that can pulverize all organic matter into a digestible mass. Like construction machinery, the swamp slugs plow an inexorable path through the bog, devouring everything in their way.

The dragonsnake, on the other hand, is a more active predator, seeking out victims that venture too close to the water's edge. The snake can rear up and slash at an animal with its fangs or its razor fins, knock it into the oily water, and then crush the prey in its coils.

We were collecting fungus specimens when the duel between the swamp slug and the dragonsnake took us by surprise. Reconstructing the event afterward, we believe the incident began because the slug had blundered into the dragonsnake's nest, chewing the beast's home as it went.

During the resulting battle, the dragonsnake managed to bore through the slug's main body and slash off great chunks of meat. But swamp slugs have few vital organs, and this one seemed unaffected by the injuries. Dripping green-brown ichor, the slug reared up and plunged down again on top of the writhing dragonsnake, opening wide its huge, lipless mouth. Once the swamp slug managed to get the snake's barbed head into its tooth-lined gullet, the battle was over.

We watched and recorded for nearly an hour as the swamp slug ponderously swallowed the entire length of the armored dragonsnake, rumbling and chewing, before it wheeled about and continued devouring its way through the bog.

Our team members stood stunned. We had never before seen such a struggle.

FIFTH WEEK SUMMARY

Ranging even farther this week into the wilderness, discovering new environments.

In some sections of the swamp, where the ground is too rocky and rugged for anything other than scrubby ground cover, clearings appear, opening up rare canyons through the canopy high above. Fog clings in these low areas, drifting over rounded boulders and dense fungus forests.

Lightning flickers deep beneath the stormclouds and mist. Above, unpredictable air currents create only occasional rifts in the cloudbanks.

For a few minutes each day, a shaft of sunlight pierces the rift in the treetop canopy to shine down on the moorish ground. As the ribbon of light touches the rounded fungus balls, the mushrooms expand rapidly and explode, showering spores across the ground.

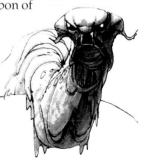

We discovered these exploding fungi accidentally when we came upon one of these mushroom

Above Dagobah's dense canopy, we found a different world entirely. Here, reptilian flying predators search for rodents rustling in the leaves. Rifts in the branches let shafts of sunlight burn all the way to the swampy ground.

covered clearings, shining our portable illuminators into the fungus forest. In every direction in which we turned our lights, detonations sent spores flying thick through the air, like a devastating battle. Already on edge from the uneasy silence of the swamp world and covered with foul-smelling and sticky spores, my team members and I fled.

Related now, in the safety of our camp shelter, the adventure seems somewhat amusing to me, but the spraying white spores and the loud explosions echoing through the misty forests made for a terrifying experience indeed.

SIXTH WEEK SUMMARY

Our short-range vehicle had so far proven mostly useless for travel through the dense tangle of the swamp. But we did manage to pilot it straight upward through a gash in the thick trees for a three-day expedition to Dagobah's astonishing canopy level.

Parts of the canopy rise above the swirling soup

of mist and break free into intermittent sunshine. Separated from the boggy, decaying landscape far below, the treetops offer an entirely different ecosystem.

When our small vehicle breached the thick murk, my team let out a collective gasp upon seeing the dazzling sunlight after so many days in the gray dampness of the lower levels. It seemed to me that I had never seen anything so beautiful. I could not remember natural light being so *bright* and so warm. Our morale jumped several notches in only a few seconds.

Under the nourishing sunlight, the stretching gnarltrees bring forth a blanket of tender leaves. Vines wind among the treetops, displaying brilliant flowers and dangling long, feathery roots to absorb moisture from the clinging mists. One species of vine-flower bears a segmented crystalline coating that acts like a prism, breaking the reflected sunlight into glittering rainbows.

Numerous small rodents scurry across the dense, matted roof of leaves and intertwined twigs, feeding on tender shoots and nesting only a few inches below the leafy surface.

Riding thermals overhead, reptilian flying creatures search for movement in the canopy and swoop down to snatch up the rodents. When shadows of the flying predators pass over the treetops, the rodents set up a chattering alarm and flee in hidden channels to their nests—as they did whenever we flew over. (Apparently they thought we were some new and enormous flying hunter.) Seen from above, the panicked rodents make a churning storm through the leaves. The reptilian flyers cannot dig deeply enough into the tangled twigs to go after their prey—but we noticed that the rodents usually did not all manage to get to safety in time.

We compared these reptilian flyers to a similar creature that inhabits the lower reaches of the swamp. Perhaps they are the same species, although with the denser foliage, the lower-level denizen grows to barely half the wingspan of its larger cousins.

In the darkest levels of the swamp, some creatures resort to bioluminescence to light their way and to attract unsuspecting prey.

Our fuel was limited, and we could not stay long above the trees. We were saddened to leave behind the sunshine. But we had our work to do.

[**Ed. Note**—*several records here are missing.*]

TWELFTH WEEK SUMMARY

Dagobah seems to resent our presence now. Though we have cataloged as many different life-forms as possible, even imaging and documenting the plants and creatures we encounter have proved too much of an effort.

There is no answer yet from the Republic on additional support-staff or new equipment. I am afraid we are not up to our assigned task. Morale is at its lowest point. Fights have broken out between some of the team members. Three of my companions are no longer speaking to each other.

Tension hangs in the air thicker than the mists.

Instead of doing our assigned research, we spend most of our days simply fighting off the encroaching jungle, maintaining our modular settlement against the constant onslaught of growing vines, creeping insects, and foliage that seems to charge forward every time we turn our backs.

The currents of the swamp change after every heavy downpour, often undermining the foundations of our sealed-off dwellings, labs, and storehouses. We have had to move camp twice in the past two weeks.

Today one member of the team died from an insect sting. In a separate file I have included images of her last convulsions, the remarkable purplish discoloration of her skin, and our utter helplessness. Our medicinal supplies did nothing to save her, and we could do nothing more than watch as she died. We buried her in the swamp, but I have no doubt that within days the various life-forms of Dagobah

This predator lunged out of a still pool and dragged one of our team members under before we could effect a rescue. The body was never recovered.

will have erased all signs of her grave.

I have sent message after message to the Republic government, explaining the wealth of possible medicinal discoveries the plants or insects of Dagobah have to offer, the opportunity for exotic pets or flora, the possibility of strange new drugs.

I have begged for assistance, but I have received only silence. Is some turmoil happening out in the civilized systems? Why would the Republic ignore us?

THIRTEENTH WEEK SUMMARY [Final Entry]

Our carefully protected food supply has begun to spoil, and this causes me greater fear than any of the previous disasters that have befallen us.

The tenaciously adapting life-forms of Dagobah have found ways to breach even our most careful seals. Much of our work now centers on finding edible plants and animals in the swamp around us, simply in order to survive.

Two more dead this week: one torn apart by a large, unseen predator, one dead from a poison plant. This latter death distresses me the most—according to all our analysis, the plant should have been edible, even nutritious. And yet it was deadly. At least the poison was fast-acting. I will have to remember it if…in case our situation becomes untenable.

I have sent out a broad-spectrum distress signal. Soon we will have to eat the native plants and hunt animals for our own food. Only five of us remain.

But we have all been highly trained. I have every confidence that we can survive.

*[**Editor's Postscript**—By the time a passing spice freighter responded to the distress signal and shuttled a rescue party down to the location of the research station, the entire team had disappeared. The modular buildings had been partially dismantled by the encroaching swamp and large animals. Some of the domes had caved in from the weight of clinging vines; all the team's food supplies had been devoured.*

The would-be rescuers collected all the data records they could find, then left the abandoned station. No sign was ever found of Halka Four-Den or the remaining members of her research team.

It seemed the Republic had forgotten all about them. With the corruption, disorder, and decay of the cumbersome old government, this was unfortunately not an unusual occurrence. We have found numerous "lost archives" in the databases on Coruscant, many telling sadly similar stories.

Though some of the Dagobah records were damaged by exposure to the harsh environment, the Republic archives still retain volumes and volumes of information on the life-forms observed and recorded by Halka Four-Den.

Other expeditions to Dagobah have been proposed, usually halfheartedly, but each one was rerouted or canceled at the last minute. Many library records have been garbled or misfiled, as if mere mention of the swampy planet is cause to draw a blanket of mystery around it. The system has been missed on any number of other surveys, records lost, coordinates mixed up. Even veteran space navigators have rarely heard of it. We hope this article will rekindle interest in the world of Dagobah. The swamp planet has made itself terribly elusive…a perfect place to hide, as if something on the swampy world does not want to be found.]

A vast number of creatures still remain to be catalogued on this world—and I do not envy any team assigned the task.

HOTH

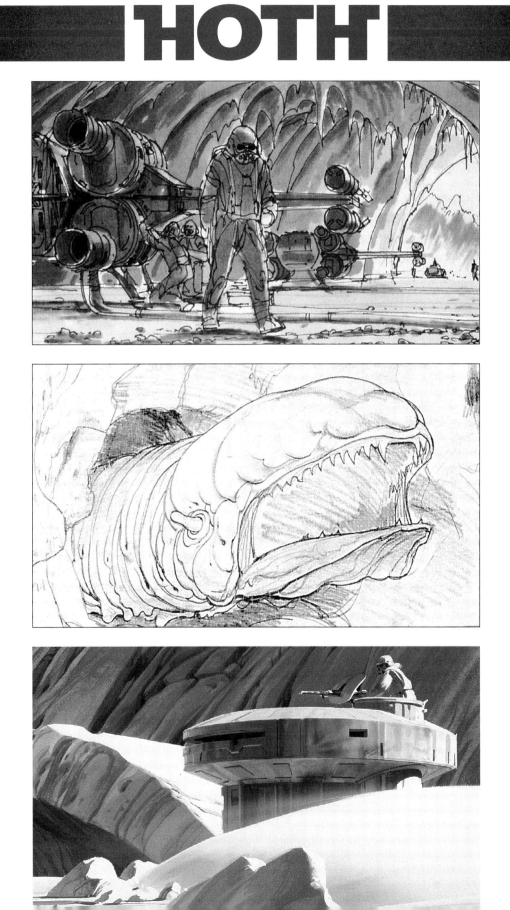

ABOUT THE AUTHOR:

Major Kem Monnon, chief of the Rebel Alliance Corps of Engineers, held the responsibility for establishing the protected Echo Base on the frozen world of Hoth. Drawing upon his uncanny resourcefulness and his ability to motivate his crews despite miserable living conditions, Major Monnon suceeded in building a secure, hidden, and defensible base. He describes the difficulties and joys encountered in establishing a secret home on the harsh arctic planet.

HOTH

Hoth is an isolated world distant from its blue-white sun, the sixth planet in the system. Tactically insignificant, unnoticed by the Imperial Navy. A perfect hiding place for a Rebel base.

Near the planet is a broad and hazardous asteroid belt, making hyperspace passage through the area extremely difficult; even travel at sublight speeds is risky for all but the most skilled pilots. Due to scattered debris from the asteroid belt, the planet Hoth itself has high meteor activity, thereby camouflaging our routine activities. All of which are great advantages, as far as the Alliance is concerned.

Hoth is far from a soft assignment, though. Daylight temperatures average only –32°C even in the temperate zone near the planetary equator. At

night, temperatures can plunge another twenty to thirty degrees, made worse by high-velocity winds tearing across the tundra. Few life-forms can survive in this environment, and those that do survive are not…pleasant.

After the destruction of our secret Rebel base on the fourth moon of Yavin, the entire Alliance scrambled to find alternative locations. I had collected a great deal of direct and anecdotal information during my years on tramp space freighters before hooking up with the Rebel Alliance. I offered my own suggestions, particularly emphasizing Hoth. The ice planet seemed a terrible option, a horrendously difficult place to establish living quarters…but it was also a place where the Empire would never suspect us. That was more important than our personal comfort. Besides, we could always wear thermal mittens and bring extra blankets.

Instead of marching in and converting the surface of the planet to our own needs, as the Empire would have done, we tried to work with the environment of a world not considered habitable by humanoid life-forms. Instead of shipping huge cargoes of supplies and prefab structures, my Corps of Engineers used the natural resources of Hoth to establish Echo Base. It was a good military tactic, efficient and leaving few traces on the surface.

Initially, we had sent a reconnaissance and survey team in a rapid low-orbital mapping expedition, scouting possible locations for a new base. Particularly close to the northern edge of the temperate zone, we found many places where volcanic and seismic activity had cracked the thick ice sheath, breaking vast networks of caverns in the ice. As soon as I saw these images, I knew these ice caves would prove ideal and adaptable for our purposes.

While the rest of the Rebel fleet made their way to the Hoth system through convoluted hyperspace paths to elude any possible pursuit, my surveyors mapped the ice labyrinths. For completeness, because I do not like surprises, they probed much deeper than what eventually became the main complex of Echo Base. The surveyors traveled far underground, where the distant sunlight barely managed to penetrate through the thick ice, leaving only a dim rainbowlike glow.

My scouts found solid rock inclusions and deep lava tubes where volcanic steam rose up to freeze against the cave walls in fantastic trees of sulfur-and-ice stalactites that hung down from the ceilings. While we did tap into some of these heat sinks as power sources, I considered the deep lava tubes too far beneath the ice to serve adequately as a

Echo Base on Hoth is a marvel of military engineering, excavated from packed snow and solid ice. The command hub *(above)* is the nerve center of the entire Rebel outpost. Rebel troops made the best of their situation, creating a tolerable home within the ice *(right)*.

supply and command base. Besides, the possibility of being trapped underground in an Imperial attack made me decidedly uneasy.

The first major part of the work of constructing Echo Base involved expansion of the natural ice caves. My Corps of Engineers worked day and night, using excavator machinery and laser cutters to blast larger grottoes and to install connections between chambers. Power conduits and communications tubes ran along the walls, mounted directly onto the smooth ice and solidly packed snow. It wasn't elegant or pretty, but it worked. We opened

Deep in the cave grottoes (above), wild tauntauns graze on lichen growths, oblivious to the struggle for freedom in the galaxy. Excavating machines (left) work to enlarge hangar chambers in the ice.

up Echo Base in record time.

Initially, our equipment could not withstand the cold. Comm units failed frequently, forcing my engineers to rely on old-fashioned messengers—non-combat-trained personnel who ran with white breath puffing from one corridor to another. Some of the lesser functionaries and diplomatic runners in exile carried recordings back and forth from deep tunnel excavations to the upper command centers, processing supply requisitions from our matériel ships, requesting design and computer assistance from other specialists in the Alliance fleet.

Large chambers in the ice caves served as main equipment rooms and hangar bays, while some of the largest items of machinery—the enormous shield generator, for instance—were located outside under thick layers of insulation to protect their fragile components from the deep cold.

By the time we opened Echo Base, we had completed the quarters and accommodations for several thousand people, including the government-in-exile of the Rebel Alliance. Representatives from the Civil and Military Government and top military advisers as well as high-level civil servants and their assistants learned to cope with the miserable conditions.

Because the structural material was solid ice, we were forced to maintain Echo Base at freezing temperatures. The walls of the living quarters were coated with an insulating plastic, which allowed the rooms to be heated to a comfortable temperature. However, several mishaps did occur when well-

Even in the bleakness of Hoth, nature has still wrought marvels, such as these glistening ice geysers, built up over centuries—destroyed in a moment by Imperial aggression.

meaning droids (hearing people grumble about the cold) increased the temperature in certain rooms, causing drastic meltdowns.

Base personnel adapted to the chill by wearing flexible insulating uniforms and comfortable standard-issue thermal suits. Some of the more temperature-sensitive inhabitants of the base found it more comfortable to remain living in their cramped—but heated—quarters inside the transport vessels parked inside the huge hangar grotto.

We did our best with the few amenities on hand; but life during wartime is hard, and no one who signed on expected a relaxing vacation.

Nevertheless, people under fire are quite resource-

The wampa ice creatures are the most fearsome predators on Hoth, vicious monsters bred for a cruel environment. Their primary food source is the tauntaun...as well as any unfortunate rider.

ful in finding ways to amuse themselves, even under strict alert conditions. For example, frequent meteor impacts have blasted circular craters in the surface ice sheets; at the floor of each crater the melted water has flash-frozen into a mirror-smooth lake. During their off-shifts base personnel supply their own recreation and exercise by ice-skating on these natural rinks.

Also, ostensibly as part of their training, new Rebel scouts put together a bizarre "tauntaun rodeo" out on the snowfields, riding the smelly, uncooperative beasts in various stunt activities.

Adapting to the environment at hand, the Rebel Alliance had found ways to domesticate the most common large life-form on Hoth, the tauntaun. Since our machinery often malfunctioned in the extreme cold, despite our best engineering fixes, we found the ornery beasts invaluable for certain activities.

The spitting, gurgling tauntauns are basically

reptilian, covered with an insulating gray-white fur that gives them the nickname "snow lizards." Their body temperature is low, and some of the Alliance exobiologists have remarked that they seem to have antifreeze for blood. They have evolved into several different species to adapt to the smallest habitable niches in the frozen wastelands.

Their cold-resistant blood allows them to survive extremely low temperatures; however, this is at the cost of shutting down many of their bodily organs. Forcing a tauntaun to perform arduous tasks in the deep cold frequently proves fatal.

Some species of wild tauntaun live on the surface, foraging across the tundra during the warmest periods of daylight, searching for edible lichens and moss on exposed outcroppings. Their strong, rough-textured lips are able to scour the hardy coatings of plant cells from the rocks. These tauntauns have splayed tridactyl feet and long claws to allow them purchase on the snow as they run. Their large hind legs make them powerful sprinters.

Beneath the insulating white-gray fur, the tough reptilian skin exudes oils and waste products from numerous tiny pores. This gives the tauntauns a distinctive and extremely unpleasant odor. I caught one of my engineers insulting a coworker by saying, "You smell like a tauntaun!" I considered that such a terrible insult that I gave him outside perimeter inspection duty for a week.

Other breeds of tauntaun look more reptilian, with narrow bodies and longer forelimbs. These types are usually denizens of the deep ice caves. They live near subterranean volcanic vents and forage among the species of foul-tasting fungus that grow in the lightless chambers.

While rounding up captive tauntauns to tame and

ride, we saw that they frequently travel in herds, moving en masse to seek any form of food, whether on the surface, in the rock outcroppings, or deep in the ice caves. From what we can tell, tauntauns will eat just about anything, including frozen carrion and small rodents they catch.

Immediately upon arriving at Hoth, some daring members of our Corps attempted to taste the tauntaun meat to see if it could become a dietary staple during our assignment on the frozen world. But they learned their lesson after only one taste. The meat was stringy, sulfurous, and practically indigestible. We would be eating prepackaged rations for the foreseeable future—and, looking at the spitting, foul snow lizards, I can't say I was disappointed.

Once the base was open for habitation and the primary routine established, the job of my Corps of Engineers was finished. But since I find sitting around on alert immensely tiresome, I was fidgeting with boredom after only a few days. I spoke to General Carlist Rieekan, the man in charge of Echo Base, and he gave me permission to continue exploring Hoth and to compile my report for possible further strategic use by the Rebel Alliance.

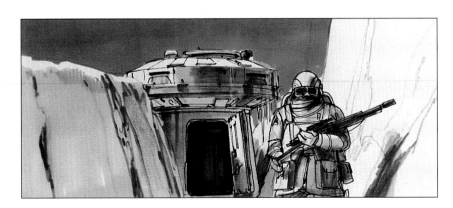

Security and watchfulness are prime concerns in a secret base. Scouts riding tauntauns or snowspeeders watch the perimeter. Even the side doorways of Echo Base are gaurded by vigilant sentries.

The stark, hostile landscape of Hoth may seem terrifying to many life-forms, but the frozen scenery has its own sort of beauty. It grows on you after a while, and I found the stark, bright *cleanness* to be refreshing after spending so much of my life in the Alliance in run-down, out-of-the-way bases or smelly spice freighters.

Once we happened to be outside just after one of the frequent, severe windstorms, right around local sunset. As the distant blue-white touched the horizon, the ice crystals that were whipped into the air from the storm created shimmering rainbows, painful to look at in the crackling cold air. The fading light refracted prismatically from great mounds of transparent ice, washing the landscape with brilliant colors. The temperature drops so rapidly at night, though, that few of the base personnel are willing to go out sight-seeing, even for a spectacle like this.

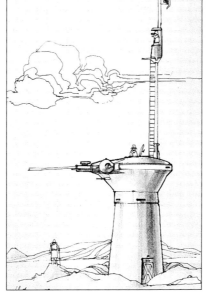

Another day, some of my people went with me to explore the flatlands north of Echo Base. As we had seen from the initial reconnaissance flights, underground springs near deep volcanic sources periodically flash into steam and spray through narrow channels toward the planet's surface. But we did not expect the weird landforms caused by this phenomenon.

When the steam strikes the subzero cold of Hoth's atmosphere, it freezes into delicate powder that slowly builds layer upon layer around the geysers' mouths. Over decades, these ice geysers build up fantastic castle-like formations, tall turrets and spiky frozen forests. The ice trees show a broad palette of colors, yellows, tans, reds, blues, and greens. I'm no chemist, but I suppose the colors come from sulfur and other mineral impurities in the volcanic springs. When the wind picks up, tiny fragments of the fragile trees break off and tinkle to the ground. It's a strange, ethereal music.

Ice caps cover most of the deep oceans of Hoth, though tidal motions caused by Hoth's three moons (and large meteor impacts, too, I suppose) crack through the frozen shelves, releasing the trapped water to gush upward, jetting high and coating the glacial wound. The intense cold needs very little time to seal these breaches, returning Hoth to its motionless, frozen state. Still, the new ice is darker and smoother, and you can see it plainly even from a low-flying snowspeeder.

In one of our far-ranging expeditions to Hoth's southern hemisphere, we found a great chasm that stretches for nearly a thousand kilometers. I thought it looked as if the ice planet had started to split at the seams, but then had thought better of it. This huge canyon is filled with water barely above the freezing point, kept liquid by the immense pressure from both sides trying to slam back together.

On the rims of the canyon, glaciers slump over the sides in a horrendous, slow-motion plunge. It looks like a time-slowed image of a huge waterfall. The great walls of ice relentlessly move, less than a meter per year according to our measurements, as they press down and grind side channels down to the open, blackish water below.

The glaciers themselves are a deep blue, veined with swirling colors from primitive algae that manage to survive by leaching dissolved nutrients and minerals from the frozen water; they must metabolize it with the dim sunlight that penetrates the murky ice.

Even locked inside the glacial prison, the algae are not safe. Wire-like ice worms burrow their way through the frozen walls, feeding on the algae. The ice worms tunnel through the glaciers, leaving honeycombed shafts along the outer surfaces of the ice, where the algae are most prevalent.

(top) Gun-emplacement crew equipped for the unforgiving cold.

(bottom) Though Hoth is a barren world, the Rebel Alliance never lets down its guard.

When the wind blows from the right direction, the tiny holes in the glaciers emit a flutelike music, rising and falling into the bleak emptiness in an eerie, lonesome melody.

The most fearsome and the deadliest inhabitants of Hoth are the wampa ice creatures. In fact, in my travels prior to joining the Rebel Alliance, any time I heard the name of Hoth spoken, these beasts were mentioned in the same shuddering breath. I thought that rumor had exaggerated their fearsomeness—but even the hyperbole of lowlife traders could not overestimate the ferocity of these monsters.

Wampas are huge, standing three or four meters tall, with yellow eyes. They are covered with wiry white fur that allows them to roam the tundra of the ice planet even during storms, perfectly camouflaged.

The snow monsters have only a very faint scent that would alert their prey—unlike the filthy taun-tauns. By the time a tauntaun can smell the wampa through its own stench, the monster is too close for the prey to escape. I suppose the lack of scent could be because the wampas keep themselves meticulously clean—but that's not likely considering the cluttered, bone-strewn lair we found.

Wampas are solitary creatures, each living in its own ice cavern. If the creatures cannot find an appropriate grotto for themselves, they are capable of ripping a new chamber from a wall of ice and snow with brute strength.

Luckily, wampas seem to be very rare. My guess would be that, because of their large size, wampas require a great deal of fresh meat. Since life is so sparse on Hoth, each wampa needs a vast and exclusive hunting domain. The creatures must spend

days wandering across the tundra, covering more than a hundred kilometers in search of food. Again, this may be an exaggerated tall tale told in a cantina over too many drinks, but I have heard poachers tell how wampas guard their territory jealously, engaging in bloody duels to protect their hunting grounds, leaving splashes of red-stained snow across the desolation.

When a wampa attacks, its intent is to stun, not kill outright (although from the few souvenir/trophy claws I glimpsed, I would say that one swipe is probably enough to slaughter lesser animals). The wampa drags its victim across the tundra back to the lair; it then suspends the hapless being from the ceiling of the ice cavern until the wampa grows hungry.

Though the ice creatures appear to be violently solitary creatures, there is evidence that they do act

Fearing an Imperial attack, all troops at Echo Base are placed on alert at the gates of the installation, manning blaster cannon (top) and defending the energy shield generator (left).

as a concerted team at times. While we were out alone far from Echo Base on our own bivouac, we slept in small thermal shelters. As the night winds gusted across the snows, we could hear a deeper, more mournful howl overlapping the sounds of the breezes. We knew it had to be wampas crying out across the vastness—perhaps seeking mates, perhaps making complicated plans.

Because of their violence, the size of their claws and teeth, and the thickness of their pelt, wampas are legendary as targets for unscrupulous big-game hunters and thrillseekers—and this is how I had heard so much about them. In my travels I had seen occasional trophies on the black market: hides, stuffed heads, and claws that commanded astronomical prices. I can remember one rugged black-market poacher loudly offering shooting expeditions to Hoth for "the best hunt in the galaxy!" —although I don't know what he would have done had anyone taken him up on the offer.

I had heard of one other ill-fated illegal poaching operation, which I told to my companions as we shivered in our shelters—and believe me, that story was on all our minds as the wampas howled at each other in the frozen darkness.

A group of failed stormtrooper cadets had set up a business as guides to take the highest-paying big-game hunters to track down and kill wampas. The profits were high and, given sufficient weaponry, the game was not too difficult. But on the fourth such expedition, the wampas fought back.

By this time the ice creatures had learned their enemies' tactics and weaknesses. The wampas found the spaceships left by the group and tore them apart during the night, leaving the hunters and their guides with no comlink and no way to get off the frozen planet. The wampas raised their howling voices in the night, terrifying the hunters,

and making them waste their ammunition by shooting at shadows. Idiots, of course. But then, these were *failed* stormtroopers.

The perfectly camouflaged snow monsters struck, attacking in unison—these supposedly solitary creatures acted together like a precision killing machine. They came seven nights in a row, and each night they took only one victim, dragging him out into the cold darkness. No amount of fighting could stop them, and even though several wampas were slain, the monsters kept coming until they grabbed their chosen human. The terrified hunters, seeing their numbers diminishing with each passing night, could do nothing.

Finally the last two survivors made a pact and turned their weapons on each other rather than become tortured victims of the wampas. Of course, as with many such tall tales, the question remains *who told the story*, if no one survived? But we could not be bothered by trifles like that as we heard the howling wampas in the distance.

All through that empty, cold night of bivouac, we posted two guards, edgy and ready to shoot at any movement outside. It was a very long night, and we were glad to get back to Echo Base, ready to spend

our time in even the most tedious chores of maintaining our defenses.

Because of its inhospitable conditions, Hoth is a great place to hide, a perfect isolated base for the Rebel Alliance. But we did not allow ourselves to grow overconfident that the Empire would never be able to locate us. Though it may have seemed unnecessary, Base Commander Rieekan insisted on a full defensive posture at all times, with no exceptions.

The other Rebel soldiers in Echo Base considered him a grim man, but Rieekan had good cause to be jumpy, unwilling to ignore warning signs until it was too late. I knew his past, and I respected him for it. I don't know what I would have done in his place, but he had already made the mistake of waiting too long—and as a result his beautiful home of Alderaan had been destroyed by the Death Star.

The hanger bay of Echo Base is a large, natural bubble in the ice, shored up with raw materials, designed for flexibility and serviceability—used to its fullest extent during the evacuation of the facility.

He won't tell you the story, keeping his sorrow to himself, but I made sure every member of my Corps of Engineers knew it. I tolerated no grumbling about his "unreasonable" demands, or his hard-driving work schedules, or his seeming paranoia about being discovered and attacked.

A native of Alderaan and a secret member of the Rebel Alliance, Rieekan had been inspecting satellite transmitters around Delaya, a nearby sister world of Alderaan, when he saw the terrible Death Star approach his home planet. Through covert operations, the Alliance had already learned of the battle station being built by Grand Moff Tarkin, and so Rieekan knew what might occur when the Death Star approached Alderaan.

But he was also terrified that if he signaled a general evacuation of Alderaan, the Empire would know its security had been breached. Why else would the people of Alderaan flee at first sight of the secret battle station, unless a spy had brought knowledge from the Imperial think tanks? That would be tantamount to admitting Alderaan's ties to the Rebel Alliance, and Alderaan had always pleaded neutrality. Torn by indecision, Rieekan held off on the evacuation, hoping that Tarkin was only

bluffing, not wishing to blow his cover.

But Tarkin was not afraid to use his new weapon, and all the people on Alderaan were destroyed. General Rieekan still bears the guilt on his shoulders. He has vowed never again to hesitate, never again to let the Empire's cruelty surprise him. He insisted on the constant defensive posture of Echo Base, no matter how unlikely discovery might seem.

We assisted in modifying snowspeeder vehicles to function at peak performance in the worst cold of Hoth, though these modifications were difficult and took some time. When the snowspeeders were functioning properly, long-range scouts flew in a wide radius around Echo Base, ensuring the security of the site.

Various "Echo Stations" were placed around the planet to monitor meteor activity and search for any sign of an unwelcome visit from our friends in the Imperial Navy.

A powerful energy field protects Echo Base from a space attack. This shield is strong enough to deflect the heaviest Imperial bombardment from orbit. Echo Base's great ion cannon is the single most powerful artillery piece in the Alliance arsenal.

One thousand Special Forces troopers are specially trained for ground defense in the frigid environment. They are armed with numerous antivehicle and antipersonnel artillery pieces specially adapted to function at low temperatures. For greater versatility, some scouts ride the perimeter on tauntaun mounts during daylight hours.

Despite our full spectrum of defenses, we maintain our vigilance, waiting, always waiting, for the Empire to find us again.

THE ASTEROID BELT

[*Ed. Note: This supplementary file, compiled by the Orko SkyMine Asteroid Processing Corporation (owned by Durga the Hutt), was originally written to describe the resources available in the Hoth system's extended asteroid belt. The appended Incident Report describes the untimely end of Orko SkyMine's Automated Mineral Exploiter project.*

The author of these reports is unknown because Durga the Hutt purged his/her/its identity following the Automated Mineral Exploiter disaster. Presumably, the anonymous author was similarly eradicated.]

Executive Summary: The Hoth asteroid field consists of the scattered remains of an ancient collision between two large, rocky planets. The impact destroyed both worlds and scattered chunks of debris in a wide swath through the system. Over billions of years, this debris has wandered into erratic orbits, forming a great hazard to all ships traveling in the ecliptic of the system—and a great mineral resource for those with the will and the wherewithal to exploit it.

Astronomical projections have confirmed that the asteroids continued to collide and grind each other down, leaving a great range of debris sizes, from microscopic dust particles, to tiny pebbles, to large boulders, and even to irregularly shaped plane-

toids massive enough to hold a scant atmosphere. Given the proper machinery and element sorters, the asteroid belt provides a wealth of material—heretofore untapped by any of the other large processing consortiums.

Since Hoth is an isolated system with little traffic, no one has bothered to map all the components of

The ferocious space slugs, whose slow metabolism allows them to survive even in near-vacuum conditions, have proven to be severe hazards to mineral exploitation of the Hoth asteroid belt. Such creatures lie in wait, lurking in crevices or mine shafts, prepared to devour any unsuspecting ships.

the asteroid belt. Because the large fragments continue to tug gravitationally at each other, consistent orbital maps are impossible to maintain.

This lack of information can only be an advantage to Orko SkyMine Corp., however. Naturally, some hardy independent miners have attempted to exploit the asteroid belt, searching the shattered rocks for precious metals and crystals. But the majority of the treasures has gone unnoticed for a great many years. Orko SkyMine could claim everything for itself.

Points of Mineral Interest: One rare finding among the asteroids is a strange transparent growth, "crystal ferns," that occurs on some rocks exposed

to hard radiation and cold vacuum. The silicon-based crystals grow several meters tall, sprawling out in delicate, weblike tangles in the low gravity. Since the crystal ferns propagate from asteroid to asteroid, broken in shards that are carried to other rocks through orbital vagaries, there is some speculation that they are actually a primitive silicon-based life-form. Such an item would be worth a great deal on the collectors' market and to those dealing in exotica.

We have received reports of independent miners and surveyors eagerly seeking forests of these crystal ferns, though they are incredibly difficult to harvest without shattering the fragile structure. Given the technical resources of Orko SkyMine Corp., though, a sophisticated solution could no doubt be found.

We have also obtained many anecdotal reports of a particularly persistent legend: Somewhere lost among the asteroids is a huge chunk of ore, nearly pure platinum that was spat out from the metallic core of one of the broken planets. This asteroid is known popularly as Kerane's Folly because it drove the prospector Kerane mad after he supposedly found it and took a sample back to verify that it was indeed the pure, precious metal he suspected—but then could never find its location again. He spent the rest of his life among the Hoth asteroids, trying without success to recover it. Other prospectors, believing the story, have continued the hunt. Perhaps with a systematic search, Orko SkyMine could rediscover this treasure.

Potential Mining Hazards: Unfortunately, independent prospectors are not the only inhabitants of the debris field.

The maze of the asteroid belt has also proved to be a favorite hiding place for notorious smugglers and space pirates. Over the centuries, the records show that many hostile criminals and their henchmen have established hidden bases inside some of the larger asteroids. They were able to elude pursuit by various Republic, Imperial, and independent planetary police authorities by vanishing into the forest of deadly flying rocks. After numerous enforcement ships were lost in fruitless pursuit attempts, it is generally acknowledged that once a refugee manages to reach the asteroid belt,

continuing the chase is futile. Such pirates may still be in evidence and could pose a threat to regular mining activities. However, given a sufficiently armed mercenary escort, Orko Sky-Mine could proceed without fear. Indeed, some of these sophisticated pirate bases could be occupied and used as processing platforms in a large-scale exploitation of the belt.

We have learned that the major pirate strongholds were formed on the largest asteroids, those harboring minimal atmospheres. The most notorious of the smugglers and space pirates was a man named Clabburn, popularly portrayed as a hairy humanoid with oily, greenish skin and no compassion whatever for other sentient beings. Clabburn would lie in wait with his attack ships along the most heavily traveled hyperspace paths on the Anoat trade corridor, attacking wealthy tourists heading for the cloud resorts on Bespin.

Upon sighting a luxury liner, Clabburn's swarm of ships would surround the target and immobilize the engines with a barrage of precision shots. Then the pirates, wearing vacuum suits, would crawl over the outer hull of the crippled ship, planting small charges that would detonate and puncture the hull. Instantly all the air inside the passenger liner gushed into space, killing the passengers without a struggle, without letting them ever see the faces of their attackers. A cold-blooded tactic, perhaps, but highly efficient. Clabburn and his accomplices could then dismantle the ship at their leisure, taking the valuables from the frozen bodies. Last of all, they would set the vessel to self-destruct, leaving no evidence of their crime.

Bounty hunters, police forces, and vengeful relatives hunted Clabburn for decades, but they could never

These sketches of the mechanical parasites, called mynocks, show these vermin in their natural configuration. In any operations in the asteroid belt, these pests must be dealt with.

110

locate his base in the asteroid belt. He kept moving from one planetoid to another, always covering his tracks and leaving unpleasant booby traps for anyone who might be one step behind him.

On first consideration, it seemed as if it would be advantageous to find one of Clabburn's abandoned bases as a central administrative site and use it for asteroid mining operations—however, the pirate made a habit of leaving behind a deadly legacy for anyone who might follow.

At the openings to his discarded bases, Clabburn planted huge wormlike guardians known as space slugs. The space slugs are hardy, primitive organisms with very low metabolisms. They subsist on virtually no atmosphere, surviving for incredibly long periods by breaking down the rock of the asteroid itself.

In low asteroidal gravity, space slug bodies can grow to enormous proportions—estimated at 750 to 900 meters. The slugs are primarily smooth and vermiform, but long root tendrils snake out of the rear portion and burrow into the veins of rock to leach nutrients.

Space slugs are plagued by large parasites known as mynocks. Common mynocks have leathery black wings and a specialized suction-cup organ for draining energy.

Frequently traveling in packs, mynocks are common throughout the galaxy, having adapted themselves to drain energy from their host. They prefer concentrated energy, such as power couplings and battery cells, but they will also digest other forms of food—from the soft inner membranes of the space slug itself to the thermal energy the creature radiates as heat.

Space slugs occasionally feast on bounty hunters or law-enforcement troops trying to track down some hidden space pirate. Unwitting intruders land inside an inviting-looking cave deep within a large asteroid, imagining it might be an active pirate base. But then the space slug closes its mouth and secretes powerful digestive fluids to break down the long-awaited meal. Because of its low metabolism, though, a space slug is often very slow to react to a ship waiting right inside its mouth, which causes it to lose many choice morsels. This could be used to our advantage should we ever encounter one of these creatures.

Granted, some of these hazards could be severe; however, we believe the potential wealth in the Hoth asteroid field cries out to be exploited. If not by Orko SkyMine Corp., then someone else will certainly fill the gap.

INCIDENT REPORT

This report lists the facts in the recent incident involving Orko SkyMine's two Automated Mineral Exploiter ships.

It is a matter of record that the largest mining venture ever undertaken in the asteroid belt involved these two automated ore-processing ships. Completely unmanned, these Automated Mineral Exploiters were programmed to detect a large mass, fly toward it, and begin to dismantle it. Equipped with detectors to search and select for high concentrations of metals, the Orko ore processors were enormous, the most expensive constructions ever undertaken by this corporation. Unfortunately, the Automated Mineral Exploiters were able to harvest only two full shipments of ore. We should point out that *mechanically,* these massive haulers performed flawlessly. Unfortunately, a simple and understandable error was made in the search programming. It is rather amusing in a way.

We have determined that due to the random vagaries of their search patterns, the two ore processors detected *each other.* Apparently each Automated Mineral Exploiter identified a large target of fabulously pure metal. The titanic ships came together and began dismantling each other for the ore. From our distant vantage on one of the former pirate bases, we could only watch as the ore processors became the largest scrap heap in this sector.

We should emphasize that other than this minor error, the Automated Mineral Exploiter concept worked perfectly. The proof-of-concept has been completed, and all blueprints remain in the databanks of Orko SkyMine Corp. Given the potential wealth of the Hoth asteroid belt, it only makes sense to begin a second attempt.

In the meantime we apologize for our error and throw ourselves at the mercy of the chairman, Durga the Hutt.

—END INCIDENT REPORT

ENDOR

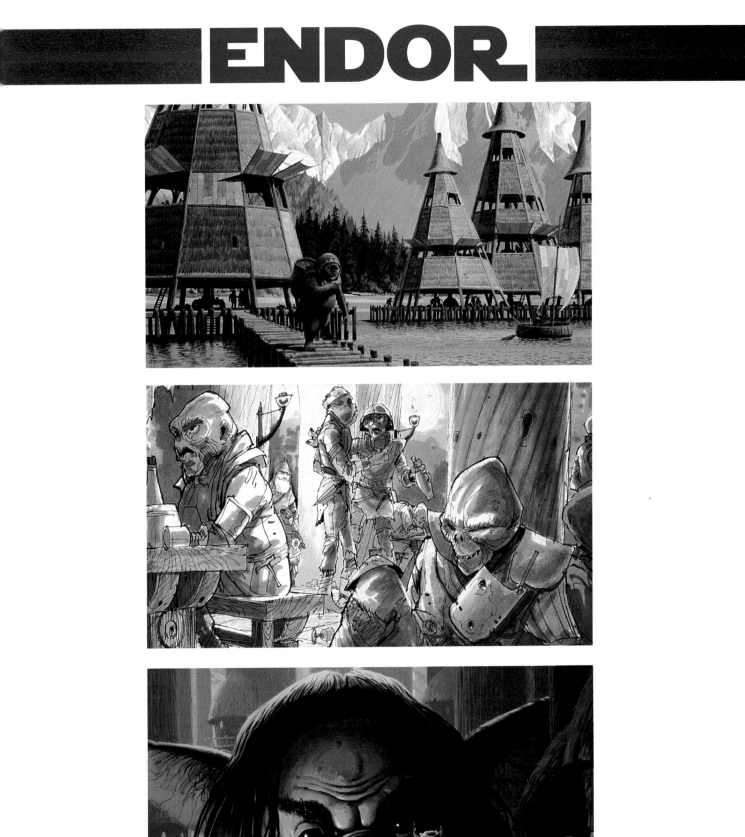

ABOUT THE AUTHOR:

Sergeant Pfilbee Jhorn served as records officer for the Emperor's second expeditionary force to the Forest Moon of Endor. Displeased with the superficial reports of the first scouting team, the Emperor requested a detailed summary. Sergeant Jhorn filed several memos before his departure, insisting that he was not qualified for the job, but these memos were misfiled and never delivered to Sergeant Jhorn's superiors. Such circumstances account for the rather bitter and resentful tone of this report.

Imperial military records show that shortly after Sergeant Pfilbee Jhorn filed this report, he was transferred to a lengthy tour of duty alone riding the solar focusing mirrors in orbit around Coruscant. Following this assignment, he was sent to Tatooine, where he served as a custodian in the Imperial desert garrison.

ENDOR

Though my superiors have not seen fit to give me full details as to the Emperor's purpose in seeking further information on the Forest Moon of Endor, I am filing this report as requested. I will state up front that, since I was never given specifics as to the information of interest, this report will perforce be broad and general. As I have had no training in planetary survey techniques, I have avoided details of a technical nature.

The trip out here was horrendous. Endor itself is a silvery gas-giant that is difficult to reach even by convoluted hyperspace paths. As shown in the attachments, the huge planet is encircled by banded high clouds and orbited by nine moons of varying sizes. The largest moon, called the Forest Moon of Endor, is the size of a small, rocky planet. As the Forest Moon is the focus of this report, I have designated it Endor for simplicity.

The Endor system is extremely remote, not just from the Core systems but also from other Imperial bases, common trade routes, and other inhabited worlds. The captain of our transport claimed that simply reaching Endor involves half a dozen tricky hyperspace maneuvers (something to do with the enormous gravity of the gas-giant and the uncharted space in the sector). The captain rather snappishly told me to leave him alone, even after I informed him that I was on a fact-finding mission for the Emperor. (His name and service number are on file, should anyone wish to initiate formal disciplinary action.) These navigational uncertainties may rule out the establishment of an important base in this system.

Given such circumstances, it is no surprise that numerous ships have crash-landed on the Forest Moon, making it something of a "desert island" in space. The lush and wild environment provides resourceful victims the opportunity to eke out an existence, but I would envy no one the job of living under these primitive conditions. Give me Coruscant any day.

However, I do not know the Emperor's purposes here. Given that Endor is isolated, yet able to support human life without expensive and difficult environment systems, this large moon may be an ideal place. My job is only to provide information, add recommendations if I feel they are relevant, and correct the numerous sketchy errors made by the initial survey team. If only they had done their job well enough in the first place, I would not have been given this redundant assignment.

(For example, the report of the first survey team stated that the only significant life-forms inhabiting the moon were the fuzzy and annoying Ewoks, who were presumed to be harmless. Not only did the survey team entirely miss the deadly giant Gorax, but also bloodthirsty condor dragons, packs of tall and timid yuzzums, and an entire settlement of off-planet marauders. The members of this first team are a disgrace to Imperial military service. Practically their only useful bit of information is that the furry Ewoks pose no serious threat and should be exterminated strictly because of their nuisance value.)

Of course, the first team's lack of thoroughness may be understandable if they were as poorly equipped as my team proved to be. When the transport ship dropped us off and shuttled our supplies down, we were appalled to find that only a group of two-rider AT-ST scout transports had been assigned to the entire task of covering a world. The food packs contained only the worst sorts of rations, leftovers from the Clone Wars, no doubt! The garment bins contained ice-assault suits decommissioned after the raid on Hoth! I had heard grumblings about incompetence, nepotism, and corruption in the Imperial Navy, and now I had no doubt.

Sworn to duty, though, my team and I set to work. We consisted of four scientifically trained troopers plus five stormtrooper escorts. We climbed aboard several jerky scout transports and clomped off through the undergrowth. I believe the AT-STs were in need of serious maintenance. The other members of my team performed the required duties, while I sat back and observed (as was my job). I took copious notes.

Much of the surface is densely covered with leg-

endary tall trees, giving it the name of Forest Moon; but other parts of Endor are rocky savannas and snow-topped mountains. Badlands to the south are dotted with sulfur springs and perilous pools. Bleak, rocky highlands are inhabited by the giant Gorax. The low gravity of the Endor moon encourages living things to become large, not just the mammoth conifer trees, but also many indigenous species.

The dense, primeval forest is the most striking feature of Endor, and most likely to cause serious difficulties for Imperial construction projects. Overhead, through the tapering treetops, the bright planet Endor fills much of the sky like a mirror, breaking through the blue of daylight or shining down like a spotlight in the night. (One side benefit of this would be the reduced cost of illumination for a security perimeter on any proposed base.)

Flowers grow high above the ground, sprouting from wind-borne seeds that have lodged in damp crevices in the enormous tree limbs. Their colors are so bright and so varied as to give one a headache, and even with my facemask filters toggled to their densest settings, the disgusting pollens still managed to penetrate, making me miserable with extraterrestrial allergies.

The thickly overgrown forest floor, with its groves of free-palms and ferns, proved extremely hazardous even for the flexible capabilities of our scout transport. If Imperial engineers think they can simply land on the moon, ignore the indigenous life-forms, and set up their base of operations without difficulty, they're in for a large, unpleasant surprise.

While our AT-STs could maneuver through some of the thickest foliage, I'd consider it impossible for a larger AT-AT to make its way beyond the largest clearings. This does not preclude, however, the use of such armored walkers for intimidation around, say, a big landing platform in the depths of the forest.

Still, even our smaller scout walker suffered several mishaps on our plodding journey through the forest: I can't begin to list all the times we stumbled in treacherous and hidden gullies concealed by the underbrush. We wasted many hours disassembling twisted metal knee joints and repairing them, occasionally even battering bent components with rocks just to make them fit back into their appropriate sockets. Naturally, our AT-ST repair kits contained none of the spare parts we needed.

The Forest Moon of Endor orbits a silvery gas-giant—called _Endor_, for you dim-witted readers—which rises high and bright every day.

The animal life on Endor is none too friendly. (I couldn't begin to say whether any of the game is edible; our old military rations were tasteless, but even that seemed preferable to eating some stringy, musty rodent grubbing in the underbrush.)

While our scout walker was being repaired—again—several of us explored the perimeter and encountered a dangerous decoy creature, which we named a tempter. The tempter lives inside a dark, hollow stump, waiting for other predators to pass by. The tempter apparently exudes a provocative smell that makes predators salivate. From the shad-

The open skies of Endor, showing only primitive trees and dirty "natural" beauty, are ripe for exploitation by anyone who can stomach this primeval world.

ows of its tree den, it opens its yawning black mouth, using its articulated tongue as a lure.

The tempter's tongue is an astonishing piece of camouflage, with a small and furry appendage that looks just like a particularly stupid rodent. The tongue appendage has its own muscles and even a dense nerve cluster that may act as a primitive sec-

but the task is far too great for our small party. I would suggest, though, that if the Emperor intends to make any substantial use of this Forest Moon, he see to it that the Ewoks are exterminated before they can cause significant damage with their ignorant meddling.

One member of our team unwisely became enamored of the Ewok society and culture. He squandered valuable time studying them and wrote copious descriptions of his impressions, though he did not bother to do a single dissection to add to our *real* knowledge of these…these creatures. I have reprimanded him severely for his misplaced priorities, but I include his observations here for completeness, though I have rewritten some of the insipid and overblown prose.

The Ewok civilization is extremely primitive and simple, with little of unique interest to warrant study by already overworked Imperial exoanthropologists. Somehow, by sheer accident, the Ewoks have performed many spectacular engineering feats, including catapults, waterwheels, and skin gliders that allow them to soar on the winds and remain aloft for a long time in the small moon's low gravity. Even the gruff engineer on our team admitted his grudging admiration for their discoveries.

It is humorous to watch the Ewoks attempt to create weapons from the crudest raw materials: stone knives, spears, bows and arrows, nets, clumsy animal traps, even catapults. Nothing the Ewoks invent would have a chance of even scratching our Imperial weaponry, though the contest (and resulting Ewok slaughter!) might be amusing to watch.

Even when viewed from the level of the forest floor, the Ewok tree villages do seem marginally impressive. It appears obvious that the tree cities grow and evolve over the generations, as the scurrying little creatures build annexes to the core group of dwellings in a cluster of the towering conifers called lifetrees.

These hardy conifer trees are long-lived and durable, able to survive the onslaughts of disease, lightning strikes, and forest fires. They continue to grow for centuries, towering up to a thousand meters tall.

The thick protective bark of the lifetree exudes a natural pesticide that drives away all but the most persistent insects. Knowing no better methods of chemistry, the aboriginal Ewoks distill an insect

ondary brain. The decoy appendage moves, making strange and tempting sounds, then ducks back into the blackness of the hollow tree.

When one of our scouts reached into the hollow trunk to secure the rodent specimen, the tempter nearly bit his entire hand off. As we struggled to free him, the gray, serpentine form lunged out of its hiding place in the trunk, hoping to finish off the wounded prey. We blasted it, then dissected the remains of the carcass.

The tempter looks like a long, blunt eel, with pale, fleshy skin covered with a thick mucus that allows it to slither into tight spots and also to strike outward, freeing itself in a flash. Apparently once it has had its meal, the tempter cleans blood and debris from the area, then lies in wait again. Once the lair in the hollow trunk is filled with bones and refuse, the tempter must move out—probably at night, under the silvery light of the gas-giant, slithering among the free-palms to find a new place to set up a trap.

We tended our wounded comrade and bandaged his arm, but his injury greatly diminished his use to us for the rest of the survey operation.

The most common creatures on Endor are the obnoxious Ewoks, feral and deceptively cute hairy things that seem to consider themselves our equals. Ewoks practically infest the forests with their tree villages. It would give me no greater pleasure than to burn down these clumsy and primitive structures, repellant from the lifetree bark for their own uses. They also use the trees as sources of wood and bark fiber for weapons, garments, utensils, and furniture; as storage places for pure drinking water; and as a good place to find medicinal plants and herbs.

The Ewoks have developed a deep and superstitious connection with the lifetrees. To cement this bond, each village plants a new seedling for each baby Ewok born; then they carefully nurture the seedling as if it were a sibling to the baby. Throughout that Ewok's life, he or she is linked to this "totem tree." When the Ewoks die, they believe their spirits go to live inside their personal totem trees. Of course it is impossible to believe such a preposterous idea, but the Ewoks as a species do not appear to possess more than a rudimentary intelligence.

In times of crisis, Ewok shamans attempt to communicate with the ancient spirits residing within the oldest trees to ask for advice. Being the village con artists, the shamans naturally insist that this is an intensely private ritual. No one else has ever heard such ancestral voices, but the gullible Ewoks do not question the sacred advice brought back by their shamans. After all, why would the spirits inhabiting their totem trees ever lie?

As for the design of the tree villages themselves, the structures at first seem to have been arranged at random, wherever the short attention of the furry creatures halted for the moment. But when our team member took the time to observe the villages thoroughly—too thoroughly, in my opinion—he noted a basic blueprint that all Ewoks seem to follow.

The central "village" of thatched-roof huts is built into the primary limbs, situated high enough above the ground that they are out of reach of most predators. Suspended bridges between trees link adjoining and distant huts; knotted rope ladders allow access up or down.

The thatched-roof huts offer plenty of warmth, shelter, and protection in the mild climate of the Forest Moon. But the whole thing could be made to go up in flames with minimal effort, simply by tossing in a few incendiary devices. In a typical tree city, the Ewok elders—funny-looking, gray-haired little beasts—order the largest huts built directly on the trunk of the tree. These central dwellings belong to the chief of the tribe, who uses the largest open areas for village gatherings, meetings, council fires, and storytelling ceremonies.

Family groups live in their own dwelling clusters on outlying trees, though separate communal huts are built for groups of unmarried females, respected elders, and visitors. A sealed cluster of structures, higher than the main tree city, is used for the communities food storage.

Unmarried Ewok males often spend a contemplative period living alone in the forest, building their own small dwellings near enough to the main tree city to assist with the Ewoks' daily work, but otherwise fending totally for themselves. Unmarried females leave gifts of food, clothing, weaponry, or trinkets on the door-steps of the solitary males as a sign of their attraction, ostensibly to tell the males how much the city misses them and wishes them to come back as part of a new family unit, preferably as that female's mate.

Ewok children _(top)_ and Ewok dwellings _(above)_ show how these primitive creatures attempt to make do with the squalor of their existence.

Such bizarre and rigid marriage customs seem like an artifact of some of the oddest practices in the early days of the Old Republic.

If the male Ewok wishes to end his solitary time, he must build an acceptable family dwelling in the larger tree city as a place for him and his mate to live. When an Ewok bachelor begins building his new dwelling, signaling that he has decided to take a mate, the unmarried females step up their work at wooing him (at least the ones who are interested). The Ewok male does not announce his choice of mate until he has completed his home; the chosen female has the right to refuse him, or the dwelling he has built. I could barely refrain from rolling my eyes at hearing such barbarities.

As with nearly all primitive races, the Ewoks developed a religious system based on superstition, worshiping the bounty around them and the forest from which they draw the necessities of their lives. Religious ceremonies are designed to please various gods of weather, deities representing the trees, the hunt, engineering prowess, fertility—as well as darker spirits who symbolized the threats and terrors of the forest.

At various times of the year, the Ewoks hold extravagant festivals of the rain and sun, springtime flowers, and fruits, as well as certain "Dark Rituals" involving bloody sacrifices. These rituals are held at night by the orange light of smoky bonfires, into which the shamans toss the green leaves of spiny hallucinogenic herbs that cause the Ewoks to have vivid dreams.

Every Ewok village appoints its own male or female mystic/shaman—the previously described con artist—who makes up answers about what the gods really want, how they can be pleased, how the Ewoks can make their prayers heard. For this "service," the village grants the shaman anything he or she could want: crystals, shells, polished skulls, and other items they find interesting. Most mystics wear a large animal skull on their head.

Some shamans are said to be "as old as the trees,"

apparently symbolizing their connection with the lifetrees and their imagined ability to communicate with the ancient Ewok spirits that dwell inside them. The shamans caper around with fetishes, beating drums and dancing. They also seem to know a few simple illusions, tricks, parlor magic. Their advice to the tribe leader is usually common sense delivered with an aura of mysticism.

Village mystics also pretend to be powerful healers, applying vile-smelling herbal medicines supposedly passed from generation to generation. Admittedly, many types of fungus, lichens, roots, berries, flowers, epiphytes, and bark may have some minimal medicinal effect, but I suspect the greatest effectiveness of these "cures" comes from the imagination and faith of the hapless Ewok patients.

Ewok villages adhere to a rigid clan system, like the Imperial military. Only, instead of molded white body armor, they use different raggedy garments for head coverings or hoods, apparently to signify an Ewok's place in the hunting order or the family unit.

Ewok warriors wear wooden chest shields, the jawbones of small animals, and sharp teeth. Others ornament themselves with feathers, necklaces made of crystals, pendants

An example of an Ewok "shaman"—the ones who talk to trees and get mysterious messages from the forest, and who call upon primitive superstitions and "magic" to defy Imperial authority.

***(pages 122-123)* An Ewok lake village in a mountainous section of the terrain. These tenacious creatures find some way to inhabit every spot of the terrain on this forest moon.**

121

of polished rock or shells, making their bodies look like a clutter of trinkets and junk. Prominent members of the Ewok village carry totems as symbols of rank. The lead warrior wears a headdress made of pale feathers, "the white wings of hope." The eldest son of the tribal leader's family wears the "red wings of courage," while the second son wears the "blue wings of strength."

Ewoks share strong family ties, appearing especially attached to their fuzzy, grublike children. The whole village fawns over newborn babies, smothering them with affection and attention, considering the care of the young a shared responsibility, even though the things look like bristly rodents to be squashed underfoot.

The Forest Moon provides plenty of food for scavengers to eat and sweet mattberries to squeeze for their juice (which is mixed with water and fermented into a bitter but intoxicating brew).

Even with their diminutive size, the Ewoks laughably consider themselves great hunters. Solitary hunters snare small animals, but occasionally an entire hunting party of Ewok warriors will set a deadly trap for larger meat animals—such as the boar-wolves.

Shaggy boar-wolves have tusk teeth, a keen sense of smell, and saberlike claws that can tear holes in trees. Though they have a penchant for howling at the silvery gas-planet in the night sky, these truly impressive predators possess an incredible patience to hide and wait out of sight once they have cornered their prey. They have fed on many Ewoks this way.

Though the boar-wolves are three times as tall as the Ewoks, the scurrying little creatures have somehow stumbled upon effective methods for fighting the monsters with spears and poison darts: The Ewoks first bait a clever trap with scraps of bloody meat from other kills and carefully hide a vine net on the forest floor. When a boar-wolf attempts to rip into the fresh meat, the net tangles around its huge armored body, enough to slow and confuse it while the Ewok hunting party charges out of the underbrush. One such kill provides enough meat to feed an Ewok tree village for days, if one could stomach the pungent and stringy meat.

In our travels across Endor, we also encountered a shallow, placid lake on which live another tribe of Ewoks. The squeaky vermin have built their huts on stilts out in the glassy-smooth water, where the water and surrounding marshes protect them from large predators. These Ewoks get most of their food by setting wicker traps for succulent crustaceans in the lake.

Older Ewoks spend their time harvesting the tough marsh grasses and flattening them to dry in the sun; they plait the dry, fibrous grasses into ragged mats, clothing, baskets, and decorative tapestries. The young lake Ewoks love to splash in the water and dig in the mud for buried shellfish, which keeps them filthy with caked dirt.

A tribe of cliff-dwelling Ewoks has made its home on a sheer rock face beside a spraying waterfall. Suicidally ignorant Ewok engineers somehow installed a primitive but intricate set of waterwheels, driven by the force of falling water. These turning waterwheels drive large wooden gears that rotate grindstones, operate conveyor belts from one part of the cliff village to another, and run a set of lift platforms up and down the cliff.

We happened to witness a revered annual event, at which representatives from the scattered Ewok tribes gather for a series of games. These "tribal games" allow them to show off their primitive antics. The Ewok revelers engage in dancing and storytelling, though some of the other activities are far more dangerous.

The most popular game among young Ewoks is to show off their prowess in tree-jumping. Ewok contestants climb to the top of the tallest lifetree, then leap off the highest limb. They must somehow catch themselves on lower limbs, jump off other

Though they show no scientific skills of their own, many Ewoks are inquisitive about technology, occasionally to their detriment.

branches, and continue to descend all the way to the ground at a breathtaking breakneck speed. Tragic accidents occur when an Ewok athlete misses a branch and plummets to the hard forest floor amid much shrieking and chattering from the other spectators. It is enough to give one a headache.

Though Ewoks enjoy tribal ceremonies, singing and playing music on primitive drums, they spend endless hours exchanging incessant stories in their bubbly, jabbering language. They have kept alive a strong oral tradition, spending many an evening's entertainment telling and retelling the exploits of legendary (and probably imaginary) Ewok warriors, great hunts against huge predators, and lone quests to other parts of the Forest Moon. Even now they are probably still telling of the marvels of truly impressive Imperial technology, which we showed them for the first time.

On our travels we found that the initial Imperial survey had missed yet another race of intelligent creatures (not that it was any surprise). These troublemakers are similar in size to the Ewoks but able to move much faster. If it is possible for a life-form to be even more unlikable than an Ewok, these creatures succeed in that area.

Some Ewoks have inadvertently stumbled upon the secret of flight through the use of crude gliders (above). Teeks (below) are fast-moving troublemakers.

Teeks are rodentlike, simian creatures that live in the forest, scavenging and stealing things from animal nests and from Ewok dwellings. The Ewoks don't like Teeks at all, considering it a sure sign of trouble even to be seen with one of the creatures.

Though Teeks are accomplished thieves and collectors of all kinds of things, they do not consider themselves dishonest, since they leave a trinket or token of equivalent value. What the Teek considers "equal value" is often very different from what the original owner of the stolen object might expect. We learned this upon finding some of our scanners and sophisticated tools replaced with dried seedpods and polished beetle shells.

Teeks have long, pointy ears and scruffy white fur, beady black eyes, and a propensity for constant chattering. A set of buckteeth makes them look stupid and goatish, but their hands are agile and fast, amazingly so. Teeks wear rudimentary clothing, with many belts, pouches, and pockets for those items they manage to snatch.

Teeks have evolved an enormously fast metabolism, which allows them to put on bursts of incredible speed, for fleeing both from enemies and from the victims of their thievery. We attempted to shoot a specimen for our collection, but each time the chattering, dashing Teeks escaped.

As my team and I continued our mechanical march across the landscape, all of our AT-ST transports broke down at the foothills of the rocky highlands. All of them at once! Muttering about low-bid Imperial contracts, we left the defective vehicles sitting at the base of a steep ridge and set off on foot. The retrieval teams would come and get us in a few days anyway, and we were sick to death of the towering forests. Give me a stark landscape any day.

To the north the dense, claustrophobic forests ended in an abrupt line of the sheer Yawari Cliffs, where the land has dropped away in a titanic slump. I could imagine ignorant Ewoks jour-

R. MCQUARRIE

neying to the edge of the cliffs from above, seeing the world below swathed in morning mist—they must have believed they had found the edge of the world.

Inaccessible, wind-tunneled caves dot the open face of soft sandstone, and we made our way to the shelter they offered. Apparently the Ewoks had invented a crude skin-glider to fly in the thermals

rising against the bright rock face and to land on broad ledges.

At the time, though, we did not know that inside some of the larger caves live the carnivorous condor dragons, flying reptilian creatures with bony ridges along their spines and grasping front claws for capturing prey in flight. The condor dragons walk on

Ewok tree cities are quaint, primitive structures built from the natural materials on Endor and inhabited by generations of these furry vermin.

two legs inside their eyrie caves, hunched over with wings curled in front of them. We know—we saw one firsthand, and it took the combined firepower of our stormtrooper escorts just to stun one so that we could examine it.

A condor dragon has a single fused fang for tearing through the thick hides of its prey, and two long lower tusks for brutal stabs and a quick kill. Large yellow eyes with round black pupils have extremely sharp vision, able to spot moving prey even through dense treetop foliage.

Agile flyers on their leathery wings, the condor dragons cry out with piercing shrieks, hoping to startle small animals from cover. Impressive beasts. The condor dragon snatches its victim, then flies back toward its eyrie cave. If the prey struggles too much during the flight, the dragon simply drops it, then swoops down to snatch the smashed body from the sharp tangle of branches below. The condor dragon will eat its fresh meat dead or alive; it isn't picky.

Back in its cave and stuffed with a heavy meal, the condor dragon falls into a stuporous sleep, curled in a dark corner, where it looks like a leathery boulder. Luckily the one we encountered had not yet recovered from its groggy slumber, and so we survived. If our timing had been different, we would have joined the bones strewing the cave floor....

Once we had succeeded in scaling the Yawari Cliffs, we found the terrain becoming worse yet, dryer and harsher, with few living plants and only poisonous insects. Rather like the stormtrooper academy on Carida.

The terrible Desert of Salma is a land of acid pools and dry lakes, where the ground is caked, dried mud. Frequent dust storms, powered by brutal high winds, scour away all trails and would have blinded us except for the sensors embedded in our visors. Many bones and mummified corpses lay buried among the baked rocks and the lifeless chemical soil. I hope some of them are Ewoks.

Beyond the blistering desert rise limestone bluffs, like bone-white mounds of ancient candlewax. Very picturesque. However, in this harsh landscape dwells the most fearsome of all creatures indigenous to the Forest Moon of Endor—the giant Gorax.

Incredibly massive, the Gorax is a true behemoth more than thirty meters high, pushing the limits of growth even

Natural predators of the Ewoks, the giant Goraxes break into even the highest of tree villages and take captives for their own amusement back to their caves in the rocky highlands.

in the low gravity of the Forest Moon. The Goraxes live in their high crags, making their homes inside immense grottoes.

The Goraxes look vaguely humanlike, with tapered primate faces and narrow chins. They make grunting, roaring noises that seem to convey raw emotion—anger, amusement, hunger—but no discernible words. The Goraxes wear fur clothes held together by large, rough stitches. For weapons they fashion stone axes from slabs of rock lashed onto handles made from entire tree trunks. Imagine what fighters they could be, if the Emperor could

figure out how to train them.

The Goraxes hang enormous ornaments upon their bodies, rings the size of docking ports dangling on their earlobes, beads the size of boat anchors in their hair. Their large, pointed ears are the size of dragons' wings, swept back and curved to be highly sensitive to the noises of smaller creatures.

The giants thrive on heat and keep a bright fire blazing in their caves at all times. Since they live out in the deep desert, the Goraxes must make frequent expeditions to the forest to gather fallen trees. Because the Goraxes live in shadowy caves, their glittering-black eyes are unaccustomed to bright lights, and they are easily blinded. Therefore, the Goraxes hunt primarily at night.

I ceased being so enamored of these monsters, though, at about the time our entire party was captured by one of the behemoths.

Although they are primitive and powerful, Goraxes like to keep pets. For instance, a Gorax will find a boar-wolf mother who has gone to ground in a cave to give birth to a litter of young. The Gorax smashes open her whelping place, kills the new mother, and selects a young boar-wolf pup it wants for its pet. In keeping with its own fondness for

bodily ornamentation, the Gorax will strap leather collars and harnesses on his pup, raising it as a hunting companion.

In search of other pets, the Goraxes kidnap Ewoks, smashing through the walls of their tree-city huts and grabbing a handful of wriggling furry captives. Unfortunately the giants have limited intelligence and an extremely short attention span. Some of their pets starve through lack of attention; others die when the Gorax grows bored and kills them.

Similarly, the Gorax took great delight in finding our bright white-armored forms scrambling among the rocks, and it managed to capture all of us. Hunting by night, as usual, one Gorax was attracted by the defensive lights around our camp perimeter. The Gorax smashed the bright lights and then chased us around the rocks, scooping up every single member of our party.

As the stormtrooper escorts rushed out, setting up tripods for their portable blaster cannons, the Gorax grabbed the struggling white captives and stuffed them into a sack at its hip. Before long, I found myself shoved in with them as well. There seemed to be no escape.

Satisfied with its night's work, the Gorax marched back to its cave, where it placed all of us in a huge hanging cage made of lashed logs. Apparently curious, the Gorax wanted to see what lay beneath the shiny white shells of the new creatures, and so the giant prodded the five stormtroopers to peel away the armor. The Gorax grew frustrated, then tore the armor away itself. None of its new pets survived the inspection.

Luckily the Gorax lost interest quickly and collapsed onto its heap of sleeping furs, snoring like a thunderstorm in the close confines of the cave. Seeing our chance, we used the laser cutters in the packs—finally, a piece of Imperial-issue equipment that actually worked!—to hack our way free of the crude cage and flee out of the winding caves to the lower catacombs.

One fearsome creature that has formed a symbiotic—or perhaps parasitic—relationship with the giant Gorax is the "rearing spider," a massive but slow-moving beast. Six-legged, with large tusks instead of piercing fangs, rearing spiders reside in the bottoms of caves inhabited by the Gorax, living on scraps discarded by the giants and disposing of the remains of forgotten pets. The rearing spiders spin large, thick webs across expanses of the caves—but these webs are primarily nests, rather than traps to capture prey. While they will attack intruders when provoked, rearing spiders mainly hide in the

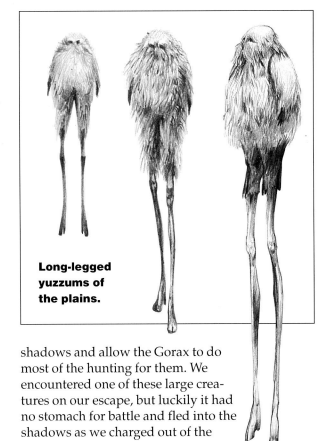

Long-legged yuzzums of the plains.

shadows and allow the Gorax to do most of the hunting for them. We encountered one of these large creatures on our escape, but luckily it had no stomach for battle and fled into the shadows as we charged out of the Gorax's lair. In the dimness of the Endor-lit night, we raced across the desolation, fleeing the land of the Gorax.

West of the densely forested terrain lie oceans and oceans of grass, plains of dry brown in summer, blankets of velvety bright green after the spring rains. The delineation between arid savanna and thick forest is very abrupt. In clumps in the hollows of rolling hills are islands of trees, a slash of dark green on the wind-rippled plains, where small animals make their homes.

We trudged out into the vast grasslands, seeking safety and shelter until the return ship could retrieve us. My Ewok-loving comrade told me that the furry vermin call this savanna the Dragon's Pelt. I told him to shut up.

As far as the eye can see, the rolling brown grasses are studded with dark lava rocks that jut like blackened teeth out of the ground. A range of snowy mountains, the Dragon's Spine, lies across the horizon in the distance, but it was much too far away for us to reach.

One night on our plodding journey we were visited by what I can only call fairylights at our evening campfires. These tiny, luminous flying creatures come out at night with buzzing, squeaking noises. Swarms of them were attracted by fires and our

Yuzzums wade through the grass, hoping to catch *ruggers*, succulent rodents that they roast over open fires on the prairie.

presence. We tried to shoo them away, but nothing seemed to work, and the things continued to pester us long into the darkness. The fairylights did no obvious harm, other than forcing us to lose sleep with their flashing, spinning, dizzying light shows.

We could not tell for certain what the fairylights eat, or even whether they are true life-forms rather than just strange bright phenomena. The lights seemed to absorb firelight as a source of nourishment, but one of my surviving companions insisted that they thrived on happy emotions and expression of warm feelings, such as laughter or giggles.

If this is so, then they got very little nourishment from me.

On the following day we ran into a swarm of yuzzums, creatures even less intelligent than Ewoks, that dwell on the plains of Endor. Standing tall on stilt-like legs above the whipping dry grasses, yuzzums wade through the savanna, looking down and searching for rodent-like ruggers running through the grass to their communal warrens.

Yuzzums have a wide mouth with protruding teeth, and a shock of dark hair on top of their heads. Groups of yuzzums stride side by side through the tall grasses, searching for a fresh rugger meal. At times, when a yuzzum manages to snatch a rodent sunning itself on a rock, he will eat the rugger raw, snapping the entire thing down his gullet, fur and bones and all.

At other times, a yuzzum hunting party will burn narcotic weeds into the holes of the rodent warrens. The small furred creatures stagger out, seemingly dizzy and delirious—easy pickings for the yuzzums to thrust into large sacks. Then the yuzzums have a rugger-roast over a crackling bonfire near one of the clusters of dark trees in the hollows. The yuzzums skewer the small creatures on sticks and, after roasting them, ritually stride about on their stilt-legs, feeding each other the sizzling meat, offering pieces to their companions and eating only what others offer to them. We found the whole ritual sickening and disgusting.

Yuzzums are partially intelligent, but seem unable to understand any life-form but their own. Which was fine, since we ignored them right back. I had, of course, heard of yuzzums before, as they were kidnapped at one time to be sold throughout the Empire by black marketeers as slaves or pets.

I recalled vividly that one smuggler had tried to pay off a long-outstand ing debt to Jabba the Hutt with a cargo of yuzzums. Instead Jabba fed the smuggler to his rancor in the pit, along with several of the yuzzum prisoners. The rancor didn't much care for the yuzzum meat, though. As I understand it, some of the kidnapped yuzzums can still be found hanging, mostly forgotten, in Jabba's dungeons.

At last we encountered civilization. Of a sort. But our choices were limited on Endor. Some of the most fearsome creatures on Endor live out on the Dragon's Pelt savanna. The reptilian marauders work together in a powerful military fashion to bring terror to the Ewoks and cause damage out of sheer spite. How could we not like them? The marauders have greasy, thick strands of hair, usually pale, sometimes dark, sprouting from the crowns of their flat heads, occasionally from the skin on their faces. Heavy protective brow ridges thrust like hoods over glittering eyes; pug nose-holes give the marauders a skull-like appearance.

They captured us, dragging us into their castle, but we could tell we were among like-minded creatures. The long-lived marauders originated off-planet and crashed nearly a century ago on the Forest Moon. As they tortured and interrogated us, we picked up a few details of their situation as well.

The marauders had once imagined themselves to be great pirates of the spaceways—but because none of them understood how to pilot their stolen ships, their reign of terror and plunder proved much shorter than they had expected. They came in a stolen ship they were barely able to pilot under the best of circumstances, and the navigator could not handle the complex gravity patterns in the Endor system (see my earlier comment).

Though the navigator survived the crash, he was executed immediately for his unconscionable failure. None of the other marauders had the slightest

131

idea how to repair their ship and get off the moon, and with the navigator dead they had no idea where to go on to from here.

Resigned to their fate, the marauders built a large ancient-style castle, which comforted them with its imposing stone walls. They cannibalized parts of their wrecked spaceship as furniture. For his throne, the marauder King Terak tore the captain's chair from the bridge of the dilapidated ship and placed it in his royal audience chamber.

Carved, horned lava-rock obelisks guard the front approach to the castle, warning off enemies and boasting of the murderous prowess of the marauders. The castle itself looks clumsy and squarish, with no finesse—but it is very sturdy, made of quarried stone blocks hauled by blurrgs, their beasts of burden.

Stones around the castle entranceway shout out with crude carved hieroglyphs, but many of the words are impossible to interpret, since few of the marauders can read or write Basic.

The castle is surrounded by a deep moat filled with black water. While constructing the castle, one of the marauders suggested installing the still functioning automatic defense mechanisms from their crashed ship for further protection against assault. A selective disintegrator field, shaped like a torpedo, targets any object that touches the water. (The marauders themselves fear this defense greatly, because they have forgotten how to turn it off!)

Terak, the king of the marauders, holds his mercenary pirates together while he searches for a new power source to be installed in their long-disassembled attack ship. He expects the solution to their exile to be a simple one, a gadget he can add to the abandoned ship so that it can take off again even after decades of disrepair.

Terak himself doesn't remember why he is searching for a power pack, but he is obsessed with get-

The marauders of Endor are creatures more akin to Imperial understanding, though pathetic in their own way. They revere their powerful technology, though they have forgotten how to use it.

ting the power—even though he would not know what to do with it if he held it in his scaly hands. However, he could be a useful ally, if the Emperor wishes to join forces (in name only) with a warlord already on Endor.

His companion, Charal, is a female shape-shifter, a Force-wielding witch who apparently escaped from her exile on a planet called Dathomir. Working by her form-changing deception, Charal fell in with the band of reptilian marauders when they were already in their last days, while they were being hunted down by combined space law forces…as was Charal herself. She intended to stay with Terak and his raiders only long enough to get herself another passage to freedom—but the shipwreck on

Endor ruined everything.

The lower-ranking marauders are staunchly loyal and subservient to their leader, but otherwise they are obsessed with rank and title among themselves. Over their decades-long exile, the marauders have made up new ranks and titles for themselves so that everyone has an impressive-sounding place—but no one exactly understands the hierarchy anymore. Nevertheless, these communal creatures prefer to be in large groups, feasting in banquet halls, playing card games with each other, even marching out to raid the Ewoks. They do not feel comfortable being alone.

Because they are stranded on Endor, and because they know no way other than preying on weaker people, the marauders regularly raid Ewok tree villages just inside the forest boundary, burning their dwellings and taking the Ewoks prisoner for use as slaves to perform manual labor. See, another reason for accepting them as allies!

When marching out for battle, the marauders wear helmets and armor cobbled together from scraps of their old protective suits, junk, metal, and thin shielding plate peeled off the abandoned ship. Inside their helmets and boots and across their chests they wear yuzzum-fur ornamentation, as well as capes and suits made from blurrg hide and condor dragon pelts. Before marching out on a great attack, the marauders blow battle horns and carry banners to symbolize their individual ranks. Despite the imposing appearance of their blockish castle and their leftover blasters and other high-tech weapons, the marauders have a very rudimentary understanding of technology, which often causes more harm than good when they try to use it.

The one technological thing the marauders understand is their weapons—most of which are simple old-style blasters and blaster cannons. They have managed to keep most of their weapons working decade after decade, though now many are cloth-wrapped, rusted, and barely functional.

As a last resort, the marauders are also proficient with long swords for hand-to-hand combat.

The marauders have successfully domesticated large two-legged savannah beasts—blurrgs—for their heavy labor. The top-heavy monsters look primarily like a bloated reptilian head standing on two meaty legs with splayed three-toed feet, balanced from behind by a lashing tail. The blurrg's mouth, huge out of proportion even to the size of its enormous head, is a constant eating machine for shoveling savannah grass, weeds, saplings, and anything else edible that gets in its way.

The blurrgs are stupid and slow, but very strong. Marauders control them with spiked chain bridles, riding on their smooth backs with stiff saddles, though occasionally the beasts fight back in a slow, reflexive way.

At first the marauders attempted to use blurrgs as attack creatures, but the creatures simply did not react fast enough, nor could they be provoked into anything more than a slightly riled stupor.

Blurrgs are so stupid they walk right into small trees, knocking them down with their massive-stone-skulled heads. A blurrg might overestimate its own strength, or underestimate the strength of the tree, and batter itself senseless trying to crash through a thicket, rather than just going around. Blurrrgs can get hopelessly tangled in the underbrush, unable to remember how to get back out again.

The marauders took us down into their dungeons, and they took all of our weapons and posses-

The marauders of Endor are a brutal lot, stranded on the Forest Moon because they do not have the skills to fix the technology they have stolen. Their leader Terak *(top)* and his shape-shifting Nightsister partner Charal *(left)* keep the rowdy marauders in line through sheer intimidation.

sions, but in the end they tortured only one of us to death. The Force witch Charal, who called herself a Nightsister, freed us after making us promise to take her with us when the retrieval ship homed in on our beacons—but Terak grew angry with her and tossed her into a cage even as we escaped into the savanna, watching the lights of the retrieval ship plunge through the evening skies.

We ran to the open doors of the retrieval ship, only three survivors out of the original nine, as the marauders pursued us, but a few blaster shots from the ship frightened them off.

We left Endor with nothing more than our memories and my report. The final decision is up to the Emperor, of course, but I hope he chooses never to return to this unpleasant Forest Moon.

Marauders often take captives, using *blurrgs*, their dinosaur-like beasts of burden. In this manner, they maintain their reign of terror and keep the Ewoks under control.

BESPIN

ABOUT THE AUTHOR:

Councilman Po Ruddle Lingsnot is an amazing success story in the annals of Cloud City: a former used-cloud-car salesman who got himself elected to the Council on Tourism and Extra-Planetary Investment, he is now an established member of the Exex, the ruling bureaucratic class in the city. A tireless promoter, Councilman Lingsnot is not content to remain in his plush offices or simply attend meetings—he is present at every vital civic event, a smiling welcome for each interplanetary dignitary who comes to Cloud City. He makes no secret of the fact that he would love to be Baron-Administratory someday. In person, Councilman Lingsnot spends his every breath extolling the virtues of the planet Bespin, as he has also done in this report describing his cloudy world.

BESPIN

The gas giant Bespin is an isolated world renowned for its productive gas-mining facilities and its peaceful relaxation environment, as well as wildly extravagant gambling in the luxury resort levels of Cloud City, which is itself the most famous floating metropolis in the galaxy. Yes, Bespin is an untapped resource, one of the best-kept investment secrets in high-rolling financial circles—a world that has something for everyone.

The planet Bespin rotates rapidly, once every twelve hours, giving two full "days" and "nights" for every standard day. The cloud layers are 1,000 kilometers thick above a metal core buried deep within tumultuous outer layers of seething high-pressure liquid and denser gases reaching temperatures of some 6,000°C. This cauldron has brewed some of the most valuable chemicals and gases in the sector, and mining activities have so far barely touched the potential of this world's wealth.

Bespin's economy has branched out in two primary directions—industrialized gas mining to exploit the rich resources of the gas giant, and lavish tourism catering to the wealthy classes looking for a truly exotic holiday.

BESPIN'S INDUSTRIAL INVESTMENT OPPORTUNITIES—TAP INTO A FOUNTAIN OF WEALTH

As proof that this is no fluke, no fly-by-night mineral strike, the resources of Bespin have been quietly excavated for many years. Our history is a saga of foresight, daring, and extravagant riches.

The legendary Lord Ecclessis Figg, well-known Corellian explorer and investor, discovered a pleasant surprise on his inspection of supposedly unremarkable Bespin: Large concentrations of pure Tibanna gas lay in the upper atmosphere. Tibanna

gas has long been treasured as a hyperdrive coolant; no better substance has ever been found to serve this purpose, and thus it has been widely sought after by entrepreneurs in every sector.

Usually found in stellar chromospheres and deep in nebular cores, Tibanna gas has always proved difficult to extract from the

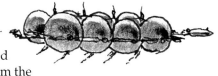

source. Unlike other concentrations, Bespin's Tibanna gas was—and is!—easily accessible. Further assays, which Figg conducted in strict secrecy, showed the clouds to be filled with extractable quantities of other valuable gaseous compounds as well, which were often flung into the upper atmospheric levels by deep storms.

Being a shrewd businessman, Figg saw his chance to become enormously rich—if he could pull his scheme off. With his flamboyant personality, Figg wooed and then married a lesser noble from the Royal House of Alderaan; she made her private fortune available to him and his eccentric pursuits. His previous ventures had been marginally successful in various parts of the galaxy, but finally he paid her back ten times over with his fabulously successful gas mining facilities on Bespin.

A technical note: When it is excited by high frequencies, Tibanna gas produces intense packets of light that can be focused into destructive blaster beams. If compressed and "spin-sealed," Tibanna gas produces four times the energy output of other competing gases for weapons production. Normally the spin-sealing process requires incredi-

On Bespin, marvelous air transportation systems are available for all of our valued tourists, regardless of body size or configuration.

ble energy, so few companies have tried it on a commercial scale—but Lord Figg also discovered that Tibanna gas from deep in Bespin is *naturally* spin-sealed. Thus, Bespin Tibanna gas is superior to all competitive products on the market.

Figg's first mining stations were simple automated containment vessels that descended into the thick clouds, filled themselves with atmospheric gases, then returned to processing ships in orbit. As with many first steps in a large operation, however, these nonselective mining stations proved very

Cloud City is a magnificent sight, particularly at dawn, when the pale sun slants through the high-rising clouds. The skyline displays a wealth of fine hotels.

wasteful, since most of the captured gas was useless.

The next foothold established on Bespin occurred when Lord Figg erected the *Floating Home* mining colony, our first permanent settlement. As a gathering point, *Floating Home* launched the boom of fortune hunters trying to strike it rich mining the gas clouds—a boom that continues unabated to this day.

Riding the wind currents around the planet, numerous other airborne mining installations were constructed—floating automated refineries, storage tanks bobbing above the clouds, and skimmer facilities to scoop gases from different levels of Bespin's cloudbanks.

For the more volatile gases and other elements extracted from Bespin's atmosphere, stand-alone floating refineries dot the clouds. These refineries are carefully isolated, given special detection and motivation systems to keep their industrial odors and noises away from populated floating cities.

The skies of Bespin are large, giving plenty of room for everyone and every purpose.

In a major mining installation such as Cloud City, the Tibanna gas is drawn up through the central core, where it is pressurized, refined, encased in carbonite, and stored. With hyperspace shipping systems in place, the freshly mined gas is efficiently distributed across the galaxy.

Since Tibanna gas is also a crucial component in the phasing chambers of high-powered blasters and turbolasers, the Empire has restricted its distribution, but Cloud City business-creatures have found

GAS PROSPECTORS

Bespin welcomes free spirits, and not all commercial exploitation is under the control of Figg & Associates. A small but important group of hardworking individualists ply the clouds as gas prospectors.

Gas prospectors pilot their own container ships, scrappy, cobbled-together vessels, sometimes assembled from components scavenged from abandoned gas refineries. These picturesque folk are a colorful, albeit infrequent, sight across Bespin's skyscape.

The prospectors search for "gas strikes," such as when a plume of deep gas spurts into the heights because of deep internal storms in the lower levels of the atmosphere.

Bespin's rapid rotation gives rise to intense storms and high winds, occasionally belching up gas products synthesized in the churning furnace far below. Often these gas geysers are detected by our orbiting satellite network, and the race is on between behemoth-sized corporate mining ships and scrambling gas-prospector crews to see who will reach the lucrative strike first.

Some gas prospectors, seeking riches from a fruitful outburst, ride extremely close to storm systems, hovering on the edges and waiting for gas eruptions. Unfortunately, the unpredictable storms frequently prove too much for the heroic lone prospectors, and many vanish without a trace. The violent storms take the prospectors, their rickety vehicles, and their gaseous cargo into the depths of the clouds.

ways to work within the law to arrange distribution through alternative channels. While it has been suspected that much of the contraband Tibanna gas used to manufacture weaponry used by the Rebel Alliance comes from Bespin, no conclusive proof of this has ever been presented.

Unfortunately, due to the too-rapid industrial expansion at the beginning of Bespin's boom years, not all of the floating installations proved profitable. Hopeful investors overestimated the de-

Tibanna gas refineries process and store this valuable substance on which the economy of Bespin rests *(above)*. Other, smaller levitating cities drift near the refineries *(left)*.

(pages 146-147) The abandoned city of Tibannopolis, a derelict boomtown in the sky, is a landmark that is often visited by young students of history.

Sky traffic patrols ensure the safety of all cloud-car passengers and pilots, especially around restricted areas such as the damaged sections of Tibannopolis.

mand for certain gases, and prices fluctuated disastrously. Independent, self-sustaining operations ran into enormous expenditures just to keep the repulsorlifts operating for huge metal constructions. Unlike space stations in orbit, Bespin's floating cities hang free in the atmosphere, requiring great force literally to "keep themselves afloat."

When such facilities went bankrupt, their owners usually shut down the repulsorlift reactors and sent the entire construction plunging into the cloud depths below.

One drifting colossus was left hanging empty, though—a huge creaking ghost town in the sky, named Tibannopolis. The ruins of Tibannopolis, tilted at an angle, still hang above the roiling, dark clouds. The energy cores of the repulsorlift generators are slowly dwindling over the years, beginning to malfunction.

Because the people of Bespin are so hardworking and resourceful, the roof, decks, and sides of derelict

Tibannopolis have been picked over. The empty structure looks like a floating skeleton, with its buckled plates and twisted support girders in a broad hemisphere and its dented ballast tanks slung below. Numerous antennae and weather vanes protrude from the joints.

The wreck of Tibannopolis is a popular place for sight-seeing, though. Daredevils frequently go there, as if they consider it the neighborhood "haunted house." On a warmer note, the empty city is also a spot frequently used by young lovers for secret trysts—what it lacks in luxury, it makes up for in privacy!

In a misty transition layer of clouds, a marvelous and surprising ecosystem thrives among floating rafts of stable algae. Sightseers might encounter exotic flying creatures *(left and above)*, many of which have never been catalogued.

NATURAL WONDERS—EXOTIC LIFE IN THE CLOUDS

With only air and mist and clouds, and its only surface deep, deep below and at immense pressures, Bespin might not seem a likely place for a broad ecology. But life is wonderful and tenacious across the galaxy, and this planet is no exception.

Rudimentary floating life—from microscopic algae clusters to huge balloonlike beldons—thrives in the temperate atmospheric levels, metabolizing the sunlight, breathable gases, water vapor, and concentrations of other nutrients. Some of the galaxy's most prominent exozoologists have come to study the creatures of Bespin, and tourists marvel at their color and their beauty.

Self-contained plankton bubbles drift about in clumps, beside wispy concentrations of algae.

The algae nodules form around ice crystals and water droplets in the clouds. The algae clusters eventually fill with air pockets, causing the greenish mass to

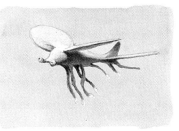

settle at an atmospheric level where their pressure is equalized. One species of floating algae, "pinks," is so plentiful that the clouds of Bespin have a distinctive rosy tinge.

Another species of algae, "glowers," inhabits the deeper cloud layers. On the night side of the planet, a purplish glow can be seen. Wind currents and convection bring wisps of mist teeming with glower-algae, causing the night sky below to look like a bizarre luminous landscape. Often at night the people of Cloud City sit out and watch from the upper decks or the lower observation lounges to see the eerie, swirling purplish clouds, backlit by occasional flashes of lightning buried under the thick mists. It is a breathtaking sight.

Lovers of flying creatures will enjoy observing the leathery,

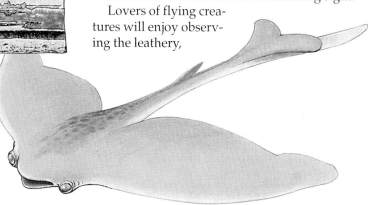

batlike scavengers, called rawwks, that inhabit many of the floating structures, especially the abandoned ruins of Tibannopolis. Flocks of rawwks cluster in open girders, nesting and reproducing. Every day they fly in great waves down to feast on floating algae beds.

In the high-pressure levels of the atmosphere, much like the deep-sea lifeforms on ocean worlds, are extremely bizarre uncataloged creatures, as well as the enormous floating animals called beldons.

Beldons are giant balloonlike gas bags that metabolize the natural chemicals at the slushy gas-liquid-solid interface far down in Bespin's atmosphere.

Beldons occasionally rise high enough to be observed in the temperate levels of the atmosphere. Anecdotal accounts from solitary gas prospectors and station managers on isolated gas refineries tell of seeing huge beldons like giant sails floating above colonies of algae, dipping down with their numerous hair-thin tentacles to feed. The most frequent sightings occur at Bespin's poles.

Beldons may be long-lived, and they may be herd animals. Only one specimen has been studied closely, found floating dead after apparently being burst apart in a lightning storm. But the carcass was so huge it could not be hauled anywhere for storage much less a thorough dissection.

It has been postulated, with a great deal of enthusiasm and only circumstantial evidence, that beldons possibly give off Tibanna gas as an exhalation product.

For this reason, the Ruling Council of Cloud City has wisely forbidden hunting beldons, lest they destroy the creatures responsible for the precious substance on which so much of our economy depends. However, tourists are welcome to take advantage of the numerous chartered expeditions that will take cloud cars through a beldon herd, if one happens to be floating high and near enough to Cloud City.

Beldons are surrounded by a small electric field, which they use to detect the approach of intruders. This electric field helps them avoid ships, approaching storms, and natural predators. When clustered together as a herd, the beldons' electrical "sensor net" can extend for hundreds of kilometers, occasionally going so far as to interfer with vehicular traffic in the area.

Beldons move about by pumping exhaust gases, self-generated electric fields, or they just drift about on the winds. Their only defense against the predators of Bespin—such as packs of flying velkers—is their massive size. Even so, one beldon will sacrifice itself to allow the rest of the herd to escape.

Velkers are V-shaped natural killers, with tough claws and armored wings evolved to tear and disable the tough outer skins of beldons. Velkers hunt in packs because it takes a large group to rip apart their enormous prey. When killing a beldon, the velkers swarm onto its outer skin and begin to systematically shred it with meter-long claws, chewing the beldon flesh with rows of mouths that line their bellies.

Once a beldon's hide is breached, it begins leaking the gas that keeps it aloft, and slowly it sinks to lower levels. The velkers continue feasting for days until the beldon descends deep enough that the velkers fly off in search of other prey. The beldon victim eventually crashes into the liquid-gas interface layer far below.

Velkers can attain remarkable speeds in flight, soaring to extremely high altitudes. The flying predators have an electrical field surrounding their bodies as well, creating discharges that can damage passing cloud cars as well as beldons. Velkers seem to thrive on energy discharges from the great storms; it may be that they reproduce during such enormous electrical disturbances.

Velkers will attack small ships that approach them too closely. A large pack of velkers has even

The silent mysterious thranta riders (above and left) often paint themselves with amazing skin patterns. Only a few lucky tourists ever catch a glimpse of their tantalizing culture.

attacked Cloud City itself, as if mistaking the giant floating metropolis for a strange beldon. However, these incidents are rare, and usually cause no damage.

Some of our most interesting creatures, though, are not native to Bespin. A small herd of the flyers known as thrantas was transplanted from their world of Alderaan as possible beasts of burden to be used here among the clouds. Thrantas are floating beasts with broad, saillike wings and body cores composed mostly of a lighter-than-air bladder. After the destruction of Alderaan, Bespin's small herd of thrantas comprises the only surviving representatives of their magnificent species.

The Alderaanian thrantas were brought to Bespin with alien riders and wranglers. The riders perform a monthly "sky rodeo" of breathtaking feats, in which the talented alien riders leap out into the open sky, falling and falling until the thrantas swoop down to the rescue. The sky wranglers ask for volunteers from the audience, but they rarely have any takers.

CLOUD CITY—THE SILVER LINING OF BESPIN'S CLOUDS

Cloud City, one of the marvels of the galaxy, is a place to invest, to relax, to entertain… it is like nothing you have ever seen before.

This glamorous and beautiful metropolis is located at the planet's equator in a "temperate" band thirty kilometers deep. The atmospheric pressure and temperature are pleasant to human life, allowing Cloud City to dispense with expensive closed environments and sophisticated life-support systems.

The entire floating metropolis is over sixteen kilometers in diameter, seventeen kilometers from the top of Kerros Tower to the bottom of the reactor stalk hanging far below. Through the core of the city runs a vast hollow wind tunnel. Side tunnels, called

One of Bespin's greatest spectacles is the great sky rodeo, where talented thranta riders perform amazing acrobatic feats accompanied by cloud-car stunt flyers.

airways, bleed out of the wind tunnel to the surface, to dispel pressure differentials. Hatches open and close as winds caress the outside of Cloud City. Inside the wind tunnel, large rudderlike stabilizers direct the flow of air up and down, to keep the city level and stable even in gusting winds.

Cloud City is safe even during occasional heavy weather. The tall buildings on the upper surface of Cloud City are designed to be flexible and adaptable, to sway with Bespin's changing winds. Sophisticated weather-watching systems and dispersed satellite buoys have been deployed at various points in the atmosphere to provide an early warning of Bespin's occasional large storms, but most of the time the environment is idyllic and pleasant.

The upper surface of Cloud City displays many landing platforms, towers, and spires. In honor of Ecclessis Figg's wife, most of the city's architecture is based on Alderaan styles—polished white synthetic stone, high ceilings, parklike recreation areas, gently curving corridors. Consistent, soothing decorations with geometric designs and lines run throughout. Plazas and open areas give the impression of empty space and freedom even in a densely packed metropolis.

The popular upper levels of Cloud City contain hotels, spas, casinos, clubs, and museums (mostly describing the triumphs of Figg & Associates and their historic mining operations). Restaurants cater to their clientele's varied tastes and biochemistries, from human to Wookiee, Ithorian, Ugnaught, Twi'lek, and other cuisines.

The upper levels are also jammed with casinos and clubs, for which Cloud City is well known. To

ensure fairness in all of Cloud City's games, the Gambling Authority conducts frequent surprise inspections to flush out dirty dealings and occasional underworld interest. Cloud City prides itself on running clean games. The Gambling Authority also imposes taxes on winnings (10 percent of house winnings, 7 percent of personal winnings), which is fed back into the city's infrastructure and maintenance to make Cloud City a clean and beautiful place to live or visit.

Though originally established as a Tibanna gas–mining station, Cloud City has been called the most precious resort in the galaxy, a place of culture, relaxation, and excitment.

Under endless skies, the open pavilions and plazas of the upper decks are places to relax, meet new friends, and enjoy the riches Bespin has to offer.

CLOUD CITY
PUBLIC SHELTER

The architecture of Cloud City is clean and smooth, with sweeping, peaceful curves as gentle as the winds. Even on lower levels, staterooms look out upon the cloud vistas or inward to fountains or entertainment centers.

The next levels contain merchant quarters and expensive housing for high-level bureaucrats. Below that are administrative offices. The Merchants' Guild boasts 100,000 members, sellers of tourist items, luxuries, foodstuffs, contraband alcohol, gems, and other trinkets.

More economical real estate extends toward the core. Levels 121 through 160 are the low-rent areas, collectively called Port Town. Port Town is the home of many unlicensed casinos and gambling establishments—cantinas—hidden among the industrial loading docks. Port Town has gained its own sort of fame as home to all manner of smugglers, bounty hunters, and information merchants.

Sadly, these unlicensed Port Town casinos frequently prey on desperate people, those unfortunates who have bribed or smuggled their way onto ships bound for Bespin, trying to parlay their meager possessions into enough money to survive. Despite many significant social welfare projects, the Cloud City Ruling Council is at a loss for a solution to this problem.

The bottommost levels of Cloud City are devoted to the service sector, factories, gas processing plants, and mining quarters, as well as the tractor beam and repulsorlift generators.

Carbon-freezing chambers are used to lock volatile Tibanna gas into transportable chunks, the best way to transport the dangerous, high-energy spin-sealed material. An object is flash-frozen and then encased in carbonite, which holds the inner temperature constant, as if in stasis. Precious carbonite, which has a variable thermal conductivity, is mined from other systems—particularly the thick outer rings of a gas-giant in the Empress Teta system.

The citizenry of Cloud City consists of humans, droids, and aliens of all species and descriptions.

Certain factions in the city government disagree over major issues, such as whether to support the Empire or the Rebel Alliance in the growing political turmoil—though all branches are unified in their interest in keeping the Tibanna gas mining operation at a low profile to maintain our privacy and productivity. Publicly, Cloud City has declared itself neutral in the matter of the Rebellion, hoping to avoid Imperial peacekeeping forces. Our neutrality declaration also reassures tourists of safety when they travel to Bespin.

Three official branches of government exist in Cloud City—the Baron Administrator, the Exex, and the Parliament of Guilds. The post of the Baron Administrator, in a tradition established by Ecclessis Figg himself on his deathbed, is filled by appointment of the outgoing Administrator (or, failing that, a majority vote of the Exex). This has led to a wide variety of skill levels among those who have held the position, from inept, to corrupt, to master leaders.

The position of Baron Administrator has been bought, gambled away, or earned through blackmail, intimidation, and even assassination. Lando Calrissian himself became Cloud City's Baron Administrator when he won the position in an incredibly high-stakes game of sabacc.

The Exex are Cloud City's distinguished executive class, who perform the rigorous and ever-increasing paperwork duties without which no great metropolis could function. The Exex are a bureaucratic aristocracy formed from the managers of the original Figg & Associates gas mining operations. Their jobs are handed down from generation to generation, further fostering the impression of a nobility.

The overriding concern of the Exex—as of politicians everywhere—is to maintain the status quo and to minimize drastic changes for the citizenry. The Exex spend much of their time and energy hosting grueling diplomatic receptions, raffling off free cloud cruises to important officials in all governments on all planets. Exex often make highly effective use of small black messenger droids, motorized boxes that seek out a certain person to deliver important messages.

The third branch of government, the Parliament of Guilds, represents the workers and craftsmen in Cloud City. Delegates from the various guilds throughout the enormous city comprise the parliament, often haggling over new terms and rights among the working people.

UGNAUGHTS—AN EFFICIENT AND ENTHUSIASTIC WORKFORCE READY TO SERVE YOUR NEEDS

Small, hardworking, and loyal, the pug-faced Ugnaughts were the primary constructors of Cloud City. Ugnaughts are renowned for their mining ability, and Lord Ecclessis Figg used them to great effect in his various operations, which was one of the keys to his legendary success.

The Ugnaughts' stocky, compact bodies are efficient energy converters. They can withstand long periods of discomfort. Their original homeworld is long forgotten by them—they were taken away as slaves and dispersed many centuries ago. In this dark time, entire groups of Ugnaughts were sold or leased as "tribes" to large corporations for work on hellish worlds.

The benevolent Lord Figg, however, made an enormous investment to exploit his discovery of Tibanna gas—he bought three entire Ugnaught tribes and gave them a huge task and a huge incentive to do it: If they would build his Cloud City, he would grant the Ugnaughts their freedom and a

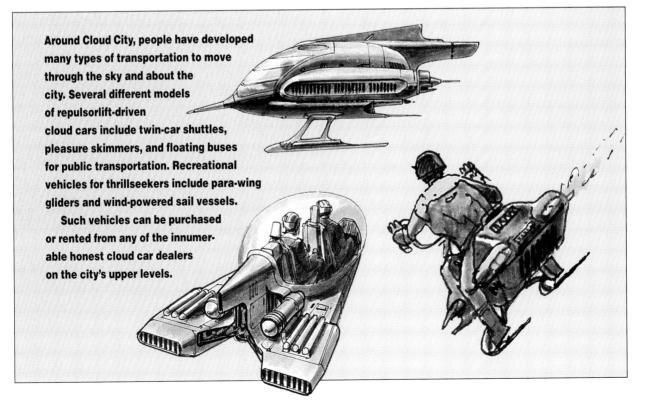

Around Cloud City, people have developed many types of transportation to move through the sky and about the city. Several different models of repulsorlift-driven cloud cars include twin-car shuttles, pleasure skimmers, and floating buses for public transportation. Recreational vehicles for thrillseekers include para-wing gliders and wind-powered sail vessels.

Such vehicles can be purchased or rented from any of the innumerable honest cloud car dealers on the city's upper levels.

place to live. The little creatures succeeded admirably, and Lord Figg kept his word.

Currently the free Ugnaughts have a lower level of the city to themselves, living in a burrow network, enclosed tunnels with dim reddish light and high humidity. They have also established access tunnels through all portions of the city, with completely concealed access hatches. The network is a veritable labyrinth of conduits, but even so, it still makes the Ugnaughts comfortable.

The Ugnaughts also have a rich oral tradition, keeping alive stories about other worlds on which they have served as slave workers. They have their own ruling councils, their own apprenticeship traditions, even representatives among the ruling councils in Cloud City. They have never forgotten Lord Figg for granting them their freedom.

Ugnaughts are fast-breeding, with a high propor-

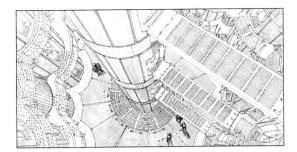

Cloud City *(left)* is also built on industry. In its lower levels, valuable Tibanna gas is spin-sealed and preserved in carbonite for shipment to meet the galaxy's needs.

The Yerith Bespin, Cloud City's finest hotel, is the favorite spot for visiting dignitaries and VIPs. More moderately priced lodging opportunities such as the Holiday Towers or the Stratosphere, are also available.

tion of females to males—all of whom are hard-working, providing a reliable and available work-force immediately on hand and at the proper loca-tion for those wishing to open a business in the city.

RECREATION OPPORTUNITES—A PLACE TO PLAY, A PLACE TO RELAX

Though Cloud City was established primarily as a great gas mining installation, it grew and gained fame as a resort and vacation spot for the rich. Now the luxury accommodations on Cloud City can be enjoyed by all sentient beings, on any budget.

Some alternative health schemes have extolled the air of Bespin for its therapeutic qualities. The wind has a bitter chemical tang from trace gases wafting to higher altitudes. Doctors still take dozens of patients out on circular platforms under floating parasols, flying into the mists of high-rising clouds. The patients lie prone on the smooth deck, wearing

only wispy sheetlike wraps, while the barge pilot flies through the chemical haze. The effectiveness of this treatment has not been clinically proved, but many visitors to Bespin are lavish in their praise of the technique.

Even while his mining operations were proving such a success, Ecclessis Figg saw an enormous opportunity to increase the offsystem money available to capitalize his investment. He remodeled and

Bespin's infrequent storms have an awesome beauty of their own—large, dark clouds and high winds that are braved only by the top-notch cloud-car pilots and skilled thranta riders.

(pages 162-163) Other sky complexes have appeared on Bespin to meet the needs of the growing tourist trade. Here travelers can relax and enjoy famous Bespin hospitality while waiting to be shuttled to Cloud City.

161

Some of Cloud City's interior decks look out upon the great wind tunnel in the central core.

promoted Cloud City as a wondrous vacation spot, with live shows, entertainment, gambling, and gourmet dining for all species. Much like the gas mining operations themselves, this idea proved successful beyond Figg's wildest dreams. Bespin's new flood of tourists was welcomed, and they continue to be pampered by the citizens and workers of Cloud City.

The city offers several dozen hotels, from the high-class Yarith Bespin atop the upper plaza to the moderately priced Holiday Towers and the budget-priced Stratosphere located in the lower tourist levels.

With Bespin's twelve-hour rotation cycle, vacationers get a full two days and nights of fun for every standard day, letting them enjoy the nightlife without missing out on sleep patterns. Tourists pay no attention to the clock, while the other inhabitants of Cloud City, such as the Ugnaughts, humans, and other species, work their own diurnal schedules.

Other than the popular casinos, for evening entertainment tourists can enjoy traditional platform danc-

Floating health spas take customers out to experience an invigorating "cloud bath" through high-rising wisps of vapor. Many believe that such gases have extraordinary value.

ing on raised stages, or riskier wind dancing. Platform dancers, or simple music appreciators, can go from small synthtone lounges to more frenetic laser-pulse dance arenas. Wind dancers climb the high towers, strap on floater packs as life jackets…and then they dance, flinging themselves into the updrafts and swirling breezes that eddy like small cyclones around the top of Cloud City. The best time for dancing is at dawn or sunset, when shifting atmospheric temperatures cause the most spectacular gusts.

During the day, cruise captains take tourist groups out on large launch platforms, treating the vacationers to daylong expeditions among the clouds, to see the transient sights and the bizarre life-forms. Tour captains usually keep a protocol droid as an assistant for translating any number of known languages. The tourists are thrilled to see the floating gas refinery complexes, the ruins of Tibannopolis, and the deep gullet of knotted storm systems in the clouds below. Bespin is full of things to see and do.

Whether for investment in industries with extremely high growth potential, or important scientific studies on the natural wonders of life in the clouds. . .or simply to relax and unwind in the gentle winds, take advantage of Cloud City's numerous recreational opportunities—Bespin is the place to be.

Get carried away on the winds!

YAVIN 4

ABOUT THE AUTHOR :

Dr'uun Unnh, while little recognized during his life, has proved to be one of the most thorough and exacting naturalists in recent history. His meticulous notes and voluminous electronic journals have described life on the jungle moon of Yavin in great detail. This article is a fictionalized version of parts of his life and his activities with the Rebel Alliance, most particularly about the base in the temple ruins on Yavin 4. With the recent resurgence of interest in Yavin 4, this article will perhaps bring Dr'uun Unnh the fame and respect he deserved during his tragically short life.

YAVIN 4

Dr'uun Unnh wrote, "The fourth moon of Yavin is small but lush, an isolated jungle world covered with dense and uncharted rain forests, dotted with deep clear lakes, and wrinkled with up-thrust volcanic mountains — a naturalist's paradise, uncataloged, a whole world waiting for the sharp eye of a trained nature lover."

And nature lover he was. The mousy, bright-eyed Sullustan saw the vast ecosystem of Yavin 4 as a challenge, and he spent his every waking moment studying new plants, new animals, trying to understand the order of the universe. In his own modest memoirs, Dr'uun Unnh said he hoped to contribute just a small dollop to the enormous knowledge base of civilization—and he did so much more.

Far from the usual paths of commerce through the galaxy, the Yavin system seemed a prime site for the Rebel Alliance to construct a new secret base. From this small jungle moon the Rebels launch-ed their successful attack upon the first Death Star, and then abandoned it in their continued flight and battle against the Empire. But Dr'uun Unnh did not live long enough to see the fruits of their struggle.

THE NEW SECRET BASE

Dr'uun Unnh had been a member of the Alliance since the early days of the Rebellion, when the growing group of dissidents needed to establish a secret base far from prying Imperial eyes. At this safe base, they could discuss strategy and lay plans for their struggle against the Emperor's New Order. They could also hide if the situation got worse.

For one of their first safe havens the Rebels chose the planet Dantooine, a mild world of empty steppes and open savannas, inhabited only sparsely by a few aboriginal tribes who wandered across the vast plains and left the civilized inhabitants alone. Here the Alliance set up primitive facilities, portable self-erecting living modules, and the best defenses they could cobble together. They used weapons stolen from smuggler outposts and gun runners, stripped-down Imperial equipment, and a small energy shield liberated from an Imperial correction facility. Dr'uun Unnh's journals of this period are fascinating glimpses of the early, tense struggles of the fight against Emperor Palpatine.

According to Dr'uun Unnh, the Rebels always considered their Dantooine sanctuary a temporary home. But over the months they began erecting more permanent structures, digging in and erecting a fortresslike setup. Their scouts and recruiters continued to spread word of the Rebellion far and wide, while other members of the Alliance, such as Princess Leia and her father, Senator Bail Organa, continued to work through political channels to overthrow the Emperor.

As time went by, the inhabitants of the Dantooine base grew lax with their own security measures until one day they were horrified to discover an Imperial observation device hidden in a cargo of equipment they had brought down to the surface. The unpacking crew reacted quickly and destroyed the tracking unit, but they could not be certain that the device had not transmitted its deadly information to Imperial listeners.

Instantly the Rebels packed up their base, collapsing the self-erecting shelters but leaving the half-built permanent structures intact. They piled aboard every transport they could find, leaving behind only a few dismantled vessels that had not yet been repaired.

The Dantooine base evaporated in a single day.

The ragtag Rebel fleet then drifted aimlessly in space, flitting from system to system, until one of their wide-ranging scouts finally located an uncharted gas-giant planet—Yavin, with its thickly forested fourth moon. This remote location appeared to be the ideal hideout.

In their desperate circumstances the Rebels took little time to make detailed maps of the moon's surface. From a cursory orbital inspection they discovered many anomalies among the jungle canopies, riverbeds, and lava mountain ridges. They found a

scattering of ancient temple ruins, all crumbling and empty, but had no time for detailed archaeological investigation.

The abandoned temples had been standing for thousands of years, resisting the encroachment of the jungles. The scouts chose the largest, best-preserved pyramid and set to work converting it into a well-defended stronghold. Teams of soldiers and the Rebel Corps of Engineers settled in to excavate and reinforce the fortifications.

With his sharp mind and lifelong store of practical knowledge, their commander—General Jan Dodonna (formerly retired) was one of the most important people in the entire Alliance. Under his

The rear of the Great Temple, an ancient Massassi structure restored and placed in service as the new Rebel base on Yavin 4.

command, the military and refugee arm of the Rebellion settled in on Yavin 4, eager to establish their new base and to begin the work of liberating the galaxy from the clutches of the Empire.

Upon Dr'uun Unnh's arrival, the Yavin moon seemed to call to him with its mysteries, its ruins, its hidden past, and its lost temple builders.

Digging through the undergrowth, the Sullustan naturalist found clear indications of a deep and widespread destruction that had taken place thou-

171

sands of years ago. He noted in his logs a question about this ancient but devastating conflict, long before Rebels and Empires and Death Stars. Though he found few details of this long-ago conflict, his best guess was that it was linked to the extinction of the temple-building race, the Massassi. (We note that his hypothesis has still not been confirmed or dismissed.)

Dr'uun Unnh's people, the Sullustans, lived in underground warrens on their native world, and he was good at digging through shadowy places to explore tunnels and caves. Due to his small stature, he was unable to help with the heavy labor of clearing the dense jungle debris that had grown over the temples, nor could he be of much assistance in repairing the collapsing wall sections of ancient stone blocks.

Collecting information was Dr'uun Unnh's specialty, and he proved his worth many times over. Before joining the Rebellion, he had studied many of the great archaeological artifacts in the galaxy, and he had also gained a broad working knowledge of natural history and alien ecosystems. The information in his head was a valuable addition to the Rebel Alliance, far more important than another shipment of weapons or heavy machinery.

When the Rebels set up their base on the jungle moon, the main priority was to make the crumbling stone structures habitable and defensible, so Dr'uun Unnh had to put his investigations on hold for a short while.

Teams of Alliance soldiers worked round the clock, clearing out weedy vegetation that had grown undisturbed for centuries in the crannies of the massive stone blocks. They chased out small rodents and giant insects that had made their nests in the darkened chambers. Dr'uun Unnh, however, took every chance he could to study the fascinating details of the jungle at every place it intersected with his work.

Outside, the Rebel Corps of Engineers erected a power-generating station, a large cluster of turbines stolen from the framework of an Imperial Star Destroyer that had been under construction at the Kuat Drive Yards. Finally, the Rebels could use laser-cutting machinery and power exfoliators to clean out the Great Temple, which they had chosen as their main base headquarters.

Chittering with amazement at the wonderful archaeological artifacts around him, Dr'uun Unnh at first had difficulty maintaining his concentration on the task at hand. He kept his datapad with him at all times, recording his impressions, photographing strange inscriptions nearly weathered away from the rock, and keeping precise before-and-after records of the modifications made by the Rebel engineers.

Despite his small stature and limited physical strength, the construction engineers frequently needed Dr'uun Unnh's services. They enlisted the compact Sullustan to crawl through tight tunnels where cave-ins had occurred, dragging power conduits behind him and mounting illumination devices to assist in the repair activities. Occasionally they had to call to him, startling him out of the close inspection of a nest or fungus he had found while performing his duties.

The greatest disaster to befall the Rebel engineers occurred when they attempted to use one of the underground levels of the Great Temple as a storage chamber. Unfortunately they had not sufficiently reinforced the ceiling and shored up the wall with plasteel girders. A massive cave-in occurred, killing eighteen Rebel soldiers and destroying a cache of valuable equipment.

When two of the levels in the Great Temple were finally cleared for occupancy and the soldiers had moved out of their temporary bivouac shelters, Dr'uun Unnh began to do further exploring, compiling an enormous database of everything he found.

Though many of the computer records were damaged in the subsequent Imperial attacks, most

Among the unique life-forms in the jungle on Yavin 4 are mucous salamanders *(above)*, tree ticks *(left)*, and armored eels (right). The naturalist Dr'uun Unnh could not begin to classify the major species here.

of the information still known about Yavin 4 comes primarily from his brave and diligent researches.

CLIMATE

Though small, the jungle moon is blessed with a mild climate and thick atmosphere. Humidity in the air is high, and as temperatures drop in the deep night, moisture condenses out of the air and settles as thick fog that clings to the canopy or penetrates to the ground below.

Because it is a moon orbiting a gas-giant, Yavin 4 experiences two different kinds of nightfall: When the moon rotates on its axis, facing away from the distant sun but still staring down upon the pale orange face of Yavin itself, the light in the air dims to a pastel glow, which Dr'uun Unnh called twilight night. When the moon goes behind the planet and the gas-giant eclipses the sun, blocking both direct light from the sun and reflected light from Yavin, the moon experiences what he called dark night.

Once every several months, because of the dance of the moon's rotation and its orbit around the primary planet, dark night lasts excessively long. The resulting deep temperature drop causes enough turbulence in the atmosphere to generate severe storm systems that rip though the jungles. During their first few months on the jungle moon, several unexpected storm periods forced the Rebels to barricade themselves inside the stone temples against the fury of the weather.

During one of these first storm cycles, Dr'uun Unnh found himself far out in the thick jungles studying the ruins of a small, isolated Massassi temple. He wrote with great emotion of how he had spent the longest night of his life inside the cold, slick temple, listening to the howling wind and feeling a chill deeper than the night eating into his bones.

Dr'uun Unnh also discovered another amazing atmospheric phenomenon, which he called a rainbow storm. He witnessed his first rainbow storm on the morning after a dark night. The sun poked around the limb of the great blurry gas-planet, and the thick jungle mists clung close to the ground. The scattered and refracted light from high ice crystals in the air combined with polarized rays coming through the upper atmosphere of the gas-giant to create whirling, scintillating showers of rainbows. Even on the small images he captured with his personal datapad, we can see how the air sparkled and flared like a blaster battle in orbit.

Dr'uun Unnh chattered excitedly to his friends about this amazing event. From that point on, some of the Rebels made a practice of climbing the newly erected observation towers to watch the rainbows pour down on them for a few minutes until the white ball of the sun separated itself from the atmospheric fringe and shone full daylight upon Yavin 4.

THE JUNGLES

Dr'uun Unnh's greatest love was the lush jungle of Yavin 4, which he called "a dense tapestry of interconnected life-forms: plants, animals, insects, all species cooperating and competing with each other in a series of checks and balances that makes the ecology of the small moon. The jungle thrives with supercharged life, as if Yavin 4 somehow has leftover energy and diverts it to the biological systems covering the moon."

Dr'uun Unnh recognized that it would take a dedicated squadron of xenobiologists and botanists years to catalog even the most prominent species. In his researches he kept a databook of common flora and fauna, trying to establish a classification framework. In one marginal note he stated his hope that, in later times of peace, someone would complete the studies in his name.

Many sections of the Yavin jungles are so dense that they proved impenetrable even for a small Sullustan. Vines interlocked, and trees grew together, walling off isolated clearings that Dr'uun Unnh discovered only by flying over at treetop level. The clearings were like microhabitats, terrariums shielded from the rest of the tangled jungle where the trapped plants and animals inbred so much that they eventually died out.

The most common large tree on Yavin 4, comprising much of the densest jungles and thickets around temple ruins, is the Massassi tree. Massassi trees have wide crowns and upsweeping branches, with a shredding purplish-brown bark that separates easily into fibrous strands (probably used by the ancient Massassi natives for fabrics, ropes, and other materials). Much of the mulch on the jungle floor is composed of decaying bark shed from these trees.

A common shrub is the blueleaf, which has thick, oily leaves and a sharp, pleasant fragrance that fills the air. Its leaves, clustered into groups of five or eight, are a bright cobalt blue. Though the blueleaf shrub grows only about a meter high, it spreads voraciously across the ground, forming dense thickets, particularly in the rich soil around fallen trees.

Other species in the rain forest include climbing ferns that sprawl across the high branches or ascend the weathered stone faces of the ancient temples; brilliant nebula orchids that display maroon, magenta, and lavender colorations similar to photographs of the Cauldron Nebula and other stellar oceans of ionized gas; and the most common dangerous plant, the touch-not, which bears leaves coated with a contact toxin, making skin blister and burn at the slightest touch. (Dr'uun Unnh learned this firsthand, to his dismay.)

The thick branches of the Massassi trees and the tapestry of climbing ferns provide the framework for an arboreal ecosystem. Slothlike woolamanders, with naked skin on their bellies and thick blue and gold fur on their backs, live in family packs among the branches, feeding on flower petals, tender leaf

shoots, and the rhizome seed nodules of nebula orchids. Large groups of woolamanders make their way across the forest canopy with an incredible racket, chattering among themselves, pelting ground-dwelling creatures—including Sullustan naturalists!—with fruit and broken branches, generally making a nuisance of themselves.

The woolamanders' main nemesis is an omnivorous tree-dwelling rodent, the stintaril, which has protruding eyes and long jaws filled with sharp teeth. Packs of stintarils swarm across the arboreal highways, never slowing down, apparently never sleeping, eating anything that sits still long enough for them to take a bite, including woolamander

young or sleeping elders.

On the ground, a large and stubborn herbivore is the runyip, an ornery, shaggy beast that roots among the forest mulch in search of buried fungi, fallen nuts, and emerging shoots. Runyips emit loud squealing noises, grunts, and sighs, as if to entertain themselves as they dig among the underbrush with their flexible noses and clawed front toes. As it crashes through the forest, a startled runyip can make a symphony that sounds, according to Dr'uun Unnh, "like a diverse musical group in the middle of an ugly accident."

Sluggish rivers slice through the jungle, moving with languid currents and teeming with so much life that Dr'uun Unnh called it a "watered-down primordial soup."

Dangling aerial roots of Massassi trees and nebula orchids trail in the surface of the river, absorbing water and precious nutrients. Clusters of algae gather around the tips, growing like hair in the current.

The angler, a spiderlike crustacean with small body and very long, very sharp knobbed legs, hangs among the dangling roots in the water. Camouflaged and perfectly motionless, the angler waits for a fish to drift within reach, at which point the angler thrusts down with its limbs like sharp pointed spears. After stabbing its prey, the angler quickly hauls it out of the water into its waiting jaws.

Tiny swimming crabs erect labyrinthine nests in the mud of the riverbanks, building small towers and curving battlements to keep amphibious predators at bay. Submerged aquatic hunters crawl along the river channel with rows of eyes on top of their heads and in front of their snouts, stalking anything that moves and lunging out to snap

The grand audience chamber in the Great Temple is the largest room at the top of the ancient structure. This chamber was enormous enough to hold assemblies of the entire complement of the Rebel base.

R.McQUARRIE

up a morsel of food with gundark-trap jaws.

Pinkish mucous salamanders swim formlessly in the water, diluted and without shape; but when they crawl out of the current and onto a riverbank they harden their outer membrane to a soft jellylike form with pseudopods and a mouth, allowing them to hunt among the insects in the weeds.

Iridescent blue piranha-beetles fly together with a high-pitched humming sound, spread out like innocuous insects while searching for prey. They subsonically contact the rest of their swarm upon finding an appropriate target. In moments a cloud of deadly sapphire beetles appears, whining a thin death cry and clicking their hard wing casings. When they set upon a poor runyip or doomed woolamander pack, the piranha-beetles cover the bodies of their victims in moments, tearing with thousands of piercing, razor-sharp mandibles, stripping every shred of meat from the carcass. Hidden in the bushes, Dr'uun Unnh witnessed the piranha-

beetles feeding once, and he hoped never to see such a spectacle again.

THE MASSASSI TEMPLES

The most intriguing highlights of the fourth moon of Yavin are the scattered monumental temples left behind by the vanished Massassi race.

The largest construction, called the Great Temple, is an enormous ziggurat, a squared-off pyramid ris-

As the orange gas gaint Yavin hangs overhead, a Rebel scout keeps watch high in an observation tower. Tall Massassi trees rise up into the sky, and the thick, unexplored jungles below hide many old ruins and mysteries—but the Rebels had little time for such investigations.

ing four levels above the ground and extending into a labyrinth of passages and underground chambers.

The Rebels primarily occupied the lower two levels of the pyramid, refurbishing large chambers and small quarters with the best materials available to them. They replaced weathered rock with sheets of seamed metal and erected temporary walls and barriers with poured paneling where ancient markings indicated that wood constructions had, under the planets conditions, long ago rotted away.

The Rebels complained that their dim quarters remained dank and unfriendly despite all the illumination sources and heaters they installed. Many claimed to hear strange noises scratching through the night silence, though nothing threatening was ever found.

To Dr'uun Unnh, though, the dim and cramped quarters reminded him of the tunnel warrens on his home world of Sullust. He always slept comfortably and woke refreshed, eager to go out and investigate further.

At the apex of the Great Temple was a single vast

room, the grand audience chamber. The audience chamber was lit by tall, narrow skylights; sunshine streamed in and illuminated polished geometric shapes and tiles of translucent precious stones. The tiles were laid out in strange but hypnotic patterns that Dr'uun Unnh had never seen before. Most of the flat flagstones were a nonreflective smoky gray; other stone lozenges of dark green and vermilion and ochre ornamented the enormous chamber. Lush green vines climbed the stone walls, spread-

(below) **The hangar bay door at the base of the temple grinds open to allow ships to emerge.**

(pages 180-181) **In the ruins known as the Temple of the Blueleaf Cluster, a strange crystalline centerpiece seems to throb with dark energy from some event in this world's past, as if trapped spirits reside in the crystal.**

ing out in verdant webs in the corners.

The Rebels did little with this chamber, merely uprooting the overgrown weeds and cleaning weathered debris, polishing the ornate flagstones. The grand audience chamber served as their meeting hall and also as the site of the brief victory celebration after the defeat of the first Death Star, at which Princess Leia Organa presented the heroes of Yavin with special medals.

Dr'uun Unnh liked to come into this cavernous chamber by himself, listening to his own words as he dictated into the datapad, collecting his thoughts in peaceful solitude. He heard his own whispers echo around the room like lost and forgotten Massassi voices spilling their secrets.

A small stairway behind the speaking platform at the end of the chamber rose to an observation platform at the roof of the Great Temple. A small group liked to stand on the platform and watch the huge gas-planet rise, when the mists rose from the jungle canopy and dissipated into the growing heat of day.

General Dodonna, however, took note of those who enjoyed standing atop the Temple and assigned them to high lookout towers erected in the jungle. These towers were made of durasteel rising tall above the canopy. It was lonely duty to be stationed with macrobinoculars, a day's worth of rations, and only a comlink for company. The towers swayed in the slightest breeze, but the hardest part by far was scaling the 812 rungs, hand over hand, just to reach the top.

The Rebels installed a modern turbolift through the center of the Great Temple. The shaft connected all the levels of the ziggurat down to the ground. The second and third levels were converted into computer processing centers, briefing rooms, and military offices, as well as recreation facilities and barracks. A large sector of the second level was outfitted as a sophisticated war room, while the corresponding sector on the third level served as the command center for the entire Rebel base.

At ground level the largest of the squarish rooms served as the launch bay and the hangar lift platform. An entire section of the floor could raise or lower shuttles and starfighters into the hangar cavity excavated beneath the main body of the temple. X-wings, Y-wings, and small supply vessels could shoot out of the long, dark hangar bay, streaking across the jungle and then up into orbit, vanishing into hyperspace.

On foot, Dr'uun Unnh explored other temple ruins in the vicinity. Directly across the forks of the river near the main base was a smaller high temple, which he named the Temple of the Blueleaf Cluster because of the unusual curved crenellations rimming the arches, as well as the ornate and deeply incised carvings around the keystone blocks.

The most frightening, yet intriguing, feature of the Temple of the Blueleaf Cluster is its main chamber, a vast echoing grotto extending to the top of the tower. In the middle of this chamber, filling the entire temple with a strange, cold, blue light, is an elongated crystal pyramid. The slick surface of the crystal felt cool and tingly, oily and charged with static electricity. To Dr'uun Unnh it seemed like a battery containing an enormous amount of power.

Looking closely at the translucent pulsating surface, Dr'uun Unnh was convinced he could see withered faces, strange alien visages like lost souls trapped within the crystal focus of power.

The frightening realization that no one knew what had caused the entire Massassi race to vanish suggested to Unnh that they should be cautious. He advised that they keep away, not understanding what awesome power might be contained within the throbbing crystal. General Dodonna agreed with him, and after the initial exploration and mapping expeditions, Dodonna sealed off the Temple of the Blueleaf Cluster, forbidding any of his troops to go there.

Across the other fork of the river stood a larger temple greatly damaged by time. Dr'uun Unnh named this crumbling ruin the Palace of the Woolamander, not because of any motif he found but simply because of the huge pack of the hairy arboreal creatures he found nesting within the ruins. The woolamanders set up a loud, howling alarm when he approached and began pelting him with rock shards and rotting fruit until he retreated. From his cursory inspection, Unnh determined that this palace held little of interest, and the structural damage and crumbling walls made the place unsafe.

After the Rebels had settled into their base and daily life gradually became a tense but well-ordered routine, Dr'uun Unnh's explorations ranged farther from the Great Temple. He knew from the tantalizing low-resolution maps taken from orbit that many other temple ruins poked through the jungle canopy, just waiting to be explored.

He took a small speeder bike, adjusted the controls so that his compact body could use it, and carried a blaster for protection (though his eyesight was poor and his aim was worse).

As a broad-based naturalist, Unnh viewed everything with far more fascination than caution, and only through sheer luck did he manage to get himself out of near-impossible situations when large animal specimens proved more interested in eating him for lunch than in providing important zoological data.

But the untamed wildness of Yavin 4 quickly taught Dr'uun Unnh a bit of common sense. He kept a tracking device mounted on his speeder bike, and he was careful to let squadrons know approximately where he intended to go and when he would return.

On one of these wide-ranging expeditions, Dr'uun Unnh discovered what he considered his most important find, according to his logs. His entry in the records he left behind said that it gave him tremendous delight, though it proved to be the end of his career, his last discovery.

Unnh came upon another quiet, sheltered Massassi temple—but this one seemed impregnable to the ravages of time and weeds, even after approximately four thousand years. This structure stood black and glittering with sharp angles and razor edges, showing the distinctive markings of Massassi architecture. It had been built on a small island in the center of a circular pond that shone like a flat quicksilver mirror, completely free of ripples. Twin lights in the sky from the orange sphere of Yavin and the distant sun cast intersecting glitter paths across the still lake.

The water in the surrounding lake was as transparent as diamond and so deep that it reflected the bottom like a lens. Just below the surface, columns of rock rose from the bottom like submerged stepping-stones, stopping just barely beneath the water. Dr'uun Unnh imagined that penitents approaching the temple must have walked across the stepping-stones, causing ripples but not sinking. To an observer on the shore, it would have appeared that the visitors walked directly across the water's surface.

On the surface of the island, mounds of pitted volcanic rock were splotched with orange and green lichen that looked like droplets of alien blood. Silence blanketed the temple and the lake, as if none of the jungle creatures or insects dared to come near the isolated site.

Between the split apex of the tall pyramid stood a colossus, a polished black statue of a dark man, with long hair swept back behind him, and the padded garments of an ancient lord. Dr'uun Unnh was convinced he recognized the trappings of one of the fearsome Dark Lords of the Sith.

The walls of the temple were made of polished dark glass. Corusca jewels, cast out from the high-pressure core of the gas-giant Yavin, studded the steep obsidian walls. Hypnotic pictographs and hieroglyphics were etched into the volcanic glass, written in a long-forgotten language. On his initial inspection, Unnh could read none of the words.

He scanned the markings and fed them into his datapad, using language-translating routines to ferret out garbled details of the history of the temples. He was astonished by the story that unfolded, lending compelling evidence to a theory that had been growing in the back of his own mind.

All these structures, according to his hypothesis, were relics left behind during an enormous conflict millennia ago that had pitted the old order of Jedi Knights against a dark offshoot that studied the even more ancient teachings of the Sith. Unnh speculated, too, that perhaps the legendary "Sith War" had been one of the reasons for the extinction of the Massassi race.

However, Unnh did not record all of his evidence, and translations of the ancient hieroglyphics found in his datapad are obscure at best, lending themselves to many different interpretations.

Dr'uun Unnh's last entries describe how excited he was by the discovery of this particular temple. Apparently he hopped aboard his speeder bike and headed back toward the main base. He made no note as he journeyed back to the Great Temple that he noticed another small metallic moon emerging from the limb of the gas-giant Yavin—the Death Star orbiting around the planet and coming into range. Nor did he note the launching of squadrons of X-wing and Y-wing fighters, streaking across the jungle canopy to do battle out in space.

The attack against the first Death Star had already begun. Rebel ships launched in parallel streaks from the lower hangar bay of the Great Temple. Swarms of TIE fighters fought the starfighters as they shot into space… .

The body of Dr'uun Unnh was found several days later when the Rebels were preparing to depart

More of Dr'uun Unnh's sketches from his datapad.

from their now discovered base and as they were taking a final tally of their losses. Preoccupied as they were with counting fallen pilots and destroyed ships, it took a long time for anyone to notice one missing member of the ground crew, a small naturalist who had been nowhere near the battle itself.

They finally located Dr'uun Unnh by the tracking mechanism he had strapped onto his speeder bike. His vehicle lay in a burned clearing out in the jungle, beneath the exploded wreckage of a crashed TIE fighter. Apparently the Imperial fighter had been damaged in space, and the pilot had unsuccessfully attempted a crash-landing. The mousy naturalist had simply been in the wrong place at the wrong time—impossibly unlucky to make up for all those times he had miraculously survived the predicaments he had gotten himself into.

The Rebels buried Dr'uun Unnh next to the

wreckage of the TIE fighter and left him to become one with the small moon he had spent so much of his time studying.

Dr'uun Unnh's personal datapad was mostly undamaged, and the other Rebel scientists carefully copied all the information that had been the Sullustan's life work. Then they packed up and abandoned the base, leaving much of their equip-

A brooding temple, surrounded by a shallow lake and crowned by the towering statue of an ancient dark lord.

ment behind. They departed the planet before Imperial forces could mount a massive counterstrike.

The implacable jungle began to retake what it had possessed before, and the fourth moon of Yavin once again became a mystery.

ALDERAAN

ABOUT THE AUTHOR:

Hari Seldona was a renowned poet of Alderaan who wrote many odes describing her great love for the peaceful, grassy world. Her popularity was such that she traveled from system to system, reading her poetry and describing her home planet, at the same time subtly criticizing the Empire. She was performing in the Corellian sector when the Death Star destroyed Alderaan—and thus Hari Seldona is one of the few natives of that world who survived.

She immediately dropped out of sight, fearing Imperial retribution. Her current practice, however, is to appear unannounced, read her poetry, and speak vehemently against the Emperor's New Order. She stirs up the crowd and then vanishes before stormtroopers can arrive. The following unsolicited article, "Requiem for Alderaan," is her chronicle of a murdered world.

ALDERAAN

While city-covered Coruscant may be the galaxy's political center, ancient and peaceful Alderaan was its *heart*. How I miss the calm, vast skies, the oceans of grass, the lovely flying thrantas.

A very old planet, calmed from the tempests of its geological youth, Alderaan had settled into a mellow climate, gentle landscapes, and a peaceful aura. A perfect place to live, to love, to ponder the universe. Perhaps the environment proved too peaceful, for otherwise the people of Alderaan might have been more prepared to see the huge sphere of death coming toward it. Perhaps they would not have been taken unaware and destroyed as they slept. Perhaps they would have fought—or perhaps not. Violence was not the Alderaan way.

As our planet fell into seismic slumber over the ages, the major mountain ranges weathered away, leaving behind breathtaking steppes and the grasslands that rippled in the breezes. In my poetry I called the constant whisper of wind the Song of Alderaan.

Alderaan provided a comfortable home during the thousands of years of human habitation. The cities were carefully manicured and tended so as to interrupt the landscape as little as possible. The people of this world tried to work *with* the landscape rather than against it.

Alderaan's open vistas proved inspirational to the galaxy's finest creative geniuses—as galactic culture has witnessed time and again. The famous Alderaan University was known throughout the galaxy for training and shaping the best minds in numerous disciplines. Many artists have claimed that the sprawling horizons opened doorways in their minds, allowing them to think vaster thoughts than they could otherwise have conceived in the confined quarters of a dirty metropolis-world such as Coruscant.

THE LANDSCAPE

Though this planet once seemed wild and empty, botanists have cataloged over eight thousand sub-species of grasses on the plains and an even greater number of native flowers.

After the warm rains came each gentle spring, the grasslands exploded with a profusion of new life. Matted carpets of short-bladed grass, tall forests of cane and grains intermingled with a glittering spectrum of colorful flowers. And the fresh smell in the air seemed headier, more stimulating than the most potent drug.

Alderaan was a peaceful world, with calm, open grasslands and quiet people.

In the late summer, when the air grew warmer and the vegetation turned golden as it dried, many flowers and grasses went to seed simultaneously. During these months, imposing "seedstorms" filled the breeze with dense masses of floating feathery seeds, like a blizzard of feathery dry snow. In years of heavy spring rains the vegetation grew thicker than usual, causing extremely heavy seedstorms. Airborne transportation on Alderaan ground to a halt, crippled by poor visibility. Clouds of windblown seeds choked domesticated flying beasts and clogged air intakes of mechanical craft. So the people remained inside with their families, watching the seed-strewn air through broad windows, enjoying this unexpected,

The open plains of
Alderaan let our
thoughts travel
unbridled, whether
on a long walk across
the grasses or
flying overhead in
a shuttlebeast.

naturally-wrought lull in their daily lives.

Wild creatures out in the grasses of Alderaan included furry, large-winged moths that nested among the bushy flowers and waving stalks. Their larvae, armored caterpillars more than a meter long, burrowed under the ground and fed upon swollen tubers in the grass roots. The armored caterpillar was known to live underground for a dozen years before it dug deep and sealed itself in a thick-walled cocoon, eventually to emerge as a furry moth. Perhaps somewhere, an alien entomologist kept a few specimens of the Alderaan furry moth; otherwise all are now lost.

These armored worms were the main food source for stilt-legged flightless birds that waded through the grasses in ranks like veteran soldiers in a well-trained infantry division. Spread out in a long, straight line, these reptilian birds moved in lockstep with their glittering eyes open, their heads tilted to listen for the subtlest of vibrations beneath the ground.

The birds swept across the prairie in a carefully regimented pattern, stopping to stab with their scissorlike bills into the packed dirt to spear caterpillars. With a honk for assistance, a stilt-legged bird could call for its companions to help wrestle the

Huge flying hotels drifted aimlessly across the continents with no destination in mind, just a place to get away from personal pressures.

prey out of the ground; they used their sharp beaks to snip the victim into equal portions. The birds gulped down the morsels, leaving the heavy shells behind like the wreckage of a small crashed ship. Then the birds lined up again and continued their march across the grasslands.

All of these creatures were burned to a cinder with one blast from the Death Star.

The wide rangelands on Alderaan were also the primary roving grounds for two domesticated food sources—grazers and nerfs. Both animals were ungulates feeding on the inexhaustible grasses and thick vegetation and continue to be raised on many worlds, so their species is one of the few that has escaped extinction.

Grazers are sluggish and methodical, massive creatures bred for their meat. Genetically altered to optimize their muscle mass, they are docile, unintelligent, and slow-moving—little more than living machines to process grass into edible meat. They have large, stupid-looking eyes and react to almost nothing. They do not panic or stampede or protect their young. They simply wander across the prairies, heads down, nuzzling the grass until they are herded off to droid-run meat-processing centers.

Nerfs, on the other hand, are rangy, supple creatures with curving, dull horns and long, rank fur that covers their muscular bodies. Nerfs are temperamental and cantankerous. They are foul-smelling and apt to spit or kick at their handlers. In fact, if their meat were not so delicious and highly prized, no one would bother raising them at all.

Alas, of all the marvelous creatures to spring from Alderaan's nurturing environment, these two are among the lowliest. I weep for all those other magnificent animals that will never again grace the galaxy.

Nerf herders were a special breed of people frowned upon by the higher cultural elements of Alderaan because they chose to live out in the open and paid little attention to their own personal hygiene. Nerf herders are known somewhat disdainfully as odorous and scruffy-looking—but I remember that when they would bring their herds in once a year to sell the expensive, delicious meat, the nerf herders lived like kings.

Alderaan developed a justly famous cuisine based not only on these two delicate meats, but also on the wealth of exotic herbs available in their coddled botanical gardens, as well as fresh edible flowers and the variety of grains.

Alderaan chefs are famous throughout the galaxy. Popular dishes include grazer fillets in tart sauce, nerf medallions simmered in wine, and slivered spiced tubers cooked in a tender roulade of grazer flank steak. Because of the high demand for the services of these chefs at expensive casinos such as Cloud City on Bespin and high-level observation restaurants on Coruscant, many of them escaped the devastation of our world, much the same way I did.

GRASS PAINTINGS

One of my fondest memories of Alderaan is of flying in an observation boat over the huge and hypnotic grass paintings that covered dozens of square kilometers out on the plains. Brilliant botanical artists used the flat grasslands as a canvas for their marvelous work, skimming low to the surface in small craft to deposit the seeds of various flowers. The artists would pick out their designs, using the flowers themselves as paint, the winds as their paintbrush, to create a natural spectacle to prove how humans and nature can work together.

The styles of these grass paintings ranged from sweeping, energetic abstract designs to realistic representations that involved such precision that many of the seeds needed to be planted by hand to achieve the exacting detail required. The natural diversity and wonder of Alderaan supplied flowers rich with all the colors visible to the human eye, as well as others that only aliens could see.

In the normal days of Alderaan, grass artists applied for a five-year license to make their huge works. The first year's growth was recognized as the work of the artist, but in subsequent years the grass painting became a collaboration between the artist and the environment itself. As the carefully planted brushstrokes grew and then went to seed, the lines blurred into a chaotic lack of focus…but with a new kind of vibrant energy that drew from the natural forces of Alderaan. Viewing the paintings always made me feel the majesty of the natural forces that shaped the face of Alderaan long before we came to settle there.

Some of the best grass artists were also skilled in meteorology, but few succeeded in the vigorous task of predicting weather and growth patterns so exactly that they could re-create specific grass paintings from year to year as their initial creations went to seed and spread out.

Here I must tell the heroic story of one rebellious but extremely talented grass painter, Ob Khaddar, who was known to be a troublemaker and a radical at Alderaan University. Upon hearing that the Emperor intended to visit Alderaan on an errand of state, Ob Khaddar concealed his dislike and successfully campaigned for permission to create a large grass painting "to honor the Emperor."

He allowed no one to assist him in the planting of hundreds of thousands of seeds from various flowers, etching out a portrait of the Emperor himself. After the warm rains of spring the broad visage of Palpatine rose from the grasses, fresh and alive—cowled but powerful, his face radiating benevolent energy, his yellow eyes filled with strength. And so when the Emperor arrived for his state visit he took the opportunity to take his entourage out on a large

sail barge to view the great portrait made to commemorate him.

But Ob Khaddar had played a final trick. On the very day the Emperor rode out to observe, accompanied by his withered advisers and his red-cloaked Imperial Guards, another set of flowers bloomed in the midst of the grass portrait. Black lilies spread their dark petals across Palpatine's face, making it look as if his skin had begun to fester and decay from within. The bright flowers of his eyes withered, leaving hollow-looking sockets.

Seeing this, the Emperor was outraged and ordered the entire plain to be torched. Stormtroopers flew over the grasses, blasting with incandescent lasers, ripping up the soil, and setting the tall grasses ablaze.

Senator Bail Organa and other representatives of Alderaan apologized profusely, though none of the Imperials could determine whether they were sincere in their shock and horror…or were secretly pleased.

Ob Khaddar himself, intelligent as well as talented, wisely disappeared before the Emperor arrived on the planet. An Imperial death warrant has been placed on him, but numerous bounty hunters have never been able to get a clue as to his whereabouts.

WATERWAYS

Alderaan had an ice-rimmed polar sea and many large, shallow bodies of water, a few inland seas but no actual oceans. The land was dotted with thousands upon thousands of lakes, chains ranging from small ponds to large bodies of water. Many of these were connected by fast-flowing clear rivers or artificial canals for luxurious slow travel. Vacation barges drifted sluggishly across the ever-changing yet always-the-same grassy landscape, listening to the Song of Alderaan.

A chain of islands in the largest inland sea held the tallest forests on Alderaan, the famed oro woods, where graceful, clean-limbed trees once climbed hundreds of meters into the air; the bark was covered with iridescent lichen colonies that glimmered in violet, cinnabar, and pale yellow. White cairoka birds fluttered from limb to limb, singing sweetly. Tiny, brilliant red deer with golden stripes rooted for shoots among the lower foliage. The oro woods were considered such a lovely oasis that the government of Alderaan decreed them a planetary treasure.

Now all this, too, is gone.

A few isolated lakes—chosen for the clarity, depth, and temperature of their water—were estab-

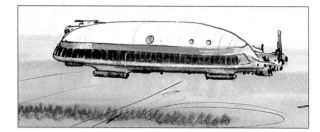

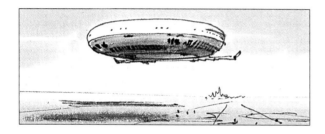

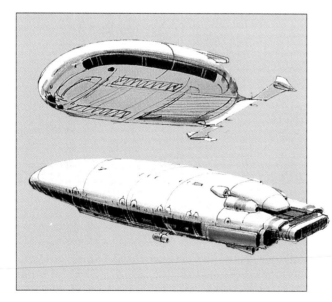

Because of the well-traveled skyways on Alderaan, a great many designs for flying crafts have been put into use, from large passenger buses to small skimmers that once cruised the skies in silence, unwilling to break the peace of this world.

lished as underwater preserves. Mon Calamari guides and fish keepers took tour groups and naturalists on diving expeditions to see the underwater habitats, to watch them feed on each other or on the numerous insect larvae that grow plentifully in the marshy weeds at the lakeshores.

Small crustacean workers built underwater mud castles where entire family units lived for generation after generation, strengthening the battlements, building protected egg chambers. Mon Calamari guides took students and tourists past these sprawling, fragile crustacean cities, but no one touched or damaged the delicate ecology.

All turned to steam with one blast from the Death Star's superlaser.

One of the natural wonders of Alderaan's waterways was a seemingly trivial phenomenon that centuries of tradition embellished into a gala celebration. The "Silver Flow" occurred like clockwork every spring.

Glimmerfish were small but incredibly fecund swimmers no longer than a finger, with highly reflective metallic scales. Females would lay hundreds of fertilized eggs up and down the shores of Alderaan's canals and rivers. When all these glimmerfish eggs hatched at once, the water became a seething, glittering mass of silvery reflections that sparkled from the sunlight penetrating the water's surface. Swarms of the tiny fish surged along with the current toward large bodies of water, where they would grow and live out their lives. Occasionally, with no cloud cover and at the height of day, the flickering light could be seen from orbit.

To the people of Alderaan the miraculous hatching of millions upon millions of tiny fish was a celebration of life and its persistence. Spectators would take boats and rafts along the canals as the glimmerfish swam by, watching the electric silver of the crowded creatures flowing beneath them. The people made the Silver Flow into one of their most popular holidays.

While the fish themselves were too small to be eaten, the celebration provided an excuse for confectioners to make small, silvery candies. Decorative laser shows dappled the night clouds with scintillating schools that looked like glimmerfish swimming across the sky.

Out in the broad lakes regatta ballets engaged colorful sailcraft and air skimmers trailing streamers in a well-choreographed dance. Musicians played on the bows of large barges as the smaller craft flitted in and out. The spectacle was popular enough that the Galactic News Service piped the annual celebration across all its networks.

This will never happen again, but archival tapes still exist for others to watch, and see what the galaxy has lost, and mourn along with me.

SKYWAYS

Because the surface features of Alderaan were so gentle, the open skies of the world became well-traveled highways. Transportation specialists of Alderaan let their imaginations run wild, designing spectacular gossamer craft, too fragile to withstand rigorous storms yet perfectly feasible in the calm, predictable air currents of Alderaan. They enjoyed the freedom of the winds, drifting wherever whim took them.

Huge sailing constructions with translucent sheets of flexible films and inflatable air bladders formed roving islands in the sky, nomadic resort hotels where tourists could relax above the serenity of the rippling grasses below. These lighter-than-air constructions moved at random over the surface, without a schedule and without a destination.

Other craft, from chartered hoverbarges to small personal skimmers, took people streaking across the sky—but the serene emptiness of Alderaan was so vast that I rarely remember seeing more than two vehicles in the same ocean of blue overhead.

For sport, some daredevils undertook the ancient hobby of constructing and piloting hot-air balloons, rising high over the unbroken terrain. Other people would tether themselves to huge kite constructions and go sailgliding, chained to the ground by a thin fiber and flying free. These daring athletes usually wore body armor and repulsorlift belts for safety.

People also rode the native flying creatures of Alderaan, particularly the thranta—an immense leathery creature whose body was primarily a giant wingspan with a central core made of lighter-than-air bladders. These creatures had long life spans and grew to unprecedented size in the unrestrained environment of Alderaan.

Many species of native thrantas drifted across the skies, skimming low and feeding on wind-blown seeds and pollens. The thrantas were docile and easily domesticated. Bearing only a rudimentary intelligence, they adapted well to captivity and seemed not to resent their role as living aircraft.

Smaller thrantas were used as personal mounts with saddles and reins adjusted so that riders could take them out on recreational rides. The larger thrantas had standing platforms mounted to their backs, where groups of people could hold ropes as a

Windows were as important as propulsion systems in sight-seeing vessels, letting passengers stare out across the unbroken fields of grass and flowers, searching for herds of wild animals.

Engines on these flying craft had been modified for efficiency and cleanliness. Because Alderaan had little industry, the skies were always a clear, deep blue, free of pollution.

thranta pilot took the creature flapping up into the sky, riding high thermals. In this way tourists could look down across the plains and observe the grass paintings or the sparse natural features.

Luckily for their species, some young thrantas were transplanted to other planets with calm atmospheres and sufficient wilderness for the thrantas to roam. Most of these attempts proved unsuccessful, except for a group of young, energetic flying creatures that have thrived on Bespin, where they still serve as an oddity, performing monthly sky rodeos. The rest of the thrantas, however, are dead in the space rubble of Alderaan.

An attempt to bring the thrantas to Coruscant ended in tragedy. Some Imperial fools hoped that the creatures could fly high above the city skyline, drifting over the glittering lights. At first the Emperor was amused by them—but the flying creatures wasted away no matter how much effort the wranglers put into tending their beasts. The noisome city air seemed poisonous to them. The close confinement of monolithic skyscrapers and the sheer number of shuttlecraft and people and industry seemed to repel them. I must confess this is my own reaction to the metropolis world, and I will never again return there by choice.

On Coruscant the thrantas' grayish, leathery skin turned blotchy. Their air bladders sagged, and they drew no strength from the specially concentrated nutrient solutions the wranglers pumped into them.

One of the thrantas brought its rider to his death as the ailing creature swooped down in the canyons of the city, plunging hundreds of stories as if in a suicidal dive toward the incomprehensibly distant ground. The remains of the thranta carcass and its rider were never found deep in the

murky underworld of Imperial City.

Now, if anyone wishes to see live thrantas, they must go to Bespin. I hope the creatures thrive there, without Imperial cruelty.

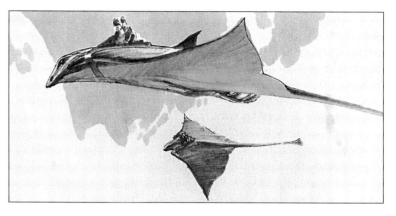

CASTLE LANDS

At the northern edge of Alderaan's great plains lay the mysterious Castle Lands: incredibly ancient ruins, towering cities made by extinct human-sized hive creatures known as the Killiks. These mysteries will never be solved, though—thanks to the Death Star.

The breathtaking Castle Lands were weathered turrets and structures densely packed into once bustling hives, built mound upon mound. The monolithic pinnacles were fundamentally similar, with only a few different designs copied thousands of times across the entire badlands. The structures were riddled with honeycombed passages, small dwelling chambers, larger communal eating areas, and egg-laying grottoes. The Killik Castles endured for millennia, barely changed—only to be destroyed in an eyeblink by a cruel superweapon.

At first glance these Castles seemed to be the work of a sophisticated species, but archaeological investigation only uncovered a deeper and deeper *alienness*. So much so that some question whether the long-extinct Killiks had any form of intelligence. Their iron-hard mounds are devoid of any technological improvements and appear to have been built entirely by insectile hand through a massive concentration of coordinated labor—however, the inner walls were decorated with brilliantly complex mosaics of colored pebbles.

Thrantas are magnificent flying creatures originally from Alderaan, though luckily they had been transplanted to other worlds before the destruction of this planet. Night riders *(left)* could see the plains under the silver wash of the moonlight.

No one has ever been able to determine whether these mosaics were some form of written communication or merely decorative art that makes sense only when viewed through multiply faceted eyes. The Killiks left no other artifacts: no tools, no machines, no vehicles, no possessions.

Many of their chitinous carcasses have been found, their glossy, greenish exoskeletons so hard that they withstood thousands of years of erosion. The Killiks had four arms, each terminating in a powerful three-fingered claw, and two stout legs that appeared capable of leaping great distances.

Across the northern steppes of Alderaan, the Castle Lands appeared in eighteen well-defined groupings, each erected at a distinct age. Archaeological speculation has it that the Killiks built their earthen cities in a certain area until either the food ran out or the population grew too large; then they abandoned their homes to swarm over the great plains until they found another site, where they erected a new city. The cycle was repeated over and over again until the Killik race finally and mysteriously died out.

Oddly, the oldest Castle structures showed the greatest technological sophistication, which dwindled with each successive generation. In progression the Killiks seemed to have lost their ability to function together as a hive organism, and their society degenerated into chaos.

Even during the centuries of human occupation, the abandoned Castles of the extinct Killiks remained in good condition—like empty, haunted spires out in the silent plains, a poignant example of how civilizations can fall…how even an abomination like the Empire is—thankfully—a mere blip on galactic history.

In the last days of Alderaan, the Killik Castles became popular retreats for those seeking places of solitude. Artists and musicians of a private, contemplative temperament often journeyed to the Castle Lands and selected any one of the similar empty towers to live in for however long they chose. They brought their own supplies and all the raw materials they needed for their craft. Traveling by silent aircraft or drifting thranta over the Castles, one could occasionally hear strains of practiced music or an unseen orator rehearsing a profound speech.

Some of the spires were revamped and modernized with plumbing, heating, power, and other amenities. Purist artists and philosophers, though, preferred to seek total primitive solitude and spend nights out under the open skies, watching the endless dizzying dance of stars and planets overhead….

So much of Alderaan's greatest cultural work was created in these isolated Killik castles that the ruins were revered with a sort of awe, as if they concentrated inspiration and deep thought. I spent many months during my own most productive period, creating sweeping verse that attempted to capture the feel of the boundless wilderness around me. Some critics have called these "Castle poems" my best work.

Alas, one artist with misguided intentions decided to paint an entire section of the spires in brilliant colors, swirling them with corkscrew designs and pastel splashes. Alderaan always did its best to foster the development and freedom of artwork and cultural enhancements of any form—and I, for one, would never dream of stifling artistic expression—but in this case the people were universally ap-

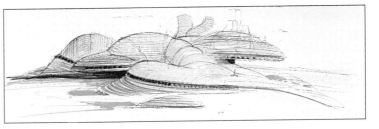

palled by the defacing of revered old structures. The Alderaan ruling council issued a decree banning such artistic pursuits from that point on.

Until the planet's destruction, the defaced spires could still be seen. The Alderaan council determined that more damage would be done by attempting to repair the unwanted painting than if they just left the eyesore as a scornful display of the excesses of certain artists.

The artist himself was not prevented from making further paintings, so long as he damaged no other ancient landmarks. Insisting that this spoiled the whole effect and crippled his artistic freedom, the artist left Alderaan and went to seek other commissions.

CITIES AND CULTURES

More than any other planet I have ever experienced, Alderaan had a worldwide conscience, an attitude among the vast majority of its population to be aware of ecological needs. They recognized that they must not ruin the environment, that their quality of life would be much greater if they found a way to cooperate with their delicate world. But all their careful plans were swept away in a single act of unspeakable brutality.

Because humans were not the original inhabitants

Crevasse City is a perfect example of how the people of Alderaan worked *with* their environment rather than against it, establishing even a large metropolis in such a way that the landscape was little affected.

of Alderaan, coming instead upon a world already littered with the debris of the Killik civilization, they developed an attitude that they were mere visitors no matter how long they remained there. Perhaps this attitude was one of the reasons why Alderaan was the birthplace of so many great artists and philosophers. It was a nurturing place, a cultural oasis that had forgotten the wealth of violence of which living creatures are capable.

The people of Alderaan were highly sensitive, paying close attention to their world and the universe they lived in. They bore within them a kernel of peace and acceptance not often found on colony planets where life is a constant struggle against the elements.

Though they passed no official laws or ordinances defining such things, the people of Alderaan long ago implicitly accepted the challenge of building their cities in such a way that it created a minimum impact on their world, finding various techniques to dig into the crust rather than erecting tall obstructions. Their cities were built on stilts out in the shallow inland seas, or wedged into crevices under Alderaan's polar ice.

Crevasse, one of the largest cities on Alderaan, was all but invisible from the air—built into the walls of a network of fissures. Once-mighty rivers flowed through these canyons, carving channels through strata laid down over thousands of years; but as the weather changed and the terrain altered, the main sources of the rivers were diverted, leaving only small streams glittering, like quicksilver threads at the bottoms of the gorges.

During the first years of human habitation on Alderaan, a collection of miners lived in small natural caves while they quarried the colorful rocks as raw material for other building projects. But as the miners discovered freshwater springs within the cliff walls, and as word got around about the beautiful sunsets, more and more people came to Crevasse.

Most of those who made their homes on Alderaan were not desperate colonists, though, but retired dignitaries and well-established businesspeople, those whose fortunes had already been made offplanet. These people wanted a pristine place they could protect and treasure.

With the morning and evening breezes, flocks of what appeared to be birds swooped over the canyons—but on closer inspection it could be seen that these were people with kite wings soaring on the thermals, gliding about and looking down on the grandeur of Alderaan's natural landscape.

Crevasse city grew with dwellings carved out of the sheer rock walls. Passages connected, making

The abandoned, petrified mounds of the extinct insectoid Killiks were among the most intriguing natural objects on Alderaan, rising from the plains in smooth, organic-looking monoliths.

199

their city larger as it spread up and down the canyon and into side gorges. To a casual observer, Crevasse—though one of the most heavily populated areas on Alderaan—looked to be a wilderness unharmed.

Another of Alderaan's large population centers, Terrarium City, has been called the City Under Glass. Terrarium's founders chose a different way to build their metropolis and yet protect the landscape at the same time.

Teams of landscape engineers excavated a natural depression in the plains, a large bowl which they sealed with a liner so that nothing could leach into the soil. They fused the surface to an impenetrable glass and then began to lay down their city in a methodical, efficient way.

They filled the huge artificial basin with a liquid polymer. Tankers came from orbit, dropping enough polymer to fill the excavated bowl until the liquid had reached a uniform height, at which the designers wished to place the city's bottom level.

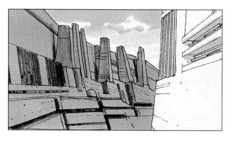

Using a fleet of modified battleships, Terrarium's designers hovered over the bowl area and played their lasers over the liquid polymer—not as destructive weapons, but as holography beams projecting a three-dimensional pattern into the transparent liquid, an image of all the preprogrammed rooms, buildings, and thoroughfares. The lasers hardened the resin in the appropriate places, crystallizing solid walls down to the tiny details of arches and windows.

The remaining polymer fluid was then drained out, pumped back into holding tanks. The first layer was allowed to dry before a capping sheet was laid on top as a roof of the bottom story, in preparation for the second layer of Terrarium City.

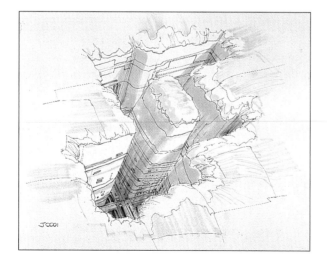

The polymer fluid was pumped in again, and this time a new blueprint was projected into the resin. Layers upon layers were patterned in an incredibly short period, with no industry, no waste, no further disruption of the world. The polymer itself was completely inert,  giving off no harmful volatile chemicals to pollute the atmosphere.

When all eighteen layers of Terrarium City had been patterned and completed, the inhabitants were assigned quarters from the blueprint maps. Each family was allowed its full creativity, because for the first month or so the polymer walls were still soft enough to allow a certain amount of carving and patterning. Several types of sonic resonators and light baths were available to texture and color the walls to the inhabitants' preferences. Groups made great entertainment for themselves by chiseling bas-reliefs into the walls and arches, expressing themselves in their own dwellings. It was a heady time, and their imaginations roamed free.

Finally the whole of Terrarium City was covered over with a transparent sheet that sealed it level with the rest of the plain. It looked like an incredibly still lake, a pool of glass from beneath which the lights of thousands and thousands of dwellings blinked, but the industry and the bustle of population remained silent from the outside, contained.

Tall pinnacle towers rose above the flat cap of Terrarium City. Slender monoliths stretched high into the sky like needles wavering in the gentle breezes. Thin cables extended from these towers out to anchor points, providing additional support to the broad rooftop layer of transparisteel.

Though their lives seemed idyllic beneath the ground in the perfectly planned Terrarium, occasionally the people needed to spend time above it—not just at grass level, but high enough to get a view from a height, to let their thoughts roam free. Turbolift shafts ran to the top of each turret. Office complexes and counseling facilities were housed in the needle towers. Lighter-than-air vehicles as well as repulsorlift craft were tethered to the towers.

The smooth lines of Alderaan architecture have been copied in many other cosmopolitan worlds, preserving yet another facet of our lost culture.

The magnificent capital city of Alderaan, Aldera, was built on an island in the middle of a circular lake, a lake formed from a fresh meteor crater breaking through into subterranean aquifers.

Because Alderaan was such an old world, very few craters remain that have not been weathered completely away. This blemish was fresh in a geological sense, and the small pointed island at its center had a poignant loneliness that seemed to ask for some greater purpose.

Visitors reached the city of Aldera by air or by boat, crossing the deep lake. Beautiful white free-form buildings stood on the uneven slopes of the island—many of them dwellings, while other prominent structures served as the cultural and governmental facilities for which Alderaan was once so well known.

Aldera housed the embassies of off-planet dignitaries, and was also the home of Senator Bail Organa. Princess Leia Organa spent many years of her childhood there. Friends of the Rebel Alliance

will recognize those names, which have since been reviled by ignoble Imperial propaganda.

Despite its other picturesque land-marks, though, Aldera was perhaps best known as the site of the famous galactic learning center, Alderaan University.

ALDERAAN UNIVERSITY

Before its tragic destruction Alderaan University was one of the oldest and most widely revered learning institutions in the galaxy. Other universities on other planets have adopted a similar model, but none was ever able to match the success of Alderaan. The university was founded long ago, one of the first structures erected on the island in the middle of the crater lake. It was originally established as a school of philosophy by the great Republic thinker Collus.

Collus originally brought with him a group of his brightest students to live in seclusion in the temperate climate of Alderaan, mulling over matters of great import (whether to the galaxy as a whole or just to the students themselves). With long stretches of uninterrupted time, the philosophers of the school of Collus pondered the inferences they drew from vast storehouses of data, statistics, and history compiled from a thousand worlds and as many civilizations.

It was here that the students of Collus understood that the Old Republic was crumbling—at least a century before the rest of the galaxy realized

it. Some of this informtion was documented but not widely released for fear of skepticism, disbelief, or outright antagonism. But the school of Collus continued to exist through the times of great upheaval, offering their assistance and wisdom whenever they felt their help would prove more constructive than destructive. Many of the galaxy's greatest moral treatises and philosophical works were penned by the students of Collus during these difficult times.

Gradually, as other powerful people began to grasp the importance of the school of Collus, other teachers came to Alderaan, building their own schools adjacent to the first learning center. They branched out in the disciplines of politics, mathematics, cultural pursuits, and the arts.

One of the conclusions that Collus himself came to before his death at an extremely old age was that knowledge without application was worthless knowledge, and that studying secondhand information without personal experience watered down any learning gained in such a manner. Philosophy studies were fine and good, because philosophy by its nature was a contemplative subject—but other disciplines required action and experience. How could a student of biology attain wisdom by looking at diagrams in books and not going into the field? How could a student of politics grasp the true mechanisms of government without setting foot on Coruscant?

Eventually it developed that while the main core of Alderaan University remained on the island

city of Aldera, various "pods" of the university dispersed to primary locations of study. Botanists and entomolo-gists spent time in directed study on lush planets such as Ithor, the home of the Hammerheads, or other tropical worlds. Meteorologists would study the immense storm systems on gas-giant planets such as Bespin. Historians would visit the ruins of the ancient library on Ossus, or Deneba, where once a great council of Jedi was convened. Political science students found jobs as government functionaries in Imperial City.

With its large numbers of young and impressionable students recently awakened to political causes

and idealistic dreams, it is not surprising that Alderaan University became a hotbed of carefully hidden dissent against the New Order. This is where many came to snoop and learn about the Rebellion against the Empire. This is where I myself was recruited as an outspoken proponent of the Alliance.

On the surface, Alderaan University retained a careful veneer of quiescence and deep study, with students focused upon their work and the lectures of their instructors. The philosophy students made no secret that they were fundamentally offended by the Emperor's New Order and the limits it placed on thought and free expression, but they restricted their discussions to theoretical pursuits. No doubt this served as a useful red herring for Imperial spies seeking access to the real ringleaders of the Rebellion.

Imperial plants tried unsuccessfully over and over again to break into any Rebel cell and find connections to the larger Alliance. But even though the students might have been as naive as they were enthusiastic, they still managed to avoid capture. Until the end, when everything was on the verge of

being cracked open—but ironically the Death Star itself ruined the crackdown on Alderaan.

One secret dissident, a friend of mine, was the bright young student musician Thelaa. She was a quiet and creative woman who came to the University from one of the backwater agricultural planets. I remember with bittersweet bemusement how she had received a great shock upon being thrown among a more cosmospolitan group of people who were interested in the larger workings of

The tall pinnacle towers of Terrarium City stretch high like needles, giving the underground inhabitants a chance for a "view from a height."

the Empire and the very nature of freedom.

Originally Thelaa's talent produced remarkable musical compositions, but then she fell deeply into her own secret cause in the name of the Rebellion. With a head of close-cropped, straw-colored hair and overlarge eyes, Thelaa projected an expression of innocence and gullibility that served her well during the several times she was routinely questioned by Imperial investigators. She took frequent sojourns alone out to the abandoned Killik monoliths, supposedly seeking hidden places where she could be inspired in her music. I know, though, what her real purpose there was.

Thelaa regularly delivered new works, much to the satisfaction of her instructors, until by a sheer fluke one of her teachers discovered that she merely copied the technically competent but generally uninspired work of a centuries-forgotten composer named Salyer!

When Thelaa refused to explain why she had passed off plagiarized work as her own, she was expelled from Alderaan University. I tried to intercede on her behalf, using my own fame to intimidate the officials—but even my entreaties had no effect. (And, legitimately, how could they ignore such an ethical violation, even had they known her true work?)

In her trips out into the wilderness Thelaa was actually running black-market weapons, which were picked up by smugglers and taken off to arm the Rebel Alliance. This was her true calling in life, and I know it made her feel vibrant and alive.

After her expulsion Thelaa fled to the isolated fortress where she had stashed her latest shipment of weapons. She was desperate, needing to get off the planet. She contacted her Rebel partners in a hidden ship in orbit—but she did not realize that on this last trip a team of bloodthirsty Imperial trackers had followed her.

After Thelaa had gone to her cache of illicit weapons, the Imperial operatives closed in on her. Thelaa spotted them before they could break into the tall cement-hard mound where she made her encampment. She kept a coded comlink channel open with her Rebel contacts as she withdrew several fully armed blaster rifles. She began shooting, but the Imperial forces were too great. They succeeded in stunning Thelaa—but only after she had managed to kill two of them.

With their new captive ready for full questioning from an IT-0 interrogation droid, the Imperial operatives were pleased to note an immense battle station arriving in orbit around Alderaan. Their smug calls to the Death Star are a matter of record. The trackers were convinced that the Empire had finally

come to crack down on the freethinking and peaceful ways of Alderaan.

But the Death Star had far more extreme measures in mind, and Grand Moff Tarkin never responded to their transmissions.

The planet Alderaan was destroyed before Thelaa could be interrogated or her stolen weapons cache recovered. Despite my sadness, I can say only that it served them right.

The annihilation of Alderaan was intended to be

a demonstration of might by Grand Moff Tarkin, an exercise of Imperial power to increase terror of the Empire and to crush the Rebellion.

It is true that the wholesale destruction of Alderaan sent tremors across the galaxy—but the result was not what Tarkin had in mind. The Death Star's vicious attack was but another demonstration of the Empire's evil, and it drove many peaceful and docile citizens into open rebellion.

From the moment of Alderaan's death, the Rebel Alliance became less a secret underground battle

Again, to avoid harming the landscape of their world, the people of Alderaan covered one of their underground cities, Terrarium City, with sheets of transparisteel.

and more an overt civil war. There could be no hope for a peaceful resolution between the Alliance and the Empire.

Though Alderaan is gone now, it survives through the wealth of art and music dispersed from star system to star system. Alderaan has become a

symbol of innocence against evil. My own memories are like precious jewels inside me, and I will devote the rest of my life to singing this requiem for Alderaan. Let no one else ever forget.

The pods of Alderaan University were dispersed like seeds on the wind, so that students taught at the ancient learning center of Collus have also carried their memories of Alderaan throughout the stars. Now, every time I hear the winds through the grasses on any world, I hear an echo of the Song of Alderaan.

The most powerful force of all, unquenchable by any Death Star's laser, is the spirit of freedom and resistance to oppression that continues to spread across the galaxy.

The glittering capital city of Aldera sat on an island in the center of a beautiful lake. Aldera was perhaps best known as the site of the renowned Alderaan University.

ART BY RALPH McQUARRIE
TEXT BY KEVIN J. ANDERSON

ADDITIONAL ART BY: